# THE BRITISH
# MALAISE

# THE BRITISH MALAISE

*INDUSTRIAL PERFORMANCE EDUCATION & TRAINING IN BRITAIN TODAY*

*Edited and Introduced by Gordon Roderick and Michael Stephens*

**The Falmer Press**
A member of the Taylor & Francis Group

First published 1982

ISBN 0 905273 21 4

Illustration and jacket designed by Leonard Williams


Printed and bound in Great Britain by
Taylor & Francis (Printers) Ltd., Basingstoke, Hampshire for

The Falmer Press
Falmer House
Barcombe, Lewes
Sussex BN8 5DL
England

# Contents

Foreword by *Sir Monty Finniston*                                         vii

Introduction
*Gordon W. Roderick* and *Michael D. Stephens*                              I

PART I   GENERAL BACKGROUND
1   The British Education System 1870–1970
    *Gordon W. Roderick* and *Michael D. Stephens*                         11
2   Britain's Economic Decline 1870–1980
    *Derek H. Aldcroft*                                                    31

PART II   THE EDUCATION AND TRAINING OF MANPOWER
3   Laying the Foundations: Schools and Industry
    *Catherine Avent*                                                      65
4   Scientists and Engineers
    *Geoffrey D. Sims*                                                     73
5   Management Training and Education
    *David T.H. Weir*                                                      89
6   Industry, Society and Education – A Multi-National View
    *Alexander Kennaway*                                                   107

PART III   INDUSTRIAL PERFORMANCE AND THE EFFECTIVE
           UTILIZATION OF MANPOWER
7   Is Manpower Planning Necessary? Is It Possible? What Next?
    *Lord Bowden of Chesterfield*                                          129
8   Trades Union Influence on Industrial Performance
    *Robert Taylor*                                                        141
9   Research, Development and Technical Decision-Making in Industry
    *T.L. Banfield*                                                        157

Index                                                                      167

# The Contributors

*Derek H. Aldcroft*, Professor of Economic History and Head of Department of Economic and Social History, University of Leicester.

*Catherine Avent*, Careers Guidance Inspector for Schools, Inner London Education Authority; member of the Finniston Committee on Education and Training of Engineers.

*T.L. Banfield*, Petro-Chemicals Division, ICI.

*Lord Bowden of Chesterfield*, former Principal of the University of Manchester Institute of Science and Technology and Minister of Science 1964–5.

*Sir Monty Finniston*, former Chairman, British Steel Corporation, past President of the Institute of Metallurgists and Chairman of the Committee on the Education and Training of Engineers.

*Alexander Kennaway*, Visiting Professor, Department of Chemical Engineering and Chemical Technology, Imperial College of Science and Technology, London.

*Gordon W. Roderick*, Professor of Adult Education and Director of the Division of Continuing Education, University of Sheffield.

*Geoffrey Sims*, OBE, Vice-Chancellor of the University of Sheffield.

*Michael D. Stephens*, Robert Peers Professor of Adult Education and Director of the Department of Adult Education, University of Nottingham.

*Robert Taylor*, Industrial Correspondent, *The Observer*.

*David Weir*, Professor of Organizational Behaviour, Department of Management Studies, University of Glasgow.

# Foreword

All industrialized countries advance the material (and cultural) interests of their citizens through complex changing patterns of economic order, and all industrialized countries have to cater to such developments within the confining context of societal characteristics which themselves may weaken the resolve of the body politic and militate against efficient industrial policies. Like all illnesses these debilitating characteristics are more readily diagnosed by others than by the patient himself. Hence the term of foreign origin – 'The British Malaise'. (This in fact is more an infectious disease than a malaise since it now appears to be transmittable to other countries of comparable if not identical societal structure.) The malaise has the symptoms of industrial lassitude and inertia, a failure to engage in industrial exercise and an over-indulgence in standards of living which can be ill-afforded; it seeks comfort and even immediate cure in quack medicines (called economic theories) rather than in a diet and regime of investment for long-term return to health.

Various reasons for the British Malaise are offered. Students of the scene – economists, educationists, industrialists, politicians, managers and managed – each lay claim to some feature of their prejudice: tradition (confusing dreams of the unrealities of a bygone age (which were none too good) with fantasies about the realities of the present); the academic system (with its preference for academic thought over action); the trade unions; the Government; the Civil Service; etc., etc., etc. The British Malaise whatever its origin(s) is a disease of industrial dyslexia – the inability to match the industrial problems of the real world with viable industrial objectives and performance.

A country which is poor in natural wealth can only meet its needs when the skills and talents of its people translate ideas and concepts into products and services which its own nationals and those of other countries want in exchange for their raw materials, products and services. The basic foundation of the British economy is and will forever be its manufacturing industries, and manufacturing industries in modern societies are complicated animated bodies of activity subject to constant mutations through new ideas, concepts, science and technology, innovation and experiments not just generated nationally but internationally as the developed nations advance and the less developed countries follow close behind.

This book deals with many of the complications of the economy but principally that part which makes industry possible. The tools of industry – its machinery and its systems – are of course man-made. The elements which can advance or regenerate the development of British industry are matters of sociological and cultural difficulty but nonetheless capable of solution through adoption of, and adaption to, relevant policies and practices generally rational and not based on emotional ideological or political dogma; through the attraction and education of recruits to industry, and training of people for and in industry; through translating research and development not just based on in-house investment in this country but through developments deriving from other countries; through the development of machine/man integration as the machine assumes greater responsibility for output (products and services) and man becomes more active in the increase of intellectual control over his machines. But above all through improving the decision-making processes by which industry either engages in or is thwarted by the hiatus between the industrialist and the investor who apply different criteria in arriving at their decisions on the same problem.

In its investment in education, in the development of skills and in the experience and ambitions of its people, in its political stability and in its freedoms, and many other aspects which go to make a good society, Britain has an advantage over many of its industrial rivals. The further development of these elements are precedent upon success in an industrially-based economy.

Being an easygoing people, perhaps the British do not realize that the Third World War has started. It is not a military combat but an economic one; it is not likely to be of limited duration with a peace treaty at its end. Great Britain is basically a manufacturing society with a superstructure of supporting wealth-creating activities. If the British wish to maintain the standards which they have enjoyed so far, or if they wish to improve upon them, they cannot remain passive or advance their industrial interests with outmoded industrial weapons.

This book performs a most useful service in drawing attention to the past, the present and the future of British industry by examining the symptoms of the country's present condition and in offering proper medicines including intellectual correctives for achieving a return to industrial health, which by the turn of this century will be sorely needed when the chance support of oil will be waning or found wanting.

Monty Finniston

# Introduction

*Gordon W. Roderick* and *Michael D. Stephens*

Let me call your attention to the fact that the terrible battle of competition between the different nations of the world is no transitory phenomenon, and does not depend upon this or that fluctuation of the market, or upon any condition that is likely to pass away. . . . We are at present in the swim of one of those vast movements in which, with a population far in excess of that which we can feed, we are saved from a catastrophe, through the impossibility of feeding them, solely by our possession of a fair share of the markets of the world. And in order that that fair share may be retained, it is absolutely necessary that we should be able to produce commodities which we can exchange with food-growing people, and which they will take, rather than those of our rivals, on the ground of their greater cheapness or their greater excellence. . . . Our sole chance of succeeding in a competition which must constantly become more and more severe, is that our people shall not only have the knowledge and the skill which are required, but that they shall have the will and the energy and the honesty, without which neither knowledge nor skill can be of any permanent avail.[1]

These words might well have been uttered by any modern day statesman or industrialist. They were in fact spoken by Thomas Henry Huxley when addressing a meeting at Manchester in 1887. They illustrate well that the times we live in differ little in some ways from those of our Victorian forefathers of the late nineteenth century; it is a matter of degree, not of kind.

The ready markets referred to by Huxley, markets established by naval power and colonization, were not to last long, for as the nineteenth century drew to its close the United States, Germany and, to a lesser extent, Belgium and France, captured markets which had traditionally belonged to Britain. Germany in particular became the bogey nation; Britain faced severe competition from her for markets, particularly in Mesopotamia, Brazil, Chile and Uruguay. 'As market after market fell into German hands there were times, particularly towards 1900, when foreign competition seemed to be a brooding menace rather than a bracing challenge and the label "made in Germany" was used as the grimmest of forebodings'.[2] Our political domination of imperial markets, though, continued to shore up our economy until finally in 1947 Britain withdrew from the Asian sub-continent.

To the average man in the street the decline in Britain's fortunes seems to have started in the 1970s following relatively boom years in the 1950s and 1960s. This view is too often shared by influential people in leading positions. For instance, writing in the *Times Higher Education Supplement*, Mr. Terence Miller, former Director of the Polytechnic of North London stated:

> It is a curious paradox that we seem able to strike this head-in-the-sand attitude at a time when catastrophe and violence, as well as poverty and the results of ignorance are almost permanently displayed on our television screens. Is this the result or the cause of the increase in the rate of decline of Britain, both economically and as a significant world power ... that has characterized the 1970s?[3]

The widespread feeling that the 'Great' has gone out of Great Britain is of recent origin at a popular level, perhaps at most it is thought to be a post-war phenomenon. It was in the early 1960s that covetous eyes were once again cast at Germany.[4] Her miraculous economic 'rise from the ashes' was observed with alarm and causes were sought for Britain's poor industrial performance – loss of Empire, obsolete industries, power of the Trade Unions, war-weariness and so on. All too few people in the country appreciated that decline had been with us a long time: 'The British economy has expanded more slowly than its main industrial competitors for the last hundred years'.[5]

Certainly loss of Empire has been a critical factor. Corelli Barnett, a leading historian, cities 1941–42 as a significant turning point in our fortunes – the fall of Malaya, Rangoon and Singapore leading to a serious loss of raw materials – but like other critics, argues that the loss of economic momentum started in the nineteenth century. Economic historians agree that British industrial performance declined relative to that of our leading competitors sometime between 1870 and 1900, but differ as to whether the starting point was in the 1870s or in the 1890s. Some critics even argue that it can be traced further back to the 1850s or even 1840s. Perhaps an extreme view is that 'the real causes of the British disease can ultimately be traced back two hundred years'.[6] It is at least reasonable to assume that the decline set in sometime in the nineteenth century. Whilst the factors responsible for our decline may still operate today, their origins are to be found in the last century rather than in the 1970s or in the post-war period.

Our national decline, then, began over a century ago, the seeds of future economic failure being sown ironically during the High Summer of our own industrial supremacy when Britain was the 'workshop of the world'. At that time acute observers were quick to point to the 'relative' decline in our fortunes which trade and productivity figures made clear. In 1880 the United Kingdom's share of manufactured goods was 41.4 per cent of the world output, whereas in 1913 it constituted only 29.9 per cent, Germany's share meanwhile increasing from 19.3 per cent to 26.5 per cent.[7] Between 1889 and 1914 Britain lost £360 million in annual manufacturing export on account of competition, a loss of about 18 per cent of the actual value of her manufacturing exports in 1913, while Germany gained £330 million.[8]

Britain mined 50 per cent more coal than America, Germany and France combined in 1870. Yet by 1900 she produced 50 per cent less than they did; while Britain's output doubled, Germany's quadrupled and America's increased by a factor of eight. Despite a very considerable lead in steel production, Britain was overtaken by America in the mid-1890s and by Germany by 1900. Germany dominated the synthetic dyestuffs industry whilst in machine tools 'the United States leapt ahead decisively'.[9] Little wonder that today we have a feeling that 'we have been here before'.

Britain, once the proud home of the Industrial Revolution, is being referred to as the 'sick man of Europe'. Terms such as 'the British sickness' and 'the British disease' have come to be synonymous with relative economic failure and an inability to match our industrial productivity to that of our competitors. Britain, once top of the world living standards league, has now dropped to below the top twenty. In electronics and machine tools, pace-setting industries, Germany's market share is nearly three times that of Britain's. Writing in 1963 Lord Snow observed:

> There is something wrong with us. For 1938 let us take the national product as 100. In the United States it has gone up to 225, West Germany 228, in the OEEC countries to 164, but Britain only to 129.[10]

Since then there has been no improvement, indeed there has been a still further relative decline. In the table of gross domestic product per head of population the United Kingdom was ninth in 1961, thirteenth in 1966, fifteenth in 1971 and eighteenth in 1976. In output per man-hour worked in manufacturing – a standard test of national productivity – the United Kingdom is bottom of the league among leading nations; the order being Japan, Germany, France, Italy, Canada, the United States and United Kingdom. In wage cost per unit of output – a key to a nation's competitiveness – only Italy comes out worse than Britain; the order being the United States, Germany, Canada, France, Japan, United Kingdom and Italy. By whatever criteria one adopts, Britain comes out badly.

Clearly there is 'something wrong'. Inevitably the spotlight focuses on management and big business. It was the same in the nineteenth century, indeed, the businessman's 'bad press' dates from the end of that century. What Professor Aldcroft has termed the 'laundry list' of causes which have been advanced to explain Britain's relative decline then could equally be taken to account for today's problems. The list includes: the handicap of an early start, obsolete technologies and industry, attitudes of labour, the educational system, governmental attitudes and, above all, entrepreneurial deficiencies. The hypothesis of entrepreneurial failure embraced many familiar accusations: amateurism, indifference and complacency, incompetent and indifferent salesmanship involving the unwillingness to try new products, a stubborn refusal to suit goods to the needs of potential clients or to engage technical salesmen with a facility in foreign languages, lack of managerial dynamism and adventurousness, technical and organizational lag within individual firms, conservatism in the face of new techniques and a reluctance to abandon individuality and tradition.

Today, in strike-prone Britain, as the industrial worker is accused of being increasingly feckless and irresponsible, industrial management is equally being pilloried on the same charges levelled against their nineteenth century predecessors – conservative attitudes, innovative lag and technical inefficiency, and poor labour relations. Addressing the Annual Lunch of the Parliamentary and Scientific Committee in 1980 HRH the Prince of Wales accused British management of being poor at communication, of being badly informed and of playing its cards too close to its chest. Much of British management, he said, does not seem to understand the importance of the human factor:

> We should pay far more serious attention to the business of training and motivating potential managers. Without this I cannot see how industrial relations will improve – a major pre-requisite for the rejuvenation of British industry.

British industry is bedevilled by the 'them' and 'us' alienation. Writing in the nineteenth century Arthur Shadwell took a serious view of the 'deep and abiding' suspicion between employer and employed:

> The habit of distrust is both a sign and a source of weakness in industrial matters ... the standing objection of workmen to innovations and improvements is rooted in it, and the very large proportion of the dispute between capital and labour can be traced to nothing but mutual distrust.[11]

Little has changed. Prince Charles stated recently that 'bloody mindedness, if it arises, must do so surely because of misunderstandings'.

The trade unions, too, of course, came in for attack in the nineteenth century and still do today.

> We are still trying to solve the problems of how to sublimate the energies of a trade union movement which grew powerful in response to the excesses of the industrial revolution, the legacy of which in terms of 'them' and 'us' attitudes can all too clearly be seen in our factories.[12]

In the nineteenth century the trade unions were accused of reduction of output, of opposition to machinery and with fomenting disputes, though Shadwell found little real evidence to support such accusations. Writing in the *Guardian* in October 1979, Peter Jenkins pointed to the negative power of the Unions:

> Their commitment to competitive collective bargaining, vested interests in declining industries and overmanned plant and their inability to reform themselves or effectively lead their members are seemingly insuperable barriers to a wealth-creating approach.

In Germany, Scandinavia and Austria, he pointed out, there has been prosperity because there has been a commitment by the workers to wealth creation as well as to welfare provision. In his speech Prince Charles said:

> The evidence is that our people like others will tolerate change if they see its necessity and properly understand its purpose and value ... the chief

executives must have a special responsibility for communicating effectively about the nature of technological changes required and proposed, the objectives being pursued and the implications for the workforce.

The 'them' and 'us' alienation has led on the one side to the 'cloth cap' image and on the other to the trappings of staff and executive status. The result is a lack of the kind of positive identification with the firm by the majority of the workers that is found in a number of other countries.

Many point the finger of blame for our economic woes at our education system which at the school level, it is claimed, puts a premium on intellectual and theoretical skills as opposed to practical skills. Management blames the education system for its irrelevance and remoteness from industry, for inculcating attitudes which give productive workers a low status and for not producing the right kind of people in the right numbers. Management complain that a career in industry is not presented in an attractive light and that management does not have a sufficiently high status in this country. In contrast the status of managers in Germany is high, reflecting a greater professionalism and technical and commercial competence. At university level the British education system is criticized for being hidebound by the attitudes that prevailed a hundred years ago when we were concerned to produce an administrative elite to serve the needs of the Empire. Its historical development has meant that an emphasis has been put on high status areas such as classics, arts and the pure sciences to the detriment of applied science and technology. During the decade 1965–75 there was a decrease in the number of engineers (mechanical, electrical and production), a switch having occurred from engineering to pure science. More recently we have seen the pendulum swing in favour of medicine, law and accountancy. Prince Charles called for improved status for engineers and criticized the view that engineers were people who wear overalls, wield spanners and generally do dirty undignified jobs:

> Until engineers are afforded the same respect and given the same status as they are in Germany, the United States and Japan we will be fighting an appalling uphill struggle and we will be left floundering and further behind.

The concern that British industry was not up to the level of competence, efficiency or productivity of its competitors led to the setting up of the Finniston Committee on the education and training of engineers. At the present time we are critically short of engineers and of mathematics and physics schoolteachers which itself is a factor affecting the rate at which we produce engineers. The freedom of individual choice has traditionally been strongly defended as a cardinal principle in English higher education; only in medicine and veterinary science is there any pretence at manpower planning. Rhodes Boyson, Minister of State for Higher Education, has stated 'There is no right of eighteen-year-olds to read whatever subject they want at whatever cost with a guarantee at the end', the implication being that higher education will be expected to adapt courses and policies to national needs. It will be interesting to see how much worse the economic situation becomes before the principle of freedom of choice will be modified or jettisoned.

In the nineteenth century a great weakness in education was the failure to produce a blueprint or plan of a cohesive system of education within which each sector would integrate with the others and which was designed to meet national objectives. Today, we seem to be repeating the error:

> In peacetime there seems to be an almost complete inability to appreciate any situation – in relation to higher education – and what plans are made deal only with numbers, space, equipment and cost, and rarely if ever with real, i.e. national, objectives.[13]

Another criticism levelled at the British is that they do not wish to work hard. In the mid-nineteenth century, hard work and discipline were reckoned to be British virtues responsible for national progress. Samuel Smiles, author of *Self-Help* (1859), *Character* (1871), *Thrift* (1895) and *Duty* (1889), stated that 'National progress is the sum of individual industry, energy and uprightness as national decay is of individual idleness, selfishness and vice'.[14] It may be that the British may not have it in them to bring about the economic regeneration of the nation. Or perhaps they have consciously made other choices. Bernard Nossiter (*Washington Post* correspondent in London) says in a book entitled *The Future that Works* that he believes Britain as a society has taken a national decision to work less hard than her competitors, produce less furiously and consume with discrimination. 'Muddling through one crisis after another has become a way of life in Britain,' says Fritz Worth of *De Welt*.[15] Another American has written:

> Always in the past British traditionalism, conservatism, a penchant for 'muddling through' has been leavened by hard common sense, a stoical determination under stress, and – at crucial moments – a saving perspicacity. There is no reason to suppose that these qualities have disappeared or that they will not again enable Britain to meet the latest crisis in its long history.[16]

But it is becoming increasingly hard to believe in the possibility of Britain extricating herself from her present difficulties without abandoning the traditional posture of 'muddling through'. Perhaps we have lost the dynamic of self help; 'The spirit of self-help, as exhibited in the energetic action of the individual, has in all times been a marked feature of the English character and furnishes the true measure of our power as a nation'.[17]

Finally, some would point the finger of blame for our economic woes at the 'establishment', i.e. the Government and the Civil Service. In explaining the 'British Disease' in the nineteenth century Professor Allen sees the 'cult of the amateur' and the misuse of the professional expert as being a fundamental fault in industry, in Government and in the Civil Service.[18] Allen firmly assigns the blame for Britain's decline to what we now call the 'establishment' (the political leaders, the Civil Service and those who sit on the boards of the chief companies). They were victims of those anachronistic institutions the English class system and the educational arrangements associated with it. Some would argue that little has changed. The Society of Public Servants complains that too many civil servants come from

Oxbridge, all read arts subjects, and have been privately educated. Campbell Christie of the Society of Civil and Public Servants claims that 'It's like choosing like, this whole generalist philosophy – for generalist read amateur'.[19] Again, the 1979 Cabinet included six old Etonians, three Wykehamists, one old Harrovian and one Old Boy of Rugby. Seventeen were graduates of Oxbridge, five were barristers, six were former Guards Officers and two were in the cavalry. Simon Hoggart, writing in the *Guardian*, commented 'Dr. Arnold would have been proud of this Cabinet which Salisbury would have chosen'.

Many see the microchip as being the panacea for Britain's ills. Britain's investment in this approached that of the Japanese and was greater than that of the French or Germans. Microelectronics would make new products and new services economic for the first time as Mr. Callaghan, when Prime Minister, told the National Economic Development Council – we could be on the threshold of the most rapid industrial change in history. But will traditional attitudes ruin such new possibilities?

Many a politician, industrialist, trade unionist or educationist seems to have a ready answer or solution to Britain's economic ills. This confidence is to be wondered at. The enigma of what went wrong in the final quarter of the nineteenth century when industrial society was far less complex than it is today is far from satisfactorily explained. One view is that 'the whole complex of circumstances that produced British pre-eminence before 1873 was fortuitous',[20] her pre-eminence, in other words, may have been based on a ready availability of capital, her position as the leading maritime nation allied to a world-wide network of markets and, perhaps above all else, on the absence of real competitors. As these circumstances changed one by one it became essential that Britain produce goods more efficiently and more cheaply than her competitors and, equally important, market and sell them more efficiently. That was the challenge that Britain failed to meet in the nineteenth century and it is the challenge that faces her today.

## Notes

1 HUXLEY, T.H. (1902) *Science and Education*, collected essays, Vol. 3, Macmillan, London, pp. 446–7.
2 ASHWORTH, W. (1960) *Economic History of England 1870–1939*, London, p. 37.
3 *Times Higher Education Supplement*, 1 February 1980.
4 It is exactly twenty years since German output per head passed the British figure. (It is now close to double.)
5 KEEGAN, V. (1980) *Three Ways of Solving Britain's Import Problems*, Guardian, 24 January 1980.
6 *Ibid.*
7 ALDCROFT, D.H. (Ed.) (1958) *The Development of British Industry – Foreign Competition, 1875–1914*, Allen and Unwin, p. 21.
8 McCLOSKEY, D.N. (1970) 'Britain's Loss from Foreign Industrialisation: a Provisional Estimate' in *Explorations in Economic History*, Summer 1970, p. 143.
9 HOBSBAWM, E.J. (1974) *Industry and Empire*, Pelican Economic History of Britain, Vol. 3, Penguin Books, p. 180.
10 SNOW, C.P. (1963) 'Education and Sacrifice', *New Statesman*, 17 May 1963.
11 SHADWELL, A. (1906) *Industrial Efficiency. A Comparative Study of Industrial Life in England, Germany and America*, Longman, Green, p. 173.
12 KEEGAN, V. (1980) *Guardian*, 24 January 1980.
13 MILLER, T. (1980) *Times Higher Education Supplement*, 1 February 1980.

14 Quoted by BRIGGS, A. in *Victorian People*, Penguin Books, 1955.
15 *Guardian*, 10 March 1979.
16 PAYNE, G.L. (1960) *Britain's Scientific and Technical Manpower*, Oxford University Press, p. 398.
17 BRIGGS, *op. cit.*, p. 135.
18 ALLEN, G.C., *The British Disease*, Institute of Economic Affairs, p. 48.
19 WHITEHORN, Katherine, *Observer*, 4 November 1979.
20 PAYNE, P.L. (1974) *British Entrepreneurship in the Nineteenth Century*, *Studies in Economic History*, Macmillan, p. 51.

*I*
*General Background*

# The British Education System 1870–1970

*Gordon W. Roderick* and *Michael D. Stephens*

What is the lesson we have learned from the band of educational experts who, last year, published the result of their visit to the United States? Was it not this – that the American people believe in education? Almost with one voice they told us that our real inferiority lay in the fact that the citizens of the United States had more faith in the possibilities of education than we have, that their whole heart .was in their work as ours has never been. This is the great difference between them and us; and it is to this belief, this ardour of faith in the efficacy of training, that the Germans and Swiss – and we may now say the Japanese also – owe largely the measure of success which has crowned their efforts.

These words have a familiar ring and might be taken to refer to Britain's present discontents, but they were actually spoken at the turn of the century by Sir Philip Magnus when referring to the 1902 Education Act. He saw this Act as one of the great leaps forward in education:

I believe that the outcome of the Act of 1902 will be to arouse in Englishmen an enthusiasm for education and a deep-seated conviction in its influence and potency which has been hitherto confined to a few specialists and faddists.[1]

Until this Act Britain had not possessed an organized system of education 'susceptible of adaptation to our varying requirements'.
A few years later, A.N. Whitehead, the philosopher, wrote:

In the conditions of modern life the rule is absolute: the race which does not value trained intelligence is doomed. . . . Today we maintain ourselves. Tomorrow science will have moved forward one more step and there will be no appeal from the judgement which will then be pronounced on the uneducated.[2]

No advanced nation was more profligate in the neglect of the abilities of its citizens than was Britain in the nineteenth century. Many of the features of the present-day educational system owe their existence to attitudes which became hardened at that time, and many of Britain's problems and discontent of today have their roots in the nineteenth century.

Most of the pioneers of the Industrial Revolution were untutored, lacking formal education, products of the ancient tradition of British craftsmanship – men such as Crompton, Smeaton, Bramah and Maudslay. The Industrial Revolution, it seemed, owed little to education systems or to direct action from the state. The key issue in education at the beginning of the nineteenth century was related to the spread of education for the 'lower orders'. In this the influence of religion was dominant. The aim was to produce a God-fearing, law-abiding and industrious workforce. During the first quarter of the nineteenth century the view became prevalent that increasing industrialization made it necessary for the industrial worker, described as a 'mechanic' or 'artisan', to have a knowledge of science related to his industrial practice. Consequently, technical education from its origins became associated in the public mind with the education of the artisan, the philosophy of middle-class education meanwhile being based firmly in the principles of the Christian religion and on a knowledge of classics. Training the mind and the formation of character were paramount objectives of the private and grammar schools, largely the preserve of the middle and upper classes, and these objectives were to be attained by instruction in the classics and through the Christian religion. The schools served as 'feeders' to the ancient universities of Oxford and Cambridge, which provided a general liberal education centred on the classics. Such an education was appropriate both for the 'gentleman' and the 'professional man', for whom it served as a cultural foundation leading to further education in law, theology or medicine. Middle class education was a continuation of the upper class pre-industrial model.

Thus, the commonly-held belief that the Industrial Revolution owed little to the ancient universities or grammar schools, or to education in its formalized setting, was justified in general terms. At mid-century the prevailing philosophy was that Britain owed her success to national character and qualities, to her craftsmen and engineers, well-endowed with natural ability. These, allied to daring entrepreneurship and unfettered individualism, had brought Britain to the top. What indeed was owed to education? Why should things not continue as before? Such arguments conveniently overlooked the advantages conferred by natural resources, geographical factors and of being a powerful maritime and commercial nation.

Even in the atmosphere of the general euphoria surrounding the Great Exhibition, one critic, Sir Lyon Playfair (first Baron Playfair) dared to draw attention to such factors. In the past, he pointed out, the ready availability of cheap natural resources had been in Britain's favour, but in future the development of transport and communication systems would tend to cancel out differences in natural resources. The race would therefore go to the nation which commanded the greatest scientific skill. Playfair's introductory lecture on the occasion of the opening of the Government School of Mines in 1851 was a prophetic warning. In it he declared that 'as surely as darkness follows the setting of the sun, so surely will England recede as a manufacturing nation, unless her industrial population become much more conversant with science than they are now'.

Following Playfair's critical observations the feeling grew gradually that without widespread systems of instruction the industry of the United Kingdom would be overtaken by those of other countries. A stumbling block to progress, however, was the belief in self-improvement and self-help; it was antipathetic to state involvement. One must not look to outside sources to provide learning opportunities, the answer lay rather in 'self-culture' through diligent and persevering effort. Many of those who advocated the virtue of self-help were also anti-state at a time when the need for state and municipal intervention was becoming increasingly evident.

Such attitudes were shared by those in positions of power and authority. Robert Lowe, the instigator of 'payment-by-results' when Chancellor of the Exchequer, expressed the view, 'I hold it as a duty not to spend public money to do that which people can do for themselves'. This became a cardinal principle of government spending on education. The belief in individualism and the dislike of state inter-ference and of centralized administration were widespread. There was a fear, too, that state support would lead to state control. The dislike of state interference was finally dispelled and overcome only by the fear of losing our prosperity. In the face of increasing intensity of foreign competition for goods and markets the state gradually and reluctantly intervened in educational affairs.

The task of educating the nation in the realities of the situation begun by Playfair in the 1850s was carried on by a small scientific lobby whose foremost spokesman was Thomas Henry Huxley. He pointed out that in the past practical men had believed that 'rule of thumb' methods were adequate as we had achieved prosperity by the use of such methods. In the future the diffusion of thorough scientific educa-tion was an absolutely essential condition of industrial progress.

Another influential figure who added his weight to the protest movement was the Earl of Roseberry:

> It was largely owing to the shrill note of warning sounded by Earl Rose-berry, who, like a prophet of old, emerges from time to time from his self-imposed solitude and silence, to arouse the people to a sense of its dangers and its duties, that something like a wave of anxiety spread over the country as to whether our educational efforts were adequate to stay the incursion of German goods into our own and neutral markets, and to maintain the position of British commerce.[3]

Official public recognition of the danger facing the country was conceded by the Royal Commission of Scientific Instruction and the Advancement of Science under the chairmanship of the Duke of Devonshire which reported in 1872. As early as the 1870s, at a time when it could fairly be claimed that Britain was still leading the world, the Commission alluded to the danger of falling behind in the competitive race, impressed, no doubt, by the constant reiteration of this theme by witness after witness. From that time on, public speeches by statesmen and industrialists, and annual reports of educational bodies, all testified to the growing awareness of the impact of foreign competition.

Huxley drew attention to the almost obsessional interest in technical education for the artisan by successive governments and the neglect of university education and of the promotion of research. Another who stressed the need for scientific research was George Gore, an industrial chemist. In a book entitled *The Scientific Basis of National Progress* he wrote:

> By the neglect of scientific investigation we are sacrificing our welfare as a nation. Present knowledge only enables us to maintain our present state. National progress is the result of new ideas, and the chief source of new ideas is original research.[4]

Others pointed to the fact that the government was prepared to support geological, biological and astronomical sciences which could still be pursued by the 'gentleman amateur' whereas the sciences which contributed most to economic progress (physics, chemistry and metallurgy) were relatively neglected.

Meanwhile, the German states, in particular Prussia, were investing enormous sums in education, right through from primary schools to the universities. In England the numerous education commissions and ensuing legislation from 1870 onwards reflected the efforts of the Victorians to get to grips with the changing situation, to make up for the previous half century of inactivity, to create some order out of the confused and chaotic state of education, and to provide the funds belatedly recognized as being essential for the support of education.

Underlying the inability to get to grips with educational problems for the greater part of the century was the poor state of primary education. Prior to mid-century, education was largely in the hands of the voluntaryists; church schools, dame schools, charity schools and Sunday schools made up the provision of schooling. Having been first in the field the Church bodies were anxious to preserve their dominant position. Consequently the progress of a state system of education was hindered by the secular-religious power struggle for the control of education. Power blocs were not confined to the Church bodies; manufacturers and landowners, too, had their own economic interests to defend whenever the state attempted to bring forth new legislation requiring state attendance.

The first intervention of the central state in the affairs of education was a government grant in 1833 of £20 000 for the 'erection of schoolhouses'. This was a far cry from continental practice, where, influenced by the ideas of Pestalozzi, German and Swiss states had established a system of popular schools based on compulsory attendance. Attendance to the age of ten was not made compulsory in England until 1880 and school fees were not abolished until 1896. A Commission set up by Lord Derby's Government in 1858 under the chairmanship of the Duke of Newcastle found a 'confusing scene'. It recommended a system of government grants supplemented by local grants. Robert Lowe, Vice-President of the Department of Education, rejected the concept of local grants and made the passing of examinations in the 3 Rs the necessary condition for a government grant. To him this was value for money. In a speech to the House of Commons he said 'If this system is not cheap, I can promise it shall be efficient; if it is not efficient, it shall be cheap'. Unfortunately, government policy and action till the end of the century in all fields of education seemed to be more often activated by a concern for cheapness than for efficiency.

Lowe's Revised Code of Regulations came into effect in 1861 and the slogan 'payment-by-results' became part of educational history. A leading nineteenth-century educationist wrote later:

'Payment by results' came to be regarded as the absolutely essential and only condition by which the state was secured in obtaining full value for its money – nothing probably has tended more to retard the progress of education in this country than this system; it was unknown in foreign countries and its injurious effects were fully realized long before it was discontinued.[5]

Elementary education was still in the hands of the voluntaryists and efforts to build schools did not keep pace with the rapid increase in child population. Many children were not on school-rolls at all and attendance generally was very irregular. William Forster's Bill of 1870, the object of which was to cover the country with 'good' schools, created school boards which were empowered to raise a penny rate to provide funds for new school buildings and thus fill the 'gap' in the provision of schools. Thus it was not until the final quarter of the century that a systematic cohesive pattern of elementary education emerged.

The inefficiency of elementary education had a deleterious effect on the quality of students entering secondary, technical and higher education for the greater part of the century. In technical education, for instance:

The students who attend even the most elementary of the City and Guilds technological classes are, in too many cases, insufficiently prepared to profit by the teaching. They are deficient in power of expression; they lack practical knowledge of arithmetic and the rudiments of science, and the necessary skill in drawing. In a word, their training in the elementary schools of the country has not produced the best results.[6]

Professor Michael Sadler, in carrying out a survey of secondary education in Liverpool in 1904, noted the elementary nature of work in technical centres. There was little advanced work, the greatest effort being devoted to the recovery of work which should already have been done at elementary school.

Secondary education, like elementary education, owed its origins to private initiatives and benevolence, but progress was stultified by the reluctance of the state to interfere and allocate adequate resources. Government action was limited to the setting up of numerous commissions, few of whose recommendations were implemented, together with the creation of a Charity Commission to oversee the considerable number of endowments, many of which were grossly abused. Although the importance of secondary education was widely recognized, inaction by central authority meant that by the turn of the century England had one of the least-developed systems among leading industrial nations:

While the development of secondary education is the most important question of the present day and is the pivot of education as it affects the efficiency, intelligence and well-being of the nation, yet its present position may be described as chaos. ... The most conspicuous fact that emerges is of how much there is yet to be done in secondary education – the short-comings are too often little less than disasterous.[7]

The Board of Education had no reservations in attributing the responsibility for this state of affairs to the dislike of state interference both by the government and by the nation at large.

> That the state has any concern with secondary education is a comparatively modern idea in England ... the term 'secondary' has been left in the air, and this is a sort of symbol of the way in which secondary education itself was for long neglected after a national system of elementary education had been established on the one hand, and on the other university education. This isolation and consequent neglect of secondary education over so long a period is at the root of the difficulties which have to be faced in the last few years in all grades of education in England.[8]

In 1868 the Schools Inquiry Commission, in a comprehensive and constructive report, advocated the placing of secondary education in the hands of specially-constituted local authorities answerable to a central statutory body under a Minister of the Crown but 'the formidable inertia of the nation reinforced by intense jealousy of state interference and dislike of public control held up much needed reforms'. The nationalization of secondary education was repeatedly postponed and a national pattern was not laid down until the Education Act of 1902.

The Royal Commission which reported in 1895 and whose recommendations formed a springboard for the 1902 Act found 'an incoherent fragmented system, an overall inadequacy of finance, dispersed and unconnected forces, needless competition between the different agencies and frequent overlapping of effort'. The supply of schools was wholly inadequate to the needs of the country; in two out of three towns there was no school above the level of an elementary school, in Liverpool, Salford and St Helens, for instance, there were no ancient endowed grammar schools, and the provision of schools was left to the generosity of public-spirited citizens, whereas there were such schools in Accrington, Burnley and Bolton. The geographical distribution of schools was irregular, as educational endowments were unevenly distributed, forming no part of a logical, natural plan of relating resources to need.

Grammar schools were very heavily influenced by the nine leading 'public schools' of the country as defined by the Clarendon Commission in 1861 – Eton, Harrow, Winchester, Shrewsbury, Merchant Taylors, St. Pauls, Rugby, Westminster and Charterhouse. With the exception of Rugby the curriculum of the schools was almost exclusively classical, mathematics having been accepted as an 'extra' in the 1820s, students wishing to pursue that study being charged additional fees. The view of the Clarendon Commissioners was that 'natural science, with slight exceptions, is practically excluded from the education of the higher classes in England'. The same attitude towards science was widespread among headmasters of many grammar schools. It was held that classics was the most appropriate study for first-class minds whereas 'modern studies' had some value for the less able.

Science, in particular, was not considered to have high intellectual or educational value. Some saw value in teaching science as something of interest to the more backward whereas others argued it only made boys more intelligent, but not more human. The consequence of these attitudes was that the majority of the able boys in grammar schools took up classics whilst very few of the abler minds took up careers in science and engineering. A study of a representative sample of the leading schools of the country shows that less than 1 per cent of boys were taking up a scientific career and only 3 per cent a career in engineering.[9]

In defending themselves against the criticisms of Royal Commissioners the schools sought a scapegoat in the Universities of Oxford and Cambridge, which, they claimed, kept a stranglehold on the curriculum of the schools. Scientific education at the Universities was totally inadequate. Furthermore, the Universities offered most of their fellowships and scholarships in classics and mathematics which clearly influenced boys in the choice of their studies and careers. In 1872 out of 202 fellowships at Oxford, only four were in science and out of 174 at Cambridge, only three were in science. The Universities blamed the schools for not sending them their brighter students to study science and for not preparing students properly in the sciences. The schools blamed the Universities for not offering more fellowships and scholarships in the sciences. Compulsory Greek, too, proved another stumbling block:

> So long as Greek remains an obligatory subject for entrance to Oxford and Cambridge any proper organization of secondary education such as is found in Germany, France and Switzerland is impossible. ... This would apply to all branches of engineering and to the higher military and naval education.[10]

Until the end of the century there were no clearly defined lines of demarcation between the various sectors of education. Elementary education and secondary education were confined to schools of various types and description, but beyond the schools there was a great deal of educational provision, much of it part-time under the auspices of various agencies. This was all part of the technical education 'movement' and was properly constituted as such when provision in each area was properly amalgamated under one committee of the local education authority by the 1902 Act. Technical education ranged from higher elementary education at one end to advanced technological instruction, trade education and technical processes at the other. The cause of technical education was hindered by uncertainty and vagueness as to its definition by its foremost proponents.

As Britain moved swiftly from a primarily agricultural economy to an industrialized state at the beginning of the nineteenth century the view prevailed that the Industrial Revolution with its specialization of processes and technological innovations demanded workmen with higher literacy levels than their predecessors, and that with rapidly changing conditions skilled workmen would require a knowledge of the elements of science. The artisan was thus seen as the cornerstone of technical education and it was the perception of his needs by the leaders of society which underpinned thinking about technical education throughout the greater part of the century. This was a major factor responsible for the low status of technical education in the nineteenth century. Unfortunately, the skilled worker often lacked the basic educational skills to enable him to benefit from the educational provision specially created for him; instead courses for artisans often attracted clerks, shopkeepers and school teachers.

The main agents for technological and technical education in the first half of the century were the mechanics' institutes, set up for the promotion of arts and science. By mid-century, most of these were mainly serving the educational, not to say entertainment, needs of the middle classes. Prompted by the fear of increasing international competition the government created the Department of Science and Art in 1853. This was to disburse certain sums for the support of science and technical instruction, part of which went to aid locally organized science and technical classes. A minute of 1859 stated 'It is to be hoped that a system of science instruction will grow up among the industrial classes which shall entail the least possible cost and interference on the part of the state'. Nearly forty years were to elapse before further government action was to follow. Meanwhile, throughout the country numerous individuals, either individually or collectively, were making very considerable contributions to the advance of technical education. In 1868 Joseph Whitworth of Manchester, the country's leading machine tool manufacturer, set up a national system of scholarships for apprentices at a personal cost to himself of £100 000. The impact of this scheme was widespread, distinguished Whitworth scholars later holding influential positions in academic and industrial life. The City and Guilds of London Institute also played a notable part in technical education, taking over the technological evening classes previously run by the Society of Arts, setting up the Finsbury Technical College (the first in the country), and establishing a more advanced institution in South Kensington which later became part of the Imperial College of Science.

The creation of new county councils in 1888 made possible the Technical Instruction Act of 1889 by which local authorities were empowered to raise a penny rate in support of technical instruction. This Act was followed in 1890 by the Local Taxation (Customs and Excise) Act, by which certain sums of money out of customs and excise duties were allocated to local authorities, either to relieve the rates or to subsidize technical education. Not unnaturally, most local authorities were happy to spend the government handout of 'whisky money', but were reluctant to raise money from the rates to pay for technical education. Local Technical Instruction Committees, which were responsible for the distribution of 'whisky money', interpreted technical education very broadly and much of the money went to schools, universities, museums and for domestic science instruction of women. It was characteristic of the way things were allowed to drift; all too often in the nineteenth century it was thought that problems could be solved by the allocation of sums of money, often derisory sums, by central government or municipal authorities.

In 1886 a Royal Commission on the Depression of Trade pointed to Britain's educational defects as being the main cause of her economic problems. It advocated that the remedy for evils due to foreign competition be found in improved technical instruction. Writing in the 1880s, Philip Magnus said:

> The prevailing opinion at the time was that technical education mainly concerned artisans, and very few persons then realized the urgent importance of providing a suitable training for the so-called captains of society, for those who would direct great engineering and manufacturing works, or for those who might assist by the prosecution of research in the processes of new industry.[11]

This was an area of great contrast between England and Germany. In his report to the London County Council, J.C. Smail, Organizer of Trade Schools for Boys, after a visit to France and Germany in 1914, defined technical education in terms of three levels – lower, middle and higher. No such clear lines of demarcation existed on a systematic basis until the emergence of the civic university colleges in the final quarter of the nineteenth century. Smail found that 'Germany possessed a national organization with definite national objectives', whereas in Britain he found overlapping between the three levels of education.

Germany dealt systematically with each problem and gave particular attention to the training of teachers for technical work and to the problem of apprenticeship. In England the system of apprenticeship left much to be desired; it had been allowed to lapse into 'one of the most unsatisfactory of vexed questions'. In Germany, training was tackled by statute; after leaving school the apprentice was obliged to attend continuation classes for up to nine hours a week, the employer being responsible for his regular attendance on pain of fine. After some years of trade experience the apprentice could enter day trade schools which served the building and engineering industries. These provided five half-yearly courses which could be taken successively or interspersed with intervals, that is, a sandwich system; such sandwich courses were hardly known in England at that time. Again in Germany the normal form of study was by day classes whereas in England it was through evening class study.

> Germany was counting at benefiting the nation by training all the workers through specialised courses whereas in Britain training is organised so that individuals may secure what they think best for their own advancement.[12]

The English system of technical education led to a mixture of types of students with a variety of aims and with widely-varying standards of attainments. In Smail's view, the system 'has led to excessive expenditure for mediocre results, excessive equipment, discouragement of teachers, falling away of students and a want of belief in education on the part of employers'. Some years later a Canadian Royal Commission on Industrial Training and Technical Education also found higher technical education neglected: 'In France, Germany, Switzerland and the United States the power and influence of technical education of the highest types appears to be greater than in the United Kingdom'.[13]

In higher education Oxford and Cambridge dominated the scene until the final quarter of the century. At the ancient universities early attempts at scientific instruction were spasmodic, leading nowhere, each innovation collapsing as soon as the innovator moved on. Improvements were not effected until Royal Commissions had reported in the early 1850s that too much power and wealth lay with the colleges which were reluctant to spend money on expensive facilities for scientific instruction. Further changes took place between 1870 and 1900 following the Devonshire Commission's strictures that funds devoted to science were 'lamentably deficient'. More staff were appointed in the sciences and whilst Cambridge introduced a Mechanical Sciences Tripos there was little technology at Oxford. But at both Universities whilst classics lost ground and sciences gained, the most prominent feature was the growth of history. A disappointing feature continued to be the paucity of fellowships and scholarships in science, a failure which was not significantly remedied over the period 1850 to 1914.

What made higher education and, in particular, scientific and technical education at university level widely available were the two London colleges – University College and King's College – and the emergence of the provincial civic colleges. These were designed to meet local industrial needs and they created their own distinctive specialisms: engineering was given considerable support at University College, King's College and Manchester; naval architecture was established at Liverpool and Newcastle; mining at Newcastle, Nottingham, Sheffield and Birmingham; metallurgy at Birmingham and Sheffield, whilst Leeds specialized in textile industries.

These colleges, of course, were funded largely through private endowments and subscriptions, government support not being forthcoming until 1889 and then only to a very limited extent. Liverpool, a particularly well-endowed college, received £500 000 for staff and buildings from private individuals between 1881 and 1914; in the same period total government support for all universities amounted to only £170 000. Although wealthy industrialists, manufacturers and merchants were prepared to endow chairs, the appointment of lecturers and demonstrators was financed out of general college funds. Such funds were rarely in a healthy state – for instance, the accumulated debt at Liverpool in 1901 was £11 000 and this meant that junior posts were spread thinly. The ratio of junior to professorial posts in science and technology in the civic colleges for 1894 was 1.7:1. A consequence of the small number of staff in each subject was that teaching duties tended to be heavy and research was neglected.

The government played little part in either the origins or the development of the provincial colleges. Government aid was concentrated on the Department of Science and Art, the Museum of Economic Geology (after 1851 the Government School of Mines) and the Royal College of Chemistry. In 1907 these two colleges were amalgamated with the City and Guilds Central Technical College to form the Imperial College of Science and Technology, a co-operative venture involving the government, the London County Council and the City and Guilds. It was the first technological university in England. This initiative paid off handsomely for the College soon became the leading centre of science and technology in the country. Its impact can be seen in the field of engineering for the number of candidates successful in the London Honours BSc in engineering rose from five in 1903 to sixty in 1910, the College contributing 50 per cent of the successes. At the heart of England's problem was the absence of a blueprint based on national objectives. The Imperial College of Science (which the government played a full part in developing) showed what could be done if problems were tackled in a systematic way.

German universities, in contrast to English, were state-sponsored. By 1880 Prussia was spending the equivalent of £350 000 on its six universities. A special feature, too, of German higher education were the technische hochschulen established at great cost; the Königliche Technische Hochschule at Charlottenburg in Berlin alone cost £450 000. These were in reality technical universities intended to impart a scientific training with its practical applications so that by this means a body of men might be educated in such a way as to make it possible for Germany to compete with the workshop-trained engineers of England. In England, there was nothing comparable with those dozen or so institutions until the establishment of Imperial College in 1907.

It was not only the universities and technical high schools which elicited admiration. The schools, too, were part of the national plan, being state institutions. Indeed, English observers repeatedly stressed that German education at all levels was characterized by a systematic thoroughness and zeal whilst 'in this country there is not the same enthusiasm for education, the same self-sacrificing spirit as may be found in Germany or the United States'.[14]

Sir Philip Magnus, Director of the City and Guilds, with his knowledge of the British system, was well placed to draw attention to the intelligible structure of the German system:

> Between the elementary school and the technical high school or university there is an intelligible and well co-ordinated system, which gives unity to the entire scheme of education. ... There is little or no overlapping. To each part of the educational machinery is assigned its special function, and no one school interferes with the work of another. ... There is also intelligent direction and control ... in this way is obtained the maximum of efficiency at the minimum of cost.[15]

His verdict about the Germans was:

> The Germans, unlike the French, the Italians, the Americans and the British have no special line of their own, but they can learn everything except the French sense of elegance. ... They can make things as solid and durable as the British and as light and convenient as the Americans... they build ships and engines as well as we can ... they weave better ... they make electrical and light automatic machines as well as the Americans and in the application of science, to which the future belongs, they easily beat both.[16]

Sir Arthur Shadwell, who wrote up his observations of the German and English educational and industrial scene in *Industrial Efficiency*, pinpointed German success as being due to order and organization. There was nothing magical about it:

> It is to the spirit of order, to the power of co-operation, to this skill in

organization rather than to any special genius, that the success of the Germans in so many varied branches of industry is undoubtedly due – qualities which are generally recognized as characteristic of the people. . . .
The foundation of German greatness, of her industrial and naval strength, were laid in her well-ordered schools and by her financial sacrifices which she made to be in advance of every civilized country in the excellence of her universities and other technical institutions and secondary schools.[17]

In 1896 Magnus, together with a number of leading industrialists, visited a number of industrial centres in Germany where,

we informed ourselves of the untiring energy of the German people, of the unquenched and unquenchable belief in the value of higher education in its application to industry, and of the startling advances which they had made in manufacturing and commercial enterprise. On our return to London we wrote a short report of our visit in the form of a letter to the Duke of Devonshire, then President of the Council. The letter was presented as a Blue Book to Parliament and was widely read and reviewed.[18]

The cumulative and impressive result of German planning and investment was that whereas the number of students of science and technology in England and Wales grew from 3000 to 4000 (25 per cent increase) during the same period the numbers in Germany increased from 15 000 to 25 000 (40 per cent increase). The universities, technical high schools and specialist academies, therefore, provided for German industry an elite corps of highly-trained scientists and technologists far greater in numbers than those available to British industry.

Nowhere was the impact of the different approaches of the two countries more clearly seen than in engineering and chemistry. In England engineering had a low status compared to most continental countries. The Census of 1841 did not include engineers among the category of 'professions' and even in 1861 only civil engineers were so included. In 1868 the Council of the Institution of Civil Engineers was pointing out that in England the profession of engineering was entirely unconnected with the government. Further, there was no public provision for engineering education, 'every candidate for the profession must get his technical, like his general education, as best he can; and this necessity has led to conditions of education peculiarly and essentially practical'.[19] Training in England consisted of a practical apprenticeship, the pupil having to pick up his theoretical knowledge by 'night study'; day-release and sandwich schemes did not exist. Pupils had to pay a premium for the privilege of being taken on; 'Young men at the age of eighteen enter the office of a civil engineer. Usually few questions are asked as to previous training . . . the pupil is a sort of nuisance in the office, only tolerated in consideration of the fee which accompanies him.[20] . . . These young men have the run of the offices, no one teaches them anything'.[21] In most parts of the continent the status of engineers differed markedly from that in England. By 1900 there were still fewer than twenty engineers in England who were entitled to be addressed as 'professor', and the total strength of the academic staff of all engineering departments did not exceed a hundred. At that time the Technische Hochschule at Charlottenberg had a staff of thirty in its engineering department whilst those at Munich, Hanover and Stuttgart had fourteen, thirteen and fifteen respectively.

Even had there been a flow of highly-qualified graduates leaving university it is doubtful whether there would have been sufficient openings in industry offering inducement. Would industry have been receptive enough and would the rewards have been tempting enough to keep engineers in England? A survey of 235 graduates of the University of Manchester around the turn of the century shows that no fewer than 20 per cent went abroad. Another study by the Liverpool University Engineering Society of its members between 1889 and 1912 reveals that thirty-nine went abroad, seventeen took up educational employment, seventeen entered public employment and thirty-four only entered industry. Clearly emigration and higher education in England in 1910 offered better opportunities for the graduate engineer.

Liverpool's engineers, for instance, whether engaged in municipal, academic or industrial life, had risen to the top through apprenticeships. Not one had received a conventional education of secondary school followed by university (as would be customary in Germany and Switzerland) and only one had been to a grammar school. In a paper to the Liverpool Engineering Society entitled *On Engineering Education* George Sander stated in 1868:

> Hitherto our workmen have been left to do for themselves ... although engaged from 6 am to 6 pm at their daily work, they manage to attend evening classes where these are available, and where they are not, they tread their way along, picking up what scraps of information they can find in the nearest lending library and by their dint of British pluck ... get sufficient knowledge to fit them for foremen and managers.[22]

Too much of the onus of obtaining theoretical training was left to the individual, with the emphasis on 'night schools' and part-time education, imposing a great strain on workers. In the opinion of many, technical training was a matter of the 'survival of the fittest'.

In the chemical industry the technical initiative passed to Germany in the final quarter of the century. The dominance was most clearly marked in organic chemicals, particularly in dyestuffs. Around the turn of the century Dr. Frederick Rose, H.M. Consul at Stuttgart, attempted to relate the German investment in higher education with the progress of the chemical industry. The field of chemical research and investigation, he said, was so dominated by Germany that 'a knowledge of German is essential – the best manuals are in German and two-thirds of the world's output of chemical research work comes from Germany'. A survey revealed that Germany possessed 4000 works-based chemists who had passed through universities or technical high schools. Some of the larger works employed between six and twenty; the Baden Aniline Dye and Soda Works alone employed more than 100 academically trained chemists.

The production of honours chemists in English universities and university colleges from 1860 to 1897 totalled only 859. In 1902 a Committee of the British Association circularized the Society of Chemical Industry. Of 502 replies 107 were undergraduates; of 167 industrial chemists forty-five had a degree. A similar survey of the Institute of Chemistry membership revealed that 30 per cent were graduates. Between 1820 and 1889 (the first year when government aid became available to universities in England) state aid to Prussian universities multiplied tenfold. In 1897 the total income of Prussian universities amounted to £563 584, of which the state gave £412 683. Sir Philip Magnus estimated that in the 1880s the total capital costs of technical high schools in Germany amounted to some £3 million with a further annual running cost of £250 000. The investment of such vast sums, a considerable proportion of which went on chemical instruction, was, in Rose's view, justified:

> Sums expended on chemical instruction have been amply repaid ... it is universally recognized that the efforts made hitherto must be increased and more carefully and judiciously applied if the German chemical industries are to maintain and strengthen their position in the future.[23]

Such was the position at the turn of the century. The First World War soon showed how inadequately prepared and inefficiently organized British industry was for supplying the arms necessary to defeat an adversary such as Germany. The War spurred the government to tackle energetically if not very effectively the problems of organizing industry and harnessing technological manpower. The spirit of urgency just as quickly evaporated with the winning of the War. Midway through the War a Committee was set up under Sir J.J. Thompson, the physicist, to examine the position of natural science in our educational system. For decades the claims of science had been met with resistance, if not hostility. The War changed that, if only temporarily. 'Not for the first time educational conscience has been stung by the thought that as a nation we are neglecting science. ... Just now everyone is prepared to receive science with open arms, to treat it as an honoured guest in our educational system'.[24] But the Committee concluded that science 'does not occupy in our system of education a place commensurate with its influence on human thought and the progress of civilization'.

Admiration for German universities, which had ceased after the outbreak of War in 1914, was replaced in the 1920s by a respect for the American universities. Ramsay Muir pointed out that Iowa, with a population of only two million, had as many universities as England and that Iowa State University was larger than Oxford and Cambridge combined. He also drew attention to their 'immense facilities for research bearing upon industry'.[25] While the total number of students at English universities increased at the rate of 1 per cent per annum during the 1930s, the number of students in science and technology declined. Between 1922 and 1938 the proportion of science students fell from 19.3 per cent of the total number of students to 16.2 per cent and the proportion of technology students from 12.5 per cent to 11.3 per cent. Of seventy-one new chairs created between 1925 and 1930 four only were in technology, whereas fifteen were in mathematics and science and thirty-nine in arts.

Although the government was increasingly compelled to assist with financing of university education in 1935 the universities were still dependent on endowments to the extent of some 14 per cent of their total income.[26] Lord Rutherford, head of the Cavendish Laboratories in Cambridge, the outstanding research centre in the country, pointed out that he could only finance two major projects because of the support given by two leading industrialists, Alfred Mond and Lord Austin. Professors of lesser repute may possibly have not been so successful in raising money. 'It is necessary,' he said, 'that our universities and other specific institutions should be liberally-supported so as not only to be in a position to train adequately young investigators of promise, but also to serve themselves as active centres of research'. In the 1930s Sir Julian Huxley pointed out that the total spent on research in this country represented only 0.1 per cent of the National Income whereas expenditure in the United States and the USSR was respectively £50 million (0.6 per cent of the national income) and £36 million, (0.8 per cent of the national income).

By 1918 the pattern of technical education had been set. It was one of part-time evening instruction combined with practical experience in industry. Day students were small in number, being only 22 000 in 1921. By 1938 these numbers had been doubled but they were still dwarfed by the numbers of part-time students – 1 280 000. The Board of Education Report in 1926 drew attention to the lack of facilities and amenities in technical education. Firms were not interested in the education of their employees, and the few firms involved were only interested in part-time evening instruction and not in the newer day-release schemes. There was little contact between schools and industry as teaching was thought by industrialists to be too academic and theoretical. The Malcolm Committee reported that 'much of the continuation school work was being vitiated by a part-time evening system which was particularly hard on the perseverance of young people already doing a full-time job in industry.'[27]

The Second World War, like the First War, provided a great stimulus to science and technology. Nevertheless, a seminal report, the Percy Report, published in 1945, pronounced that there had been a failure to secure the fullest possible application of science to industry, this failure being partly due to deficiencies in education:

> The annual intake into the industries of the country of men trained by universities and technical colleges has been, and still is, insufficient both in quantity and quality. . . . In particular the experience of War has shown that the greatest deficiency in British industry is the shortage of scientists and technologists who can also administer and organize and can apply the results of research to development.[28]

It called for comprehensive provision of training, more co-operation between industry and education and a greater commitment to research.

Two years later a government report pointing first to the by now familiar complaints of sporadic developments varying with locality, the dominance of evening classes, and the use of unsuitable and ill-equipped premises, said that as far as technical education was concerned 'our fortunes tomorrow depend upon the extent to which our plans for technical and commercial education are placed today in the forefront of our reconstruction programme, and the vigour and vision with which they are carried through'.[29]

The growth of technical education had to a large extent been an *ad hoc*, empirical process. As a result, technical establishments ranged in size from very small units to large city colleges. The 1950s and 1960s witnessed many attempts to come to grips with technical education and to elevate its status. In 1956 the government introduced an authoritative White Paper. In introducing it Sir Anthony Eden, Prime Minister, said 'The prizes will not go to the countries with the largest population. Those with the best system of education will win'. A system of regional colleges of technology and of advanced colleges of technology was introduced, the latter becoming upgraded to full university status. The maintained sector of education received a further boost by the creation of polytechnics in the 1960s and by the later creation of institutes or colleges of higher education. Whether such moves have solved Britain's problems remains open to doubt.

Britain's technological manpower problems continued to be a constant source of worry in the 1950s and 1960s. The number of qualified scientists and engineers in Britain in 1956 was only 0·6 per cent of the working population as compared to 0.9 per cent in the United States. The real weakness lay in technology, for the proportion of scientists in the British figure amounted to 44 per cent whereas the corresponding proportion in America was 30 per cent.[30] The bias in favour of science was partly explained by the high status attached to mathematics and physics at the time. This is reflected in the high proportion (42 per cent) of scientists being mathematicians and physicists compared to 24 per cent in the United States.

Again, the essential problem came back to one of social attitudes. The social evaluation of industry in Britain differs markedly from that in many other nations:

> To be a high industrial executive in America is not only eminently 'respectable' it is 'socially desirable'. It is the prevailing opinion that business attracts the best talent from educational institutions whereas in Britain there is a strong tendancy for the best students to find their way into the Civil Service and the professions generally.[31]

Owing to early specialization in schools, youngsters of fourteen were being asked to make often uninformed choices at an early age. These were frequently made under the undue influence of masters who were themselves products of an educational system which rated humanities and pure science more highly than technology. Often antipathetic to industrial careers they inflicted their prejudices on the young and were not the best propagandists for technology. A survey of schools carried out by the Oxford University Department of Education in the early 1960s found that:

> the public image of science and technology current among sixth formers is largely based on a quite unusual degree of ignorance about the nature of technology. ... The popular assumption is that boys in this country tend to enter higher technological education only when they cannot get a place in the faculties of pure science; in other words that applied as opposed to pure science is getting the 'rejects'. ... The evidence from the inquiry seems in this case to support the popular assumption. To an extent unusual in Europe, boys from the top grades of our sixth forms cluster in the

faculties of pure science, while engineering and technology courses draw on the lower grades. . . . Nowhere does technology fail to attract the best brains to anything approaching the same degree as in this country.[32]

The problem of scientific and technical manpower was further adversely affected by other factors. Just as there was in the nineteenth century a 'brain drain' of scientific manpower so there was emigration to Canada, North America and Australia in the 1950s and 1960s. Beneath the new found glamour attached to science, reasons for the Brain Drain were not hard to find; lack of facilities, outdated equipment, loss of time in waiting for technical workshop services. The University Grants Committee reported in 1956 that:

> In some universities, laboratories are still housed in huts erected for emergency purposes in the 1914–18 war and scientific research is still carried out in ill-lit basements and cupboards.

One potential source of untapped manpower lay in the female population. The Robbins Report on Higher Education pointed out in 1963 that only one in four university students was a woman. Since then the proportion has increased, but women represent less than 0.5 per cent of all qualified engineers and among 10 000 members of the Institution of Production Engineers in 1959 there were only six women. The recent Finniston Report, which underlines the dangers caused to the British economy by the ignorance and neglect of the engineering profession by society and its leaders, devotes only $1\frac{1}{2}$ pages to the problem of attracting more women into engineering: 'Our adoption of the masculine when referring to engineers is not just a stylistic convenience,' says the report. 'Engineering has been recruiting from only half the population'.

The recognition of the association between science and technology on the one hand and national prosperity on the other, now widespread, has been the result of Britain's declining economic power as George Gore predicted in the late nineteenth century. In a debate in the House of Lords in the mid-1960s Lord Todd said:

> As a nation we decline to believe in the technological revolution . . . we have to change the climate of society at least enough to respect those who make the wealth.

In the 1960s there was a feeling that Britain was at last on the road to the technological revolution which would herald in the new millenium. There was intensive campaigning in favour of science and technology in the 1950s and 1960s led by influential figures such as Lord Snow and Lord Bowden who filled the roles undertaken by Playfair and Huxley in the nineteenth century. There was further inspiration from Mr. Harold Wilson, when leader of the opposition. In a speech to the Labour Party Conference at Scarborough in 1963 he said:

> Our failure to develop science and technology is leading to a mass sell-out to foreign concerns. . . . Britain, once the workshop of the world, is becoming the dumping ground for the products of overseas industries that are just that bit quicker in getting off the mark than we are.

Two years later in his Reith Lectures Sir Leon Bagrit stated:

> It is essential for our future national prosperity in Britain that we should modernize this country by spreading an understanding of the most advanced forms of technology as rapidly as we can . . . we must make sure that our universities, our technical colleges and schools are mobilized to produce the people with the backgrounds, the training and the inclination which is necessary to bring this about.

A key to all this is, of course, education. Have we yet learned the lesson? In the 1970s Britain had one of the lowest per capita educational investments among EEC countries; Brussels figures for 1975 (in European Units of Account) show the United Kingdom as 215.4, France as 247.4, West Germany as 291.1 and Denmark as 414.

### Notes

1 Presidential Address at the Annual Meeting of the Association of Technical Institutions, Manchester, 27 January 1905.
2 WHITEHEAD, A.N. (1916) quoted in ARGLES, M., *South Kensington to Robbins*, Longman, p. 137.
3 MAGNUS, Sir P. (1910) *Educational Aims and Efforts, 1880–1910*, Longman & Co, p. 119.
4 GORE, G. (1882) *The Scientific Basis of National Progress*, Williams & Norgate, p. 1.
5 MAGNUS, *op. cit.*, Longman, Green & Co, pp. 3–4.
6 MAGNUS, *op. cit.*, p. 220.
7 Board of Education, Annual Report, 1909–10.
8 Board of Education, Annual Report, 1908–09.
9 See RODERICK, G.W. and STEPHENS, M.D. (1979) *Education and Industry in the Nineteenth Century*, Longman, p. 46.
10 MAGNUS, *op, cit.*, p. 10.
11 MAGNUS, *op. cit.*, p. 230.
12 Trade and Technical Education in Germany and France, report by SMAIL, J.C., Organizer of Trade Schools for Boys 'On Trade and Technical Education in France and Germany', London County Council (1914).
13 Quoted in SMAIL, *op. cit.*, p. 7.
14 MAGNUS, *op. cit.*, p. 28.
15 *Ibid.*, p. 123.
16 *Ibid.*, p. 122.
17 SHADWELL, Sir A., quoted in MAGNUS, *ibid.*, p. 93.
18 Report on a visit to Germany with a view to ascertaining the recent progress of technical education in this country. Eyre & Spottiswood (1896).
19 Report on the Education and Status of Civil Engineers in the United Kingdom and in Foreign Countries. Published by the Council of the Institution of Civil Engineers (1870), p. VIII.
20 'Young Englishmen and their parents crowd the doors of the offices and workshops, offering premiums of £300 to £500 for the mere permission to pass three years inside the magic gates, which must be passed to gain an entrance into the profession' (1870) Report, p. 201.
21 (1870) Report, p. 201.
22 Transactions of the Liverpool Polytechnic Society, 26 (1868), pp. 38–9.
23 ROSE, Dr. F. (1901) *Chemical Instruction in Germany and the Growth and Present Condition of the German Chemical Industries, Diplomatic and Consulate Reports*, Cd. 430–16, Foreign Office, p. 75.
24 National Science in Education, Report of the Committee on the Position of Natural Sciences in the Educational System of Great Britain (the Thomson Committee) (1918), pp. 2–4.
25 MUIR, R. (1927) *America the Golden: an Englishman's Notes and Comparisons*, London, pp. 27–31.
26 BERNAL, J.D. (1942) *The Social Function of Science*, Routledge, p. 420.
27 Report of the Committee on Education and Industry (1926–28), HMSO.

28 Ministry of Education, Higher Technological Education (1945), HMSO.
29 Ministry of Education. Further education: the scope and content of its opportunities under the Education Act (1947), HMSO.
30 PAYNE, G.L. (1960) *Britain's Scientific and Technical Manpower*, Oxford University Press, p. 31.
31 British Productivity Council, Education and Management. (1956), p. 8.
32 Department of Education (1963) *Technology and the Sixth from Boy*, Oxford University Press, pp. 1–2.

# Britain's Economic Decline 1870–1980[1]

*Derek H. Aldcroft*

## Introduction

There can be few topics more depressing than Britain's recent economic growth performance. However one juggles with the figures one cannot escape the conclusion that, in comparison with virtually all the major and minor industrialized or developed nations, Britain has had a deplorable track record since the early 1950s, and, even with the current windfall of North Sea oil, the position to date is still deteriorating. It is difficult to realize nowadays that this country was the pioneer of modern economic growth in the later eighteenth and early nineteenth centuries. Not that economic growth then was particularly spectacular compared with what was to follow in other countries at a later date, but at the time it certainly appeared impressive against the backdrop of a millenium of near stagnation and the slow development of Britain's closest competitors. This initial lead gave Britain a high standard of living and for a century or so she had the highest level of per capita income in the world, with the possible exception of Australia.

So much for the happy part of the story. The unfortunate thing is that Britain could not maintain her initial momentum in the face of developments elsewhere. Somewhere in the final quarter of the nineteenth century the British economy began to run out of steam just at the time when the growth potential of other countries, notably Germany and the United States, and to a lesser extent Japan, France, Italy and Sweden, was coming on stream. The extent and causes of the slowing down or 'climacteric' in growth before 1914 are still the subject of lively debate, but there can be little doubt that the British economy did falter in the decades prior to the First World War with the result that Britain's market shares began their long-term decline. Moreover, it has been recognized that in this period the economy suffered from certain structural weaknesses which were to act as a drag on performance into the twentieth century. The war of 1914–18 had, on balance, adverse effects and since that time the economy has continued, with short intermissions, notably in the 1930s, on a steady downward trend.

In long-term historical perspective Britain's post-war growth performance, at least until the early 1970s, has been fairly respectable. But in comparison with nearly all other modern industrial countries it has been a near disaster, with a rate of growth in total output of about one half the general average. Thus, from being one of the richest countries in Europe at the end of the Second World War, Britain had, by the later 1970s, become one of the poorest in terms of per capita income, and if past relative performance continues she is destined to be overtaken eventually by any and every country which steps over the threshold of modern economic growth. It is indeed a most remarkable achievement, the more remarkable when one considers the enormous comparative advantages, in terms of production equipment, skills, technological know-how, commercial and financial services and the like, which this country possessed in 1945. In Professor Pollard's words: 'There has been no failure like it known to world economic history. The decline of Spain, Portugal, Geneva or Venice, in their time, perhaps the closest parallels, took over a century in each case to accomplish what we have achieved in thirty years'.[2]

### The growth failure

A century or more ago Britain had one of the highest income levels in the world – perhaps only exceeded on a per capita basis by Australia and for rather special reasons. It can scarcely be doubted that in the early nineteenth century she stood alone in terms of per capita income given her enormous industrial lead. Today, of course, the position is very different. After possibly one of the largest relative declines in economic strength ever recorded, Britain now has one of the lowest income levels of the major industrial nations.

Measuring growth and welfare is not an easy task, especially over long periods of time. The farther one goes back in time the less reliable are the data, while problems of inter-country comparisons are notoriously difficult even for the contemporary period. There is also the additional difficulty of deciding what data to use to serve as reliable indicators of progress and performance. Probably the most useful in this context is some measure of income or output per head which, while lacking distributional properties, does provide a broad picture of the aggregate pattern of change over time.

In fact there is little need to quibble over much about the problems of measurement or the indicators selected in the British context, since whatever the basis of measurement employed one comes up with the same depressing result: that for a century or more Britain's economic performance has not matched, or even closely approached for much of the time, that of her major competitors.[3] In two recent articles on long-term growth in sixteen countries (which accounted for some 60 per cent of world output in the 1970s), Maddison[4] found that Britain had one of the lowest rates of growth in total output and in output per head since the 1870s. At that time Britain produced a fifth of the output of the group of countries and ranked second in terms of the level of per capita output. By the 1970s however, she accounted for less than 7 per cent of the combined output and her ranking had dropped to fifteenth place.

The data in the following tables amply demonstrate Britain's changed position.

Taking the century as a whole (1870–1976), Britain's rate of growth of total domestic output per head was less than three quarters of the average for the 16 countries (see Table 2.1). A breakdown into sub-periods reveals that only in one instance, the period 1929–50, did this country manage to exceed the combined rate for the

Table 2.1  Rates of growth of total GDP, population and GDP per head 1870–1976

|  | Total GDP | Population | GDP per head |
|---|---|---|---|
| UK | 1.8 | 0.55 | 1.3 |
| USA | 3.5 | 1.60 | 1.9 |
| France | 2.2 | 0.31 | 1.9 |
| Germany | 2.5 | 0.43 | 2.0 |
| Italy | 2.3 | 0.70 | 1.6 |
| Japan | 3.8 | 1.12 | 2.6 |
| Belgium | 2.1 | 0.63 | 1.5 |
| Netherlands | 2.7 | 1.27 | 1.4 |
| Canada | 3.8 | 1.76 | 2.0 |
| Australia | 3.2 | 2.03 | 1.1 |
| Switzerland | 2.4 | 0.83 | 1.6 |
| Austria | 2.6 | 0.48 | 2.1 |
| Sweden | 3.0 | 0.64 | 2.3 |
| Denmark | 2.9 | 0.99 | 1.9 |
| Norway | 2.9 | 0.80 | 2.1 |
| Finland | 3.1 | 0.94 | 2.2 |
| All countries | 2.8 | 0.94 | 1.8 |

Source   Maddison, A. (1977) 'Phases of Capitalist Development', *Banca Nazionale del Lavoro Quarterly Review*, 121.

Table 2.2   Gross domestic product per head at US 1970 prices 1870–1976 ($000s)

|  | 1870 | 1913 | 1929 | 1950 | 1960 | 1970 | 1976 |
|---|---|---|---|---|---|---|---|
| Australia | 1341 | 1942 | 1757 | 2364 | 2801 | 3814 | 4280 |
| Austria | 412 | 1059 | 1130 | 1133 | 1992 | 3000 | 3713 |
| Belgium | 951 | 1487 | 1781 | 1925 | 2441 | 3759 | 4515 |
| Canada | 619 | 1466 | 1644 | 2401 | 2892 | 4042 | 4882 |
| Denmark | 536 | 1315 | 1499 | 1923 | 2445 | 3642 | 4082 |
| Finland | 399 | 743 | 928 | 1364 | 1999 | 3201 | 3814 |
| France | 670 | 1219 | 1547 | 1752 | 2504 | 3917 | 4697 |
| Germany | 523 | 1048 | 1212 | 1343 | 2607 | 3846 | 4359 |
| Italy | 537 | 756 | 883 | 981 | 1616 | 2575 | 2869 |
| Japan | 273 | 517 | 756 | 624 | 1300 | 3261 | 4155 |
| Netherlands | 954 | 1254 | 1654 | 1858 | 2550 | 3760 | 4304 |
| Norway | 489 | 854 | 1186 | 1866 | 2408 | 3582 | 4549 |
| Sweden | 416 | 998 | 1436 | 2234 | 2924 | 4263 | 4748 |
| Switzerland | 806 | 1345 | 1996 | 2337 | 3145 | 4155 | 4199 |
| USA | 774 | 1815 | 2362 | 3223 | 3720 | 4789 | 5385 |
| UK | 956 | 1468 | 1582 | 2061 | 2598 | 3233 | 3583 |
| Average | 666 | 1205 | 1460 | 1836 | 2478 | 3677 | 4258 |
| UK as % of average | 143.5 | 121.8 | 108.4 | 112.3 | 104.8 | 87.9 | 84.2 |

Source   Maddison, A. 'Phases of Capitalist Development', *Banca Nazionale del Lavoro Quarterly Review*, 121, p. 126.

sixteen countries (see Table 2.3). In all other periods her performance fell well below the average, though until the 1960s it hovered within the 70–80 per cent range.

The most dramatic deterioration undoubtedly occurred after the Second World War. At the end of the reconstruction period, in 1950, Britain's international growth ranking, though certainly somewhat lower than in the 1870s, was still reasonably respectable since the level of domestic product per head was about 12 per cent higher than the average for all the countries listed. Apart from the United States, she was surpassed only by Australia, Canada, Sweden and Switzerland, and then fairly modestly. Yet a generation later, in 1976, she had dropped to fifteenth place (Italy being at the bottom) and her level of domestic product per head was only 84 per cent of the combined average. The really big collapse occurred in the 1960s when Britain's growth rate was only 55 per cent of the average, while even for the period as a whole (1950–76) it was only 60 per cent.

If we compare the UK with the whole of Europe (both West and East) the post-war collapse appears even more pronounced. Using data compiled by Bairoch[5] (see Tables 2.4 and 2.5), it can be seen that the level of per capita GNP in Britain remained constantly above the European average, at around 180 per cent, throughout the period 1860–1950. This more favourable outcome reflects of course the poor show-

Table 2.3   *Annual growth rates of the volume of GDP per head: UK and sixteen countries 1870–1976*

| Period | UK | Average of sixteen countries | UK as % of sixteen countries |
|---|---|---|---|
| 1870–1913 | 1.0 | 1.4 | 71.4 |
| 1913–1950 | 0.9 | 1.1 | 81.8 |
| 1913–1960 | 1.3 | 1.6 | 81.3 |
| 1913–1976 | 1.4 | 2.1 | 66.7 |
| 1929–1950 | 1.3 | 1.1 | 118.2 |
| 1950–1960 | 2.3 | 3.0 | 76.7 |
| 1960–1970 | 2.2 | 4.0 | 55.0 |
| 1970–1976 | 1.6 | 2.4 | 66.7 |
| 1950–1970 | 2.3 | 3.5 | 65.7 |
| 1950–1976 | 2.1 | 3.3 | 63.6 |
| 1960–1976 | 2.1 | 3.5 | 60.0 |
| 1870–1950 | 1.0 | 1.3 | 76.9 |
| 1870–1960 | 1.2 | 1.5 | 80.0 |
| 1870–1976 | 1.3 | 1.8 | 72.2 |

Source   Derived from data in Table 2.2.

Table 2.4   *Volume of per capita gross national product at market prices: UK and Europe (in 1960 US dollars and prices) 1830–1973*

| | 1830 | 1860 | 1913 | 1929 | 1950 | 1970 | 1973 |
|---|---|---|---|---|---|---|---|
| UK | 360 | 584 | 996 | 1038 | 1352 | 2079 | 2284 |
| Europe | 240 | 310 | 534 | 571 | 749 | 1828 | 2077 |
| UK as % of Europe | 150.0 | 188.4 | 186.5 | 181.8 | 180.5 | 113.7 | 110.0 |

Source   Bairoch, P. (1976) 'Europe's Gross National Product: 1800–1975', *The Journal of European Economic History*, 5 (Fall), p. 307.

Table 2.5    Annual growth rate of the volume of per capita gross national product at market prices: UK and Europe
1830–1973

|  | 1830–1913 | 1913–1950 | 1950–1973 | 1830–1973 | 1913–1973 |
|---|---|---|---|---|---|
| UK | 1.23 | 0.83 | 2.31 | 1.30 | 1.39 |
| Europe | 0.97 | 0.92 | 4.53 | 1.52 | 2.29 |
| UK as % of Europe | 126.8 | 90.2 | 51.0 | 85.5 | 60.7 |

Source   Bairoch, P. (1976) 'Europe's Gross National Product: 1800–1975', *The Journal of European Economic History*, 5 (Fall), p. 309.

ing of Eastern Europe in the first half of the twentieth century. However, between 1950 and the first half of the 1970s this country's lead dwindled rapidly, to about 10 per cent above the European level, and since then the position has deteriorated further. This sharp decline came about as a result of the rapid acceleration in growth throughout Europe in the post-war period. Until 1913 Britain's growth of GNP exceeded that for the whole of Europe, while even in the period 1913–50 it was still some 90 per cent of the latter. By contrast, during the most recent period, 1950–73, it was only just about half that of the European continent.

The main focus of attention in this paper is with the events of the recent past, that is the period since the Second World War. There are several reasons for so doing. In the first place, the author has already dealt with earlier periods elsewhere and it would be pointless to traverse the same ground again. Second, though Britain's relative decline began a century ago, it should be recognized that, given the commanding lead established by this country in the first half of the nineteenth century, it was inevitable that some loss of output and trade shares would ensue as other countries began to industrialize in a serious way. Third, the magnitude of the post-war decline would seem to provide ample justification for concentrating one's attention on this period. And finally, while there may well have been weaknesses in the British economy before 1939, and before 1914 for that matter, the present writer is not fully convinced that one can simply explain away the dismal record of the more recent years in terms of root causes, though no doubt these did have some lagged effect. However, given Britain's relatively strong position at the end of the Second World War it would seem more plausible to argue that the responsibility for the recent growth failure lies primarily with the post-war generation of British people and that to attribute it to the mistakes of our forefathers is merely shifting the burden of guilt from those on whom it should rest. After all, whatever the mistakes of the past, a generation is a reasonably sufficient time-span in which to revitalize or strangle an economy. The British have undoubtedly demonstrated their skill in the latter respect.

### The supply problem

It is far easier to outline Britain's growth problem than it is to provide a rational and logically balanced explanation for it. Not that there is any shortage of explanations, ranging from hard-line economic variables to sociological interpretations including such intangibles as the British Disease and the British National Character.

No doubt there are many relevant factors but the difficulty lies in the lack of specification as to their individual quantitative importance. Moreover, much of the reasoning has often involved a degree of circularity. A further difficulty lies with the time period under discussion. From the end of the reconstruction period, *circa* 1950, to the early 1970s, most major industrial countries enjoyed 'super-growth', moderate inflation, low unemployment and buoyant trade. This favourable environment deteriorated rapidly after the strong boom of 1972–73 and the rest of the decade was characterized by high inflation, rising unemployment, lower growth and periodic shocks largely generated by energy problems. Clearly, therefore, the period as a whole cannot be regarded as a unity though one should be wary of over-emphasizing the break in trend in all respects. It is true that Britain, along with other countries, operated in an increasingly hostile environment in the 1970s. On the other hand, the problems of the 1970s may have had a greater impact on a relatively weak and vulnerable economy, such as that of the UK, while domestic policies may also have aggravated the country's economic position.

If one approaches the growth problem from the supply side – namely factor inputs (capital and labour) and productivity, the proximate reasons for Britain's slow growth can be fairly readily identified. It can first of all be located in the industrial and services sectors which accounted for the bulk of total output. Agriculture was only a very small component of national income at the beginning of the period – and an even smaller one at the end – while its post-war performance was eminently respectable in comparison with that of other countries.[6] The strong growth in productivity contrasts sharply with that in the industrial and service sectors.

The central fact to emerge from Table 2.6 is that the growth in labour inputs and also output per employee were much lower in the industrial and service sectors in Britain than in other countries during the period 1950–76. Industry, which Cornwall regards as the main engine of growth,[7] had a relatively weaker growth performance and employment actually fell slightly, whereas the service sector made a significant addition to its workforce and had a better relative performance in output and productivity growth. The low overall rate of employment growth in the non-agricultural sectors *vis-à-vis* other countries may be attributed to three factors: a low rate of population growth, the limited influx of foreign workers and the small net contribution made by agriculture. Most other countries secured greater gains, either individually or in combination, from these three labour supply augmenting factors than did Britain.

Was Britain's development therefore retarded by a shortage of manpower? It has several times been argued that elastic labour supplies are favourable to growth. Kindleberger, for example, using the Lewis model, maintains that many European fast-growers benefited considerably from good supplies of labour.[8] Knox goes further and asserts somewhat dogmatically that the differences in the growth of the non-agricultural labour supply between Britain and other major industrial nations were so great as to render further discussion of the low UK growth rate almost superfluous.[9]

Table 2.6  Rate of growth of GDP, output per employee and employment by sector 1950–76

| | Gross domestic product | | | | Output per employee | | | | Rate of growth of employment | | | |
|---|---|---|---|---|---|---|---|---|---|---|---|---|
| | Agriculture | Industry | Services | Total GDP | Agriculture | Industry | Services | Total GDP | Agriculture | Industry | Services | Total GDP |
| Austria | 2.2 | 5.7 | 4.6 | 5.1 | 6.0 | 5.2 | 2.9 | 5.1 | −3.8 | 0.5 | 1.7 | 0.0 |
| Denmark | 0.7 | 4.1 | 3.8 | 3.6 | 3.7 | 3.6 | 1.6 | 2.8 | −3.0 | 0.5 | 2.2 | 0.8 |
| Finland | 1.4 | 5.3 | 5.0 | 4.7 | 5.6 | 4.1 | 1.9 | 4.3 | −4.2 | 1.2 | 3.1 | 0.4 |
| France | 1.4 | 5.7 | 4.6 | 4.9 | 4.7 | 5.0 | 2.8 | 4.4 | −3.3 | 0.7 | 1.8 | 0.5 |
| Germany | 2.0 | 6.2 | 4.9 | 5.4 | 5.8 | 5.4 | 2.9 | 4.7 | −3.8 | 0.8 | 2.0 | 0.7 |
| Italy | 2.2 | 6.6 | 4.4 | 4.9 | 5.6 | 4.3 | 1.8 | 4.2 | −3.4 | 2.3 | 2.6 | 0.7 |
| Japan | 2.5 | 11.6 | 7.8 | 8.7 | 6.2 | 8.3 | 4.0 | 7.2 | −3.7 | 3.3 | 3.8 | 1.5 |
| Netherlands | 3.0 | 5.7 | 4.2 | 4.5 | 4.8 | 5.3 | 2.0 | 3.5 | −1.8 | 0.4 | 2.2 | 1.0 |
| Norway | 0.8 | 4.6 | 4.9 | 4.3 | 4.3 | 3.7 | 2.3 | 3.4 | −3.5 | 0.9 | 2.6 | 0.9 |
| Sweden | 0.8 | 4.1 | 3.9 | 3.5 | 4.6 | 3.9 | 1.6 | 2.8 | −3.8 | 0.2 | 2.3 | 0.7 |
| USA | 1.8 | 3.7 | 3.8 | 3.3 | 5.1 | 2.8 | 1.4 | 1.8 | −3.3 | 0.9 | 2.4 | 1.5 |
| UK | 1.9 | 2.3 | 2.4 | 2.4 | 4.0 | 2.6 | 1.3 | 2.3 | −2.1 | −0.3 | 1.1 | 0.2 |
| Arithmetic average | 1.7 | 5.5 | 4.5 | 4.7 | 5.0 | 4.5 | 2.2 | 3.9 | −3.3 | 1.0 | 2.3 | 0.8 |

Source  Maddison, A. (1979) 'Long Run Dynamics of Productivity Growth', *Banca Nazionale del Lavoro Quarterly Review*, 128 (March).

That Britain's employment grew slowly there can be no doubt, but to sustain the above argument one would first have to demonstrate that the British economy was seriously hampered by a scarcity of labour. It is true that labour bottlenecks did occur at the peaks of the cycle, while there have been numerous studies suggesting that Britain suffered from shortages of skilled labour, notably in engineering, and also managerial talent. But it would be difficult to lend support to a generalized labour supply thesis in the British context for the following reasons. First, even in the boom periods, although labour supplies were sometimes tight there were other and more important constraints on growth, namely capacity bottlenecks due to low investment and, more important, the constraint imposed by the deterioration in the balance of payments. Unlike Germany and Japan, Britain, as Thirlwall has demonstrated, usually hit a balance of payments ceiling before one of capacity, though it may of course be argued that the long-term solution to the former was partly dependent on some capacity adjustments. Second, since manufacturing industry is generally reckoned to have been seriously overmanned in this period there was obviously a ready solution to any serious labour supply problem. A serious demanning exercise would not only have released labour but it would also have pushed up productivity to the benefit of Britain's competitiveness in overseas markets and in terms of import substitution. Third, it would be extremely difficult to invoke the labour supply thesis for the 1970s when high unemployment levels indicated substantial labour reserves.

If we glance again at Table 2.6 it becomes clear that the main source of rapid growth in most European countries, especially in industry, was derived from productivity improvements rather than labour inputs. Employment growth accounted for only 17 per cent of the combined GDP growth of 4.7 per cent per annum and 8.3 per cent in the case of Britain. Several countries, moreover, had below average employment growth yet did well in terms of output growth. Austria is a good example since there was no overall increase in employment and only a relatively modest rise in the industrial sector, yet that country's growth performance was above average. A purely mechanical arithmetic exercise would suggest that had Britain's total employment grown at the same rate as the average, 0.8 per cent per annum instead of 0.2 per cent, the effect would have been to raise the GDP growth rate to 3 per cent as against 2.4 per cent a year, assuming no change in productivity. This may appear a strong assumption, yet there is no valid reason to suppose that larger labour inputs would automatically have resulted in higher productivity growth; indeed, they may well have depressed it by weakening further the incentive to invest and innovate in labour saving projects. Conversely, had Britain achieved a productivity growth rate similar to the average for the twelve countries, then her GDP growth rate would have worked out at 4.1 per cent per annum, or not far short of the 4.7 per cent recorded by the twelve countries.

In this aggregate analysis we have of course ignored one important feature and that is the distributional shifts of employment between sectors. It is the growth of non-agricultural employment which is of special significance in this period and many European countries gained in this respect from having a large quantity of manpower in low productivity agriculture which could be transferred to other sectors of the economy without detriment to agricultural output. The service sector in particular benefited from this outflow of labour since because of the poor productivity growth in many branches of this sector labour inputs were a more important source of growth than in manufacturing. If Britain had had a similar reservoir of labour on which to draw so that employment growth in both industry and services could have matched the average, then both these sectors would have expanded at about 3.6 per cent per annum. The assumption here is that there would have been no constraints on utilising the additional labour to achieve the higher growth which is clearly not very plausible. While this is certainly an improvement, we may note that industrial growth would still have been nearly two percentage points below the average. Moreover, it is clear from the experience of Austria, the Netherlands and Sweden that low employment growth, and in industry in particular, was no bar to high productivity growth and fast overall growth. This point is given added weight in the British context in view of the degree of overmanning and inefficiency in many branches of industry.

It would be rash to argue that a larger non-agricultural labour supply would not have made any additional contribution to Britain's growth. Probably its greatest impact would have been in the service sector. But for reasons already stated, we doubt whether it was the key to Britain's post-war growth problem. Higher growth could have been achieved within the existing labour situation. The real source of the lag is to be found in the low rate of productivity growth and ultimately in the level of investment and innovation especially in manufacturing industry.

It is a well-known fact that Britain has had a low rate of investment; throughout the post-war period the share of total income invested has been well below that of the major industrial nations. Even more relevant is the fact that the capital stock per employee has grown very slowly and, as Table 2.7 demonstrates, there is a close association between investment per head and productivity per worker. Countries with the most rapid growth in plant and equipment per employee tended to have the fastest rates of productivity growth. This reflects not only the direct effects on productivity from using more capital per worker, but also the higher rate of technical

Table 2.7   *Productivity and capital stock growth, 1963–74*

|  | Rate of growth of output per employee | Rate of growth of capital stock per employee |
|---|---|---|
| Belgium | 4.3 | 3.8 |
| Canada | 2.2 | −0.3 |
| Denmark | 2.9 (1965–74) | 2.6 (1965–74) |
| France | 4.1 | 5.6 |
| Germany | 4.2 | 4.6 |
| Italy | 5.3 | 5.0 |
| Japan | 11.3 | 10.2 |
| Netherlands | 4.1 | 4.5 |
| UK | 2.7 | 2.0 |
| US | 1.4 (1963–73) | 0.5 |

Source   Stein, J.P. and Lee A. (1977) *Productivity Growth in Industrial Countries at the Sectoral Level, 1963–1974.*

innovation associated with rapid capital accumulation. Conversely, countries which accumulate slowly will tend to have an ageing capital stock, they will derive less benefit from innovation and therefore they will experience low productivity growth and reduced international competitiveness. This in turn will adversely affect trade performance and eventually lead to a balance of payments growth constraint. In other words, export-led growth can only be enjoyed by those countries which are able to supply goods to the world market on competitive terms.

Not only has capital investment grown more slowly in Britain but on average workers in this country have had considerably less equipment per head to operate than their European and Japanese counterparts. There are also indications that the existing capital stock in Britain is not used as efficiently as it might be. Furthermore, there may well have been a misallocation of investment resources in the post-war period especially in so far as a large amount of capital has been directed to the public sector where the returns are low compared with manufacturing. On average some 40–50 per cent of gross fixed investment has occurred in the public sector with public corporations and local authorities accounting for the bulk of this share. In 1970 public corporations alone had £12.3 billion worth of investments or £6400 per employee, as against £21.8 billion and £1160 per head in the private sector. Yet in terms of employment creation and income generation per pound of investment the private sector was five to six times more productive than the public corporations.[10]

While it would be misleading to argue that such disparities in performance fairly reflect the degree of misallocation of resources, the data do raise some doubts as to whether the public sector (where market signals are only partially operative, and sometimes non-existent) has not absorbed too large a share of total investment. We shall return to this question in the next section.

For the moment there is one final question to be raised in this section, and that is why investment in Britain has been so low. The most obvious, but by no means only, reason is the steady deterioration in profitability. Several countries have experienced declining rates of return on assets, especially in recent years, but the extent of the downward shift has been considerably more pronounced in Britain.[11] Moreover, throughout the post-war period the percentage return on assets has been much lower than in many other countries, for example, Germany, Japan and France, and by the 1970s it had reached miniscule proportions. The relative deterioration may of course partly reflect the low rate of investment and innovation and also inefficient use of the existing capital stock.[12] A further factor however is the high proportion of corporate sector income going to wages and salaries. The wage–income ratio has been rising steadily in most countries in the post-war period but the upward shift has been most pronounced in the UK. By the mid 1970s the wage–income ratio in Britain had risen to around 82 per cent (as against 71 per cent in the early 1950s) compared with an average of 72 per cent for seventeen industrial countries. According to Paldam, capital's share of income may now be too low to generate a full employment rate of growth of between 3–4 per cent per annum.[13]

The proximate cause of Britain's growth failure in the post-war period can therefore be attributed to an inadequate rate of investment rather than a shortage of labour. This in turn led to a slower rate of innovation and productivity advance than in fast growing economies with attendant consequences in terms of international competitiveness. Competitiveness here is taken to include price and non-price factors both of which deteriorate as investment and innovational response fail to keep up with competitors. Ultimately, failure on the supply side generates a balance of payments growth constraint (see below).

The distribution of investment between sectors may also have been non-optimal in that too great a share went into slow growth sectors and into public sector activities including defence where the returns were low and the innovational spin-off was limited. The low rate of accumulation in the private sector can be attributed in part to the sharp decline in corporate profitability as capital's share of income was squeezed by the rising wage and salary bill.

Two major influences have had an important bearing on the final outcome: government policy and management. Both of these have had adverse consequences. Government policies for the most part were not conducive to a high growth economy, while management's innovational response left much to be desired. These two themes will be discussed in the following sections.


### The policy dimension

No discussion of post-war economic performance would be complete without reference to the role of government policy. The state is now the chief economic agent in the economy of Britain; it dispenses a large share of the nation's resources and it is responsible for the overall management of the economy. On balance the influence of government in economic affairs has tended to increase in the post-war period, though the extent of intervention has varied somewhat depending on which political party has been in power. However, it is doubtful whether the economic policies of any government in this period can be regarded as particularly beneficial from the point of view of economic growth. While the record in terms of employment and stability – at least until the early 1970s – was certainly better than before the war, the consequences of policy in general were detrimental to economic performance and tended to hinder industrial regeneration. Professor Pollard, one of the severest critics, sums up the position as follows:

> ... while Montagu Norman had only 11 years (c1920–1931) to damage the British economy, the Treasury have had over 30 years since the end of the last war. In that period, they have transformed the strongest, the technologically most advanced and most promising of European industrialized economies into the weakest, poorest and most backward. It is an achievement of economic mismanagement unparalleled in the annals of the civilised world. [And the] tragedy is that even today, after over 30 years of the most resounding failure, neither the Treasury nor those who achieved high honours in advising them, seem to have the slightest inkling that there is anything wrong or that they have anything to apologise for.[14]

Whether all the blame for economic failure can be heaped upon the policy-makers is debatable, but there can be no doubt that they have a lot to answer for. We cannot of course examine every aspect of policy in this essay. What we shall do is focus attention on the main implications of macro demand management; in so doing we shall demonstrate not only the adverse consequences in terms of economic performance, but also show that heavy reliance on demand management resulted in a neglect of supply and structural policies to the detriment of the long-term growth potential of the economy.

For much of the period the primary emphasis of economic policy was directed towards demand management. It was basically an employment policy though from time to time it had to be tempered as a result of consequent strains on the balance of payments. Though somewhat modified during the course of the 1970s, under the pressure of serious strains following the crisis and collapse in economic activity after 1973, it was not fully abandoned until the Conservatives came to power in the spring of 1979. It remains to be seen whether this marks a significant turning point in the orientation of economic policy.

The obsession with general demand management policies, both among Treasury officials and politicians, is understandable for two main reasons. First, recollections of the inter-war unemployment situation provided the main thrust for employment stimulation measures. Second, the apparent success of the policies in terms of employment generation and stabilization (though on close inspection the latter remains more doubtful), at least for much of the 1950s and 1960s, ensured that they would be continued. The success was more apparent than real, however, for in part it stemmed from the favourable economic climate of the period to 1973.[15] What was not realized was that such policies entailed serious long-term consequences for the growth of the British economy.

At first glance an employment-determined management policy might appear to be favourable from the point of view of economic growth. In fact, however, it was quite the contrary from the long-term point of view. It involved maintaining the employment level above the natural or sustainable rate and this led, at times, to a rate of growth higher than the equilibrium rate, that is a rate consistent with stability. It was essentially a short-term policy which entailed reflationary boosts to the economy whenever unemployment rose to a critical level, only to be followed by restrictive action once the demand stimulus gave rise to external constraints in the form of balance of payments difficulties. Moreover, the stimulus to activity generally took the form of consumption-led booms rather than investment ones which, given Britain's trading elasticities, not only exacerbated the balance of payments position but also created capacity problems.

Some of the employment-generating measures were ludicrously excessive given the economy's underlying capacity and external constraints. Maudling's dash for growth in the early 1960s, the Heath–Barber boom nearly a decade later, and even the Butler consumer boom of the mid-1950s, were patently excessive; they ran up against capacity bottlenecks but, more important, they led to a rate of growth which was not consistent with external equilibrium. Following Thirlwall's rough approximation for sustainable growth consistent with external stability, that is the export growth rate divided by the elasticity to import ($\frac{x}{\pi}$), the upper bound for the growth in total ouput probably lay within the range $2\frac{1}{2}$–3 per cent per annum.[10] In both the early-1960s and again in the early 1970s GDP growth at the peak (1964 and 1973 respectively) was running at around 6 per cent, at least twice the sustainable rate. Clearly such rates could not be maintained for long without serious external strains and for some years afterwards policy had to be directed towards rescuing the balance of payments by deflationary action. In the latter instance the oil crisis intervened to exacerbate the payments situation though this should not be allowed to obscure the fact that the initial deterioration was caused by irresponsible fiscal and monetary policies which in this case also had serious inflationary implications.[17]

The erratic nature and frequent changes in the direction of policy were not conducive to long-term business investment. Between 1950 and 1975 there were no less than forty-seven changes in consumer credit restrictions, rental deposits and tax levels largely for purposes of demand management, which led to market instability and adversely affected key industries such as cars and consumer durables.[18] The capacity of industry was not sufficient to cope with a sudden rise in consumption, and by the time stimulus to investment came on stream, the policy direction was on the point of being reversed. Demand stimuli tended therefore to result in spillovers into imports.

Surprisingly, little was learned from these episodes; the policy mix continued as before and, as we shall see later, no attempt was made to determine the sustainable growth rate or shift to a supply orientated policy in order to try and raise the rate. First, however, we must look at some of the broader implications of policy management.

Both employment – generating policies and associated welfare measures have involved a rising tide of government spending in the post-war period. Nearly all sectors of government spending have increased faster than total output though the biggest expansion has been in transfer payments. The growth in public spending has been associated with a shift of resources away from manufacturing into the service sectors of the economy, and particularly the public sector which has been the main employment generator in the 1960s and 1970s. Taking the period 1950 to 1976 employment in manufacturing fell slightly whereas in services it rose by one per cent per annum.

A more detailed breakdown of employment shifts since 1961 is given in Table 2.8. Between 1961 and 1978 there was very little growth in total employment but while mining, manufacturing and associated industries (transport and energy) all lost workers, services taken as a whole increased their employment by nearly 29 per cent. Most service activities, apart from distribution, increased their share of the labour market but the largest expansion occurred in public sector employment, both central and local and especially the latter, which rose by no less than 58 per cent (excluding the Armed Forces and public corporations). Inclusive of the latter categories then, total public sector employment rose by nearly one third and by 1978 accounted for almost as many workers as manufacturing. Private sector employment as a whole declined by over one million during this period.

From a welfare point of view the growth in non-manufacturing employment may

*Table 2.8    Employment by sector in UK 1961–78 (mid-year estimates in 000s)*

| | 1961 | 1978 | percentage change 1961–78 |
|---|---|---|---|
| Total employed labour force | 24 457 | 24 928 | 1.93 |
| H.M. Forces | 474 | 318 | −32.91 |
| Civilian employment | 23 983 | 24 610 | 2.61 |
| Agriculture, forestry & fishing | 1098 | 653 | −40.53 |
| Mining and quarrying | 728 | 344 | −52.75 |
| Manufacturing | 8636 | 7423 | −14.05 |
| Construction | 1658 | 1658 | 0.0 |
| Gas, electricity, water | 389 | 349 | −10.28 |
| Transport & communications | 1724 | 1527 | −11.43 |
| Other services | 9749 | 12 547 | 28.70 |
| Total Central Government | 1773 | 2309 | 30.23 |
| of which: National Health Service | 575 | 1175 | 104.35 |
| Total Local Authorities | 1870 | 3013 | 61.12 |
| of which: Education | 785 | 1566 | 99.49 |
| Health & social services | 170 | 334 | 96.47 |
| Total Central & Local Government (excluding Forces) | 3169 | 5004 | 57.91 |
| Public corporations | 2200 | 2061 | −6.32 |
| Total public sector (excl. Forces) | 5369 | 7065 | 31.59 |
| Total public sector (incl. Forces) | 5843 | 7383 | 26.36 |

Source    Semple, M. (1979) 'Employment in the Public and Private Sectors, 1961–78', *Economic Trends*, 313 (November), pp. 90–108.

be regarded as advantageous at a time when employment elsewhere was stagnating, and indeed but for the resilience of the service sector the employment figures for the 1970s would look horrendous.[19] Nor would it be sensible to argue that all the growth in service employment was bad for growth or that it was all determined by government policies. Quite clearly the post-war period has seen a rapid growth in many types of private sector service employment (for example, leisure activities, finance etc.) in most developed economies, reflecting the changing pattern of consumer preferences. Some of these activities moreover (finance, insurance and banking in particular) have been important exporter earners. Similarly, the large expansion of public sector employment can be seen as a response to the growing demand in high income countries for more collective goods, especially welfare security and education. Moreover, while the shift in the share of resources towards the service sector may simply reflect the change in consumer preferences, it does not automatically follow that the private sector, and more particularly manufacturing, has been starved of resources (or 'crowded out') either by service sector growth as a whole or by public sector growth in particular, if at the same time manufacturing was shedding labour because it was becoming more efficient. In fact manufacturing productivity did for a time rise quite sharply though significantly output growth did not keep pace, a situation not dissimilar to the inter-war period when large-scale manpower shedding took place in some of the older basic sectors. The current debate on microchip technology suggests that within the next few decades manufacturing's share of employment will drop even further as the new technology leads to much greater efficiency. The same may be true for some of the service trades with alarming implications for employment prospects.

Notwithstanding these reservations, it may be argued that the shift of resources to the service sector, whatever its determinants, has adversely affected the growth of the economy. For one thing it involved a movement of resources from high to lower productivity growth sectors thus dampening the overall rate of productivity growth. Though productivity levels and growth rates vary considerably between service sectors it is generally accepted that on average both the level of productivity and the potential for productivity growth are lower in services than in manufacturing, though this position may change in the future. Eltis gives two illuminating examples of the inefficiency of public sector employment growth. In the hospital services there was a 51 per cent increase in the number of hospital administrators between 1965 and 1973 but an 11 per cent drop in the number of beds administered. It also took longer for patients to gain admission to hospital, while the real cost of administering each bed rose by 60 per cent. Similarly, in state education employment rose by 54 per cent between 1964–74 yet only 51 per cent of those employed were engaged in teaching, the remaining 49 per cent consisting of administrators, cleaners, cooks, school meals supervisors, clerks, as well as a host of ancillary workers engaged in a variety of non-teaching duties of a vaguely-specified nature.[20] A similar situation exists in many branches of higher education and in local government which are overloaded with superfluous administrators and underemployed ancillary workers.

Secondly, it has raised the volume of non-marketable and non-exportable output while at the same time generating an increased demand for imports on behalf of workers engaged in non-exporting service trades, thus weakening the balance of payments. Third, the rapid rise in service employment, especially in the public sector, may have deprived industry of some of the best brains for creative innovation and management, though the total employment impact on manufacturing has not been serious. For example, the civil service has competed for the country's top talent while defence research has absorbed many key scientists and technologists on work which has relatively little civilian spin-off. Finally, it has created financial problems for both the public and private sectors, a subject which we shall have cause to refer to later in this section.

The main question however is the extent to which public policy has been responsible for lowering Britain's rate of growth. There are several different aspects which are relevant in this context not all of which can be discussed in detail here. In so far as one of the main problems since the war has been the low level of investment it is important to determine the extent to which public spending has affected the investment rate. In a recent study of several countries D. Smith found a positive association between growth and exports and investment and public consumption.[21] Britain's weak performance in exporting arose mainly because of supply constraints which in turn were generated by the low level of investment. At the same time the level of domestic investment was also related to the rise in public consumption, with each 1 per cent increase in the share of public current expenditure (excluding transfers) in national income leading to a 0.2 per cent drop in the rate of economic growth. Since from the mid 1950s the share of narrowly defined public consumption in national income rose by some 4.2 percentage points the overall effect may have been to lower the long-term sustainable rate of growth by between 0.6 to 1 per cent per annum. If so, this would provide further confirmation of the point that demand management policies designed to stimulate growth at $3\frac{1}{2}$–4 per cent a year when employment conditions were weak soon ran up against capacity shortages, not to mention balance of payments constraints, since they diverted resources away from productive ends. Capacity growth in export-earning and import-substitution activities was stifled, while demand generation via public consumption not only contributed little in terms of marketable and exportable output but actually eroded the balance of payments through rising imports.

The impact of total public spending (that is including transfer payments) – running at between 45–50 per cent of total income in the 1970s – on investment has been less pronounced which, as Smith notes, suggests that it may be less harmful for the government to raise taxes and make transfer payments rather than consume resources directly. However, even this course of action has serious implications. It tends to foster consumption at the expense of investment and the balance of payments as income is transferred from savers to those with a high marginal propensity to consume, while it increases the taxation burden of the productive sector in order to finance the transfer payments and an enlarged administrative network. Moreover, the productive sector may be squeezed in two ways: directly by the new financial burdens imposed by the state, and indirectly through enhanced wage pressures as workers try to off-load their share of the burden on to employers. The average worker and taxpayer has, in practice been unwilling to accept the growing burden of state expenditure involved in providing more collective goods and services, which has increased at a faster rate than total income. Indeed, the increased social wage-expenditure on social services and payments financed by the government via deductions from wages, far from being met by any trade-off in the form of lower pay demands, seems to have had the opposite effect as workers attempted to maintain a steady growth in real disposable income in the face of a rising tax burden. Between 1952 and 1975 the amount the government took in tax and insurance contributions from the average worker's pay packet rose from 3 to 23 per cent; these deductions were positively related to higher wage levels especially in the period 1963–75, with every 1 per cent increase in the rate of deduction by the state leading to a 0.85 per cent impact on wage rates. Since the actual wage changes could hardly be justified by the underlying trends in profitability and productivity the ultimate effect of tax-financed spending was to squeeze further the surplus of the productive sector.[22]

In the long-run therefore, a policy designed to raise the share of the public sector – whether via direct public consumption or transfer payments or both – must inevitably reach limits beyond which it will undermine the economic base of the economy by imposing too large a burden on the productive sector. An economy cannot in the face of a dwindling surplus from this sector hope to maintain, let alone increase, the size of its non-productive sector without serious consequences. The long-term implications of such a policy have been outlined clearly by Eltis:

The fact that a growing share of resources to the non-market sector makes economic and social sense does not mean that the rule that the non-market sector must be financed from the surplus of the market sector can be broken. This rule must always be followed by any society which seeks to avoid economic breakdown. A failure to finance the non-market sector from the surplus of the market sector can only result in balance of payments collapse as efforts are made to use the resources of foreigners to provide what a population is unwilling to pay for, or physical shortages of capital as society consumes its seed-corn in the form of extra social services, and so fails to maintain the employment creating capacity of its capital stock.[23]

Thus apart from the domestic implications arising from the shift in resources, the main problem is ultimately the balance of payments. Unless manufacturing can dramatically improve its efficiency, or unless the service sector can take over the exporting role of industry which seems highly unlikely given the market structure of many services, especially public sector ones,[24] then a continued shift of resources towards services and especially those provided by the public sector, provides the recipe for a built-in collapse of the balance of payments. The temporary relief afforded by oil exports only serves to conceal for the time-being the deteriorating position of the non-oil balance.

Before moving on to consider the financial implications of government policies in the 1970s, it might be helpful to provide a more detailed illustration of the consequences of one particular item of state spending. In the previous section we expressed doubt about the large proportion of investment resources absorbed by the public sector on the grounds that it was not as productive as private sector investment. Whether this created financial problems for industry in terms of 'crowding out' is a moot point, at least in the early part of the period, though the rather bigger state funding demands of the 1970s certainly did not ease the financial burden of the private sector (see below). However, one particular field of government spending – that on defence – can be shown to have had several adverse consequences in terms of industrial development. In view of the present government's commitment to increase defence spending by 3 per cent annually over the next few years it may be worth looking at this aspect in greater depth.

It is not without significance that the most successful capitalist economies in the post-war period have been those with small defence industries.[25] The two notable examples are Germany and Japan which have had low defence budgets though these have been rising in recent years. Conversely, the least successful economies, the American and British, have had the largest defence budgets in terms of their incomes. In 1974, Britain's military spending as a proportion of GNP at 5.24 per cent was the second highest after the US, while her R&D military expenditure was higher than that of any other European country and probably ranked third or fourth in the world. Some 7 per cent of manufacturing industry is devoted to defence with some of the largest and well-known firms in both the private and public sector – Plessey, GEC, Racal, Vickers, Ferranti and the British Aircraft Company – heavily involved in defence work.

While it would be too simplistic to equate low investment rates with high defence spending (the British case) and conversely, high investment ratios with low defence capability (Japan and Germany in particular), there can be no doubt that Britain's heavy commitment to this sector, both in the post-war period and in the historical past, has not been particularly beneficial from the point of view of the civilian economy. In a forcefully argued essay Mary Kaldor has recently demonstrated how the structure of the military contracts market has led to an ossification of parts of British industry, a characteristic which extends back to the later nineteenth century. The concentration of several large firms on meeting the specific require-ments of military orders led to a neglect of the commercial application of their innovations which thereby retarded the restructuring of their activities and inhibited entry into new fields. This failure meant that in time these companies became increasingly dependent on defence contracts which absorbed some of the best engineers and scientists and 'channelled technical innovation . . . along a dead end, towards the grotesque combination of complexity, sophistication and conservatism that characterizes much of modern technology'.[26] The commercial civilian spin-off in terms of innovational response has been very limited partly because companies have become obsessed with the technical perfection of specific product requirements, while the total market in the UK has often been too small and specialized either to provide the conditions for entry into volume production for the civilian market, or the technical back-up for those industries which have potential growth possi-bilities. Thus, companies producing electronics have not been able to escape from specialized low-volume production into the mass market for civilian products, while in aircraft production the only really successful commercial venture was the Vickers Viscount. Government inspired efforts to utilize defence-inspired know-how for civilian purposes led to the fiasco of Concorde which proved to be one of the most expensive and least commercial prestige projects of the century.

In view of the events of the more recent past it is important to consider in further detail some of the financial implications of government policy which in one way or another have tended to reduce the growth potential of the British economy. The 1970s were a difficult decade for most countries. Compared with the boom decades of the 1950s and 1960s growth was slower, unemployment higher, inflation much higher, not to mention the severe shocks imposed by energy problems. However, the key issue has been the inflationary pressures and their effects on investment and growth.

The background to the inflationary difficulties of the decade is complex though it can be argued with some degree of certainty that the origins of the problem are not to be found in some exogenous shock such as the oil price hike of 1973–74, but were the outcome of prior overloading of the governmental financial machine.[27] Employment creation was again the main policy objective. In an effort to increase the rate of growth and relieve unemployment the Heath Government resorted to high public spending and a lax monetary policy which provided the basis for double digit monetary growth throughout the 1970s. This fed through into inflation, led to high interest rates and involved tidal waves of gilt sales in an effort to finance the public sector borrowing requirement which rose from almost nothing in 1970 to £10.6 billion in 1975–76.[28] Subsequently the efforts to contain these problems led to retrictive policies including monetary targeting and high interest rates, though there were temporary relaxations. In the early part of the period there was also a severe balance of payments crisis generated by the oil deficit.

The climate of the 1970s was hardly conducive to rapid investment and growth. Apart from the increasing uncertainty created by the events of the period, much of the time was spent in trying to contain the inflationary pressures which meant restrictive policies and high interest rates. These were only partly successful since government spending and debt funding continued at a high level. Thus, with a declining return on private assets, together with the heavy financial demands of the government and high interest rates, it has been increasingly difficult for companies to raise new finance on terms which would be profitable. Indeed, given the unusual conditions in the financial markets, firms lucky enough to have spare cash often found it more profitable to invest it in gilts or place it on loan than to reinvest it in their businesses. Whether in a narrow sense it can be argued that the private sector was 'crowded out' by the government's financial demands is debatable, but it is certain that the overall effect was to make the raising of new finance more expensive.

Perhaps a more serious consequence was the squeeze placed on company liquidity by the flow-on effect of large wage awards in the public sector. One reason for the continued high level of government spending was the readiness of public authorities (both central and local) to implement high wage awards. The reason for this was not wholly political but partly stemmed from the fact that most public sector authorities are not subject to market forces as is the case with the private sector. Thus it is relatively easy to concede high claims which can, up to a point, be financed fairly readily from taxation or borrowing in the case of the central government, or from the rates in the case of local authorities. While some moderation ensued for a time in the middle of the period as a result of the Labour Government's incomes policies, the private sector was forced to keep pace with claims in the public sector. This had a serious effect on company liquidity, particularly recently when companies have been borrowing heavily to finance inflated wage bills, which in turn has exacerbated the problems of controlling the money supply. At the same time of course it has reduced the ability of firms to compete in the world market.

It is unfortunate that the inflation of the 1970s, which was largely though not entirely domestically generated, was not dealt with more effectively. Though the main policy objective in the later 1970s was that of controlling inflation – and to this end traditional demand management policies gave way to monetary control – the authorities baulked at taking quick and rigorous action for fear of the unemployment consequences. Even more unfortunate, and ironic too, is the fact that the Conservative Government, elected in May 1979 on a promise to combat inflation by firm monetary control, should find itself unable to get to grips with money supply growth after more than a year in office. Thus the new growth constraint continued into the 1980s.

It has not been possible to consider every aspect of government policy in this section and the main focus of attention has been on macro-management. However, enough has been said to indicate why post-war policies have not been conducive to a high rate of economic growth. Indeed, both directly and indirectly they have been instrumental in reducing the growth of productive capacity and undermining the balance of payments. And, far from encouraging any restructuring of the industrial sector, they have in fact had the opposite effect with manufacturing diminishing in size over time. The fact that the balance of payments no longer poses a serious growth constraint – at least for the time being due to North Sea oil – should not allow us to forget that the non-oil account is in a very weak state, accentuated in part by the strong oil balance. It is ironic that at the very time when the external constraint was in the process of being eased a new growth constraint – inflation – should appear on the scene. However, this too can be regarded largely as a product of imprudent government policies stretching over most of the 1970s.

Until very recently official preoccupation with employment and welfare objectives gave rise to policies which were largely incompatible with rapid economic growth. 'The over-anxiety of successive governments to improve the record of economic growth has been essentially counter-productive'.[29] In fact, not only did they adversely affect long-term investment and growth but they became increasingly ineffective in achieving their original aims of maintaining employment and stability. Government attempts to spend their way into unrealistic employment and output targets by means of demand management policies led to ever-increasing inflation peaks and higher unemployment troughs through successive stages of each cycle as the power of the instruments weakened over time.[30]

Rather more serious from the long-term point of view was the fact that obsession with demand management policies deflected attention away from the supply side of the economy. This is partly understandable since it was less easy to devise a coherent policy framework for supply management and any policies tended to have a long gestation period. By contrast, demand management was relatively easy to comprehend, policies could be formulated and applied quickly and the results were not too long in forthcoming. This proved an attractive package for officials and politicians with limited economic knowledge and short-term horizons.[31] But the orientation of official policy was also conditioned by the objectives in hand – employment and welfare at the expense of price stability and external equilibrium. The latter were treated as residual objectives to be dealt with from time to time when things really got bad, by methods which only tended to make matters worse for the future rather than providing long-term solutions. Had price stability and external equilibrium been regarded as key objectives – as they were in Germany for much of the post-war period – then the authorities might well have been forced to pay closer attention to supply matters, such as competitiveness, innovation, structural change, etc., solutions to which would eventually have permitted a faster sustainable rate of growth.

Supply considerations were not of course totally absent from the policy agenda but there was never any real attempt to formulate a coherent and rational plan of campaign, merely a hotch-potch of measures and subsidies, often in response to some crisis or impending collapse or determined by prestige considerations, which were either of the wrong sort or proved to be abortive failures. In total they achieved very little in terms of improving economic performance largely because many of the policies were never designed with this purpose in mind and therefore could only be regarded as supply orientated in a negative sense. For example, large sums of money have been pumped into declining or ailing sectors (shipbuilding, steel, cars, though significantly little into textiles) largely for purposes of job preservation, or alternatively, into prestige projects, Concorde for instance, the spin-off from which was very limited indeed.[32] Shipbuilding provides a good illustration in both respects: the notable reluctance of British governments, unlike their French, German and Japanese counterparts, to support risky but potentially-worthwhile innovations, their main contribution being confined to rescuing ailing yards which tended to remain in a sickly state even after the rescue operation had taken place. And 'when they did support the building of a single ship, it was the uneconomic and originally very conservatively designed QE2, fitted with Parsons-designed engines which failed on sea trials'.[33] By contrast, very little state assistance was available for purposes of propagating innovational opportunities in potential or fast-growing industries – note for instance the parsimonious attitude towards micro-chip technology despite Britain's serious lagging in this field. If it is accepted that governments should play an active part in industrial development then its role should be directed towards selecting and fostering innovations and growth industries of the future, not in propping up weak sectors whose long-term viability is beyond redemption in their present form and – in some cases – in any form. Whether, as Mottershead queries, governments can utilize sufficient resources to exert significant leverage on the main economic variables is another matter, but the fact remains that Britain's industrial policies to date have been mainly 'limited to a peripheral role of tidying up at the edges of the economy, rather than providing any central thrust to alter and improve industry's performance and that of the economy as a whole'.[34] There are, of course, many other ways in which governments can provide valuable assistance towards industrial reconstruction – for example retraining programmes – but we cannot enter into detail at this stage.

A broader attempt to get to grips with the supply side of the economy was made in the planning exercises of the 1960s and early 1970s. It was a very half-hearted attempt which ended in ignominious failure, partly because no real consensus emerged as to what should be done, and hence the plans took the form of a patchwork quilt rather than an integrated strategy. Moreover, planning began at an inauspicious time when there was little hope of achieving the targets set, which provided a convenient excuse for abandoning the plans rather than reworking or modifying them. The British experience contrasts sharply with that of France where planning became a way of life and plans were not scrapped as soon as short-term difficulties emerged.

In fact, as Michael Shanks notes, planning was really a prestige gimmick in this country and was never really accepted as a serious branch of policy.[35] Real policy, as far as the British authorities were concerned, was demand management, which had little to do with long-term supply considerations, involving as it did short-term expediency and improvization to outside pressures. Not surprisingly therefore, the policy-makers never attempted to specify what the sustainable rate of growth of the British economy was, let alone implementing any concerted and consistent action designed to raise the rate over the long-term. The failure to face up squarely to the real growth issue, coupled with an almost pathological obsession with demand management policies, have proved to be costly in terms of economic growth.

## Managerial response

The policy mistakes of past governments, and particularly the failure to develop a supply-orientated strategy, would not have been so serious if, as Freeman has pointed out, 'British industrial management had been as strong and efficient as German industrial management in coping with the problems of international competition and the associated technical change. But this is manifestly not the case. In sector after sector long-term weaknesses have become apparent which require concerted long-term strategy to rectify'.[36]

It has been a favourite pastime of the British people to castigate managers and businessmen, to regard them as the villains of the piece; they become the convenient scapegoats when things go wrong, or the wicked capitalists when profits seem too high. Britain does not respect its businessmen as the Germans do theirs, nor has this country got its folk-hero businessmen of the type revered in the United States. One of the reasons for the low status accorded to entrepreneurs is the fact that the British have never fully reconciled themselves to the virtue of the profit motive, profits being regarded as somewhat sinful. Be that as it may, it is easy to become conditioned by such attitudes and to attribute the blame for Britain's poor economic performance to the weak response on the part of management. How far this blame is justified is the question we shall try to answer in this section. We can of course only touch upon selected aspects of the subject and much more work needs to be done at the micro level before a final answer can be provided.

Numerous studies over the past few years point to the fact that the key weaknesses in British industry relate to investment, innovation and productivity, the last being basically determined by the first two. A low rate of investment and a lagging in innovative activity, the two playing an interacting role, have resulted in a low rate of productivity growth and thereby a reduced competitiveness of British goods both in the domestic and overseas markets. The price factor has not been the only problem affecting Britain's competitive strength; indeed, in certain periods Britain probably had a price advantage arising from exchange rate movements, especially in the period after the 1967 devaluation and again following the floating of sterling in 1972. Perhaps an equally if not more important factor, and one which has gained increasing recognition in recent years, is the importance of non-price factors in Britain's ability to market goods: that is the type, quality and technical merit of British products have often been inferior to those of our competitors. The latter defects may, as with the price factor, stem from deficiences in investment and innovation, the combined effect of which has led to supplying Britain the wrong goods in the widest sense of the term.

The overall loss of competitive power is a two-edged weapon: it reduces the ability to sell abroad and it increases the propensity to import foreign goods, both facets of which are amply demonstrated by the steady loss of export shares, and the rising share of manufactured imports over the last two decades. Britain's trade elasticities reveal the loss of competitive strength: they have deteriorated steadily over time and the world's income elasticity of demand for British products has been consistently lower than Britain's income elasticity of demand for the goods of other nations. It is therefore not surprising that Britain's trade account has been a perennial source of trouble in the post-war period. Moreover, it is very difficult for a country, even when presented with some windfall stimulus, to escape from this unfavourable situation except by its own exertions. The export bonanza following the sharp decline in sterling after the float of 1972 did not feed through into the domestic economy in any meaningful way.

Several studies have emphasized the importance of productivity growth and innovative capacity in determining competitive strength. Thus an examination of eighty-two separate industrial sectors, carried out under the auspices of the Department of Employment, revealed a strong association between the growth of exports and higher rates of output and productivity growth. Industries whose productivity rose fastest were able to remain internationally-competitive and enjoyed higher rates of export growth which fed through into output and employment. And in turn, fast-growing output tends to stimulate further productivity growth thereby closing the virtuous circle. Unhappily, many British industries have become locked into the vicious circle of low productivity and low output growth,[37] a situation stemming largely from the low level of investment and the slow pace of innovation.

The importance of technical innovation as the main source of competitive strength has been forcefully argued in a recent study on Britain's industrial performance by the Science Policy Research Unit of Sussex University.[38] Innovative activities were found to be closely associated with export shares in chemicals, durable consumer goods and capital goods, especially the latter where quality rather than price has often been the overriding factor. Apart from aerospace and other public defence related sectors, Britain has few comparative advantages in innovation and during the last two decades Britain's innovative effort has declined noticeably compared with that of other countries, with a consequent widening of the gap. The most disturbing aspect is that in recent years the volume of resources devoted to industrial innovation has declined sharply, as the figures for R & D expenditure demonstrate. It is true that total R & D as a percentage of GDP has compared fairly favourably with that of other major countries but this is largely because of the high proportion of government-backed research on defence and related activities, the relative importance of which has tended to increase in recent years as industry-financed research has declined. In fact in the period 1967–75, Britain was the only major OECD country in which industry-financed R & D activities declined in absolute terms. The decline was fairly widespread, with the exception of chemicals and pharmaceuticals, though by far the worst performance was recorded by mechanical engineering where R & D manpower almost halved and industry-financed R & D expenditure as a percentage of net ouput fell from 2.7 to 1.9 per cent. It is not surprising therefore that mechanical engineering has been one of the weakest performers in international markets in more recent years.

Experience indicates that those firms and industries prepared to commit themselves heavily to innovation will in general be successful, while those which fail to do so will eventually lose their market share and decline. The evidence to date suggests that the innovative response of British industry as a whole has been considerably weaker, especially in recent years, than that of its competitors. There have been notable exceptions but these only serve to prove the rule. Chemicals and pharmaceuticals have held their own on balance largely because of their heavy commitment to research and development of new products. The British achievement in coal-cutting machinery provides a marked contrast with the rest of the machinery sector. It has had an excellent export record as a result of the vigorous enterprise of the principal firm, Anderson Boyes which, in collaboration with the National Coal Board, perfected its short-wall coal cutters, 42 per cent of which were exported in the period 1945–70. British exports of underground coalmining machinery have held up well compared with those of Germany in more recent years, 1965–77, whereas those of the machinery sector as a whole declined from 65 to 45 per cent of the German total.

Similarly, the experience of the textile machinery industry provides further confirmation of the importance of adapting to changing conditions. In general this industry scarcely ranks as a success story with its share of world trade falling from 30 to 11 per cent in the period 1954–75, whereas the German share remained fairly stable at 30 per cent and the Swiss share rose to 15 per cent in the 1970s. Even more disturbing is the fact that by the 1970s many British textile companies were buying foreign machines, not because of the price advantage but primarily because of the technical superiority of the imported products. The failure of many textile machinery-makers to adapt or improve their products to meet changing market demands, or to produce entirely new generations of machinery, is exemplified by the disastrous record of British Northrop which originally pioneered the automatic loom in Europe, and is adequate testimony to the fate of a once successful industry. Those firms or sectors which did make the effort, for example Wilson and Longbottom in developing several specialist looms, had a much better chance of survival.

If the rate of technical innovation is an important determinant of economic success it is important to stress, as Pavitt does, that innovation does not necessarily take place automatically in response to economic growth or a high level of investment. Favourable economic conditions will no doubt induce a greater innovative effort and many new innovations will involve substantial investment. Furthermore, a rapid rate of investment itself will give rise to new developments and improvements in product processes, though the line of causation may often be reversed in cases where the rate of product innovation is high, as in the electronics industry, with the result that investment opportunities and the level of investment will be determined largely by the rate at which new innovations are adopted. Whatever the line of causation it is ultimately the choice of technique which is crucial and the correct choice will depend not only on a firm's in-house technological capability but ultimately on the general level of managerial competence.

Britain's poor track record in innovation can therefore be seen 'as the consequence of an accumulation of discretionary decisions reflecting the conservative characteristics and lack of professional competence of British managers, engineers and workers; relatively little search (i.e. innovative) activity, bad choices, and slow adaptation and learning'.[39]

Not only has British management a poor record with regard to innovation but there is plenty of evidence to suggest that it does not make the best use of the resources which it already has. It is true that manufacturing industry's low level and rate of growth of productivity compared with its major rivals reflects the low capital stock per worker and the slow pace of innovation. Yet industry surveys point to the underutilization of existing resources, with the result that the productivity of factor inputs is low in comparison with that of identical inputs in other countries. The studies are too numerous to quote in full and three examples – clothing, engineering and motor vehicles – must suffice.

A report by the Clothing Industry Productivity Resources Agency covering twenty-two firms in the clothing industry found a number of common weaknesses, including excessive employment especially of indirect staff, poorly-designed wage systems, ineffective quality control, and badly-organized sewing rooms. The average number of support workers in relation to production operatives was as high as 58 to every 100 compared with only 29 per hundred in the one West German company which was studied. It was found that productivity increases of up to 100 per cent were possible in some companies, the average for the group being 42 per cent.[40]

Similar scope for significant productivity improvements were found to exist in many engineering firms after a research team from the University of Birmingham's Department of Engineering made a study of the distribution of time spent by operatives and machines during a working day in forty engineering and metal working firms over the period 1968–72, and a series of follow-up case studies of forty-five firms between 1970–74. On average operatives spent 16 per cent of their working time 'waiting' and 48 per cent in actual production activity, while the machines were idle for no less than 50 per cent of the time. With only relatively small-scale reorganization and technical improvements labour productivity could have been improved instantly by over one-third and capital productivity by at least 100 per cent.[41]

The third example, that of motor vehicles, is all too familiar given the industry's declining fortunes in recent years. The decline has been dramatic since in 1955 Britain had the highest labour productivity in Europe though well below the level achieved in the United States. By the early 1970s, however, output per head was not only below that of 1965 but it was nearly a third lower than that of France, Germany and Italy. In some cases differences of up to 80 per cent were found in the number of man-hours required to assemble similar cars. One of the problems in the British car industry has been underinvestment in capital equipment, particularly in volume car production where annual throughput has been low by international standards. Additional and important factors have been excessive overmanning and the associated failure to secure maximum output from the existing stock of production factors. Thus although labour costs per hour tend to be lower in Britain the unit costs per car assembled are high because of low factor productivity.[42]

The weight of evidence now accumulated in numerous reports and studies seems to leave little doubt that there have been serious failings on the part of British management over a wide sector of the industrial economy. The more difficult task is to explain why this should be so; why, in comparison with other countries, should Britain have been burdened with so many 'sleepers' and so few 'thrusters' in industrial management. It would be tempting to attribute the difference in experience primarily to the more hostile economic environment in this country which has not been conducive to rapid investment and innovative activity. As we argued in the last section, this has certainly not been a negligible factor, but there is the awkward problem of explaining why some sectors and firms, for example GEC, Racal and BTR, have managed to thrive through adversity, while others – such as Dunlop, Courtaulds and Turner and Newall – even when presented with new opportunities, have not been able to launch themselves on to a sustained growth path. The 'thrusters' are few in number and it is possible that they would have succeeded whatever the climate given their able management. There is also the possibility that the swarms of imitating entrepreneurs so familiar to Schumpeter require a favourable environment in which to flourish, but it is a tenuous point which is difficult to verify one way or another, and in any case the line of causation can easily be reversed.

This point may be taken further with somewhat more rewarding results. A recent study by Dunning of the UK's international direct investment throws some light on the relative locational advantages, or rather disadvantages, of the UK for economic enterprise.[43] During the last two decades the UK outward/inward capital stake in manufacturing has risen considerably, in contrast to that of total investment. This partly reflects the tendency for British firms to supply overseas markets from foreign bases (in contrast to West European experience) where they are more efficient, as the relative attractions of the UK as a locational base deteriorate.

Data on profitability show that UK firms operating abroad have had a better record than British firms in the UK, while in the last sixteen years the profitability of both foreign investment by UK firms and investment in the UK by foreign firms has consistently exceeded that of domestic investment by British firms. By the 1970s, UK firms abroad were even outperforming foreign firms in this country in chemicals and electrical engineering. As Dunning observes, this lends some support to the view that the deterioration in the UK economic environment, rather than a lack of technological or managerial expertise, has been responsible for Britain's weak economic performance. But the evidence is by no means unequivocal. Some firms did thrive in the UK environment while foreign firms did better than domestic ones. Moreover, that the UK firms locating abroad were more successful than their domestic counterparts may simply reflect the fact that these were the more enterprising ones which took advantage of the best opportunities.

Notwithstanding the above comments, there are still strong grounds for arguing that, for one reason or another, Britain has suffered from a shortage of the right managerial talent in the post-war period, and most comparisons with other countries tend to be unfavourable. In the 1950s the Industrial Management Research Association was receiving reports from its members that 'not enough men were available with drive and academic qualifications', and that industry tended to choose men for their character rather than their qualifications.[44] The Association, while questioning whether firms were 'choosing too few of the aggressive and sometimes difficult people who provide stimulus, pep and drive', admitted that it was often necessary to create teams of ordinary men since it was not possible to get first rate men for every job.[45] Though industry has been frequently criticized for not recruiting sufficient numbers of men qualified in engineering or some branch of science, one of the problems, then as now, was that of finding enough applicants with such qualifications who were likely to be suitable material for managerial posts. Whether science or engineering graduates make better top managers than those trained in arts, law or accounting is, as Coleman points out,[46] a debatable point, but the scarcity of the former did raise a problem for middle management recruitment and particularly for the production side of industry. Arts graduates did not prove entirely satisfactory substitutes since it was said that they often took years getting over being at the university and 'are commonly not only unabashed but even slightly proud of their complete ignorance of the sciences and this is true of their dons.[47]

Similar problems still appear to exist today. One of the main criticisms emerging from the study of the Sussex Research Unit is the lack of professionalism among British managers.

> While much of British industry has been run by managers possessing few, if any, formal technical and managerial skills, our major competitors' industries have been controlled more often by trained managers possessing a range of such skills. It might be that, as in English cricket, in British industry the days of the amateur are numbered.[48]

Elaborating on the same theme Nuala Swords-Isherwood raises some of the wider educational and social issues relevant to management:

> The major and significant differences between British managers and their rivals in most other countries are in their professionalism, in the number of engineers amongst them, and in their social class. The educational system in Britain is such that the most favoured subjects of study are not those most directly relevant to industry. It has been geared to non-industrial pursuits, and the pinnacle of achievement has been as far removed as possible from production. Signs can still be seen in the unpopularity of industrial careers, with consequences for the quality of industrial entrants, for their competence and for their status. The vicious circle once established is difficult to change, although there is some suggestion that such changes are occurring.[49]

The consequences of Britain's managerial limitations are plain enough and need not be elaborated in detail. Businessmen have concentrated on short-term gains at the expense of long-term growth strategy, they have had a predilection for the quiet life rather than the risk and uncertainty involved in change and they have shown a marked reluctance to keep abreast of the technological frontier. The cumulative effect of the lag in innovation has meant that Britain's product range has steadily but inexorably slid downstream, into less sophisticated, lower unit value goods which face increasing competition from producers in the lesser-developed countries and which are not particularly marketable in the high income countries. Moreover, the conservatism of management has been matched by an equally, if not more, conservative attitude on the part of organised labour, the one reinforcing the other. Austen Albu, commenting on the failure of management in shipbuilding and marine engineering to 'buy out' the restrictive practices of the unions which often made the introduction of new processes unprofitable, notes how 'a vicious circle has been created of initial management conservatism and resistance of workers to change, which in practice reinforces that conservatism. The end of the process has been the unwillingness of better-qualified and more entrepreneurial engineers to enter the industry or, if they do, to leave it for other employment, so reinforcing its decline.'[50]

Why British management should differ from that in other countries is not an easy question to answer. One suspects that it has something to do with society's attitudes, priorities and social values, though it is impossible to estimate in any meaningful way the impact of such influences. General impressions, though inevitably imprecise, do suggest that British people do not rate the pursuit of economic progress as highly as the Americans, Germans or Japanese, and that enterprise and profits are not held in such high esteem as in some other countries. In short, it amounts to a non-growth mentality in a society whose cultural values have shifted in other directions.[51] How one changes these values is difficult to say though it is interesting, by way of historical illustration, to show how the cultural aspect can work in reverse. In the later eighteenth century the Scots directed their attention towards economic effort partly because of the cultural vacuum created by theological disapproval of the creative or imaginary arts. In other words, Calvinist theology became an incentive to action rather than contemplation.[52] It is perhaps too much to hope that divine providence will intervene with a repeat performance two centuries later.

## Conclusion

It is relatively easy to identify the main economic trends in Britain over the past century. Briefly, it can be summed up as a period of almost continuous relative economic decline, and one that has accelerated significantly in the post-war period. Although Britain's economic problems predate the Second World War it is clear that the track record in the more recent period has been conditioned more by contemporary events and actions than by the mistakes of the historical past. The economic variables responsible for the poor performance can be readily stated: namely low investment, slow productivity growth and a noticeable lag in the rate of innovation. These have combined to weaken Britain's competitive strength thereby giving rise to the familiar balance of payments problem. The reasons why these variables behaved in the way they did is still a matter of debate but we would argue that government policy and managerial performance have been largely responsible. Economic policy in general has been detrimental to growth because of its short-term volatile nature and its concentration on demand management at the expense of the supply side of the economy. The rising share of state activity has also had long-term adverse consequences as far as growth is concerned. Management must also share the blame through its conservatism and limited time horizons which have slowed down the rate of investment and innovative activity, though it is also possible that business leaders have been unfavourably influenced both by the economic environment and by the social values and attitudes of a society which has lost its aptitude for economic progress. Economists often fight shy of social explanations because they cannot readily be identified or quantified. Unfortunately it is not possible to explain all economic problems in economic terms without a degree of circular reasoning. It is instructive to note that Sir Alec Cairncross and his co-authors in a recent survey of British manufacturing were ultimately faced with a puzzle in this respect:

> Is it really inescapable that productivity in Britain – and the standard of living – should fall further and further behind the level in the rest of Western Europe: that while our neighbours move up to the American level we alone of the major industrial countries lag behind? Most people feel that anything our continental neighbours do we could do too. Then why don't we? If it is not the government's fault, whose is it? Perhaps we don't rate the importance of faster growth highly enough and we are not prepared to acquiesce in an order of social values that would give higher priority to sheer efficiency and making money? If so, it will be interesting to see what happens when European incomes are twice as high as in Britain and mobility within the Common Market increases.[53]

## Notes

1  This essay is part of a larger study on *Britain's Economic Growth Failure, 1950–1980*, to be published by Harvester Press.
2  POLLARD, S. (1976) 'The British Economic Miracle', *Economics*, p. 1.
3  'No matter what statistics are chosen, the reality of the relative economic decline of Britain is abundantly clear'. CARRINGTON, J.C. and EDWARDS, G.T. (1979) *Financing Industrial Investment*, p. 20.
4  MADDISON, A. (1977) 'Phases of Capitalist Development', *Banca Nazionale del Lavoro Quarterly Review*, 121 (June) and MADDISON, A. (1979) 'Long Run Dynamics of Productivity Growth', *ibid.*, 128 (March).
5  BAIROCH, P. (Fall 1976) 'Europe's Gross National Product: 1800–1975', *The Journal of European Economic History*, 5.
6  Centre for Agricultural Strategy (University of Reading), *The Efficiency of British Agriculture* (Report No. 7, 1980).
7  CORNWALL, J. (1977) *Modern Capitalism*.
8  KINDLEBERGER, C.P. (1967) *Europe's Postwar Growth: The Role of Labor Supply*.
9  KNOX, F. (1976) *Governments and Growth*, pp. 70–4; Cf. NALDOR, N. (1966) *Causes of the Slow Rate of Growth of the United Kingdom*, p. 30.
10  CARRINGTON, J.C. and EDWARDS, G.T. (1979) *Financing Industrial Investment*, pp. 84–5.
11  The data are too extensive to quote here: see HILL, T.P. (1979) *Profits and Rates of Return*, pp. 122–5 and MANISON, L.G. (1978) 'Some Factors Influencing the United Kingdom's Economic Growth Performance', *IMF Staff Papers*, 25, pp. 713–4.
12  Since the mid 1960s there has been a secular fall in output per unit of capital. MANISON, *loc. cit.*, p. 719.
13  PALDAM, M. (1979) 'Towards the Wage-Earner State', *International Journal of Social Economics*, 6, pp. 45–61.
14  POLLARD, S. (20 July 1978) in a Letter to *The Times*.

15 ALDCROFT, D.H. (1980) *The European Economy, 1914–1980*, pp. 252–3.

16 THIRLWALL, A.P. (1980) *Balance of Payments Theory and the United Kingdom Experience.*

17 The broad definition of money supply (M3) exploded upwards and in the two years from December 1971 rose by no less than 60 per cent. MAUNDER, W.P. J. (Ed.) (1980) *The British Economy in the 1970s*, Heinemann Educational Books, p. 41.

18 MAUNDER, P. (Ed.) (1979) *Government Intervention in the Developed Economy*, p. 142.

19 If employment in the service sector of OECD countries had not continued to rise after 1973, unemployment by the later 1970s would have risen to 33.7 million as against 18.2 million. M. Lengellé maintains that a standstill in the growth of service sector employment would have aggravated the economic crisis and provoked a slump of similar magnitude to that of the early 1930s. LENGELLÉ, M. (1979) 'Development of the Service Sector in OECD Countries: Economic Implications', in LEVESON, I. and WHEELER, J.W. (Eds.) *Western Economies in Transition*, p. 155.

20 ELTIS, W. (1979) 'How Rapid Public Sector Growth Can Undermine the Growth of the National Product', in BECKERMAN, W. (Ed.), *Slow Growth in Britain*, p. 126.

21 SMITH, D. (1975) 'Public Consumption and Economic Performance', *National Westminster Bank Quarterly Review*, (November).

22 THORNTON, J.S. (1979) 'The Wage/Tax Spiral in the UK', *The Business Economist*, 11.

23 ELTIS, *op. cit.*, p. 121.

24 See SARGENT, J.R. (1979) 'UK Performance in Services', in BLACKABY, F. (Ed.), De-industrialisation, Heinemann Educational Books, p. 108.

25 This section draws heavily on the very succinct essay by Mary KALDOR on 'Technical Change in the Defence Industry', in PAVITT, K. (Ed.) (1980) *Technical Innovation and British Economic Performance.*

26 KALDOR, *op. cit.*

27 See PARKIN, M. (1980) 'Oil Push Inflation?), *Banca Nazionale del Lavoro Quarterly Review*, 183 (June).

28 Moreover, funding this by the issue of high coupon securities entails a heavy debt servicing burden for the future especially if inflation is reduced. Overall, the rate of interest on the national debt rose from 4.5 to 9.5 per cent between 1970–71 to 1979–80 and will probably exceed 10 per cent in the early 1980s, thereby adding possibly another £1 billion to the PSBR. See RIPPON, G. MP in a Letter to the *Financial Times*, 5 August 1980.

29 CAIRNCROSS, Sir A., KAY, J.A. and SILBERSTON, A. (1977) 'The Regeneration of Manufacturing Industry', *Midland Bank Review*, (Autumn), p. 18.

30 See BRITTAN, S. (1977) *Economic Consequences of Democracy*, p. 100.

31 To be fair, most economists, while recognizing the importance of technical change, have fought shy of formulating supply management policies, and have been content to interpret their responsibility in traditional demand management terms. Thus, conventional thinking gets built into the system out of which it is difficult to break. The only group with a recognizable supply policy orientation is the Left of the Labour Party but unfortunately their policies command limited acceptance since they are associated with the extension of public ownership, among other things.

32 Subsidies to privately-owned firms between 1974–75 and 1977–78 (at 1977 survey prices) totalled £1849 million, MAUNDER, P. (Ed.) (1979) *Government Intervention in the Developed Economy*, p. 155.

33 ALBU, A. in PAVITT, K. (Ed.) (1980) *Technical Innovation and British Economic Performance*, pp. 176–7.

34 MOTTERSHEAD, P. (1978) 'Industrial Policy' in BLACKABY, F. (Ed.) *British Economic Policy 1960–1974*, p. 483.

35 SHANKS, M. (1977) *Planning and Politics: The British Experience, 1960–76*, p. 89.

36 FREEMAN, C. 'Government Policy' in PAVITT (Ed.), *op. cit.*, p. 312.

37 WRAGG, R. and ROBERTSON, J. (1978) 'Britain's Industrial Performance Since the War', *Department of Employment Gazette*, (May).

38 PAVITT, K. (Ed.) (1980) *Technical Innovation and British Economic Performance.*

39 PAVITT, *op. cit.*, p. 9.

40 *Financial Times* (21 March 1980); for further examples see ALDCROFT, D.H. (1979) *The East Midlands Economy*, p. 45.

41 See GOMULKA, S. in BECKERMAN, W. (Ed.) (1979) *Slow Growth in Britain*, p. 176. and LAWRENCE, P. (1980) *Managers and Management in West Germany*, p. 129.

42 CAIRNCROSS, *loc. cit.*, p. 10.

43 DUNNING, J.H. (1979) 'The UKs International Direct Investment Position in the Mid-1970s', *Lloyds Bank Review*, 132 (April).

44 Cf. COLEMAN, D.C. (1980) *Courtaulds: An Economic and Social History*: Vol. 3, *Crisis and Change 1940–1965*, p. 300. Coleman notes that the chairman of Courtaulds, Hanbury-Williams, and some of his closer colleagues, tended to be impressed by the 'right sort of people' or 'good chaps'.

45 The senior management of one firm often described themselves as 'a triumph of mediocrities'. Industrial

Management Research Association, Meeting on Recruitment of Staff, London, 9 June 1955. *Ward Papers*, Business History Unit (LSE).

46 COLEMAN, *op. cit.*, p. 229.

47 Ward Papers, W/1/55–59. Box 4, Slip 262, 24 September 1956. I should like to thank John Martin of Leicester Polytechnic for references to the Ward Papers.

48 ROTHWELL in PAVITT, *op. cit.*, p. 306.

49 *Ibid.*, pp. 93–5.

50 PAVITT, *op. cit.*, p. 181.

51 A personal experience of the different attitudes to business, while impressionistic, is nevertheless illustrative. On visiting Germany one of the first sites to be shown by German hosts is more than likely to be some vast chemical, steel or other industrial complex presented with great pride. Foreign visitors to this country would tend to be shown (by their English hosts) some medieval church, baronial estate, workman's cottage or taken to a museum. An industrial complex would be last on the list, if at all, and then it would be denigrated as an aesthetic monstrosity or environmental hazard!

52 CAMPBELL, R.H. (1980) *The Rise and Fall of Scottish Industry, 1707–1939*, p. 28.

53 CAIRNCROSS, *loc. cit.*, p. 18.

# 2
## The Education and Training
## of Manpower

# Laying the Foundations: Schools and Industry

*Catherine Avent*[1]

There has probably never been a time when so much has been spoken and written about contacts between schools and industry, about the standards of young people leaving schools and their employability and about the image which wealth-creating industry seems to have among teachers. There are many reasons for this, particularly the impetus given to careers education and guidance in the last decade: reports have been issued on the subject from the Department of Education and Science; and the vast expansion of higher education consequent upon the recommendations of the Robbins Report (1963) has meant that employers are recruiting young people directly from school, with lower attainments and potential than was the case in previous generations. This has led to complaints on the part of recruiting and training managers that young people do not have an appropriate basis of communication skills, numeracy and attitudes suitable for industrial employment. So we start with an established public concern about the relationships between the schools and industry.

Representatives of many professions can be heard lamenting the apparent prejudice of secondary school teachers, pupils and parents against entry to their occupation! This is nothing new. People claim that teachers portray industrial employment as dirty, noisy, dangerous, involving long or unsocial hours, short holidays, low pay, strife and hassle! Stories are constantly told of parties of school pupils visiting factories and then being warned that if they do not do well in their examinations their fate will be to join an apparently disconsolate workforce! There are probably no more environmentally-unpleasant factories than there are schools with buildings put up during the last century, and certainly most influential people in industry and commerce are parents for part of their working lives and have direct experience of the good buildings provided for many schools and the exciting range of subjects within the curriculum. So it is important at the beginning to set on one side the old-fashioned images which schools and industry may have of each other . . . this of course would be easier if the media did not so consistently portray images of

---

[1] The opinions expressed in this chapter are the author's own, and are not necessarily those of the ILEA, by whom she is presently employed.

blackboard jungles and dark satanic mills.

There is no doubt, however, that many young people say that their teachers positively discouraged them from considering careers in industry and in particular of taking the necessary education to fit them for a branch of the engineering profession. A great deal more contact does take place nowadays at local levels and in many areas teachers and industrialists meet regularly to discuss, for example, the industrial applications of mathematics at different levels so that boys and girls in the classroom can be given exercises based upon industrial problems. Any such contact must increase mutual understanding. It is dangerous to speculate about attitudes but it can fairly be said that wherever good contact is made between teachers and representatives of other professions there is a likelihood that more sympathetic attitudes will result.

It is hard to tell why some careers have apparent glamour in the eyes of young people. Architecture has always had a more attractive image to those with little experience of it than, for example, surveying or civil engineering; medicine attracts more applicants than dentistry; and veterinary science has reaped the harvest of popular books and television plays.

Research into the attitudes of school pupils has been undertaken for many years and perhaps the earliest relevant to this theme is that of Donald Hutchings at Oxford who surveyed the attitudes of sixth form boys in 1963. Amongst the most prestigious professions and those thought to offer good pay and attract intelligent recruits were – in the eyes of these boys – a career as a doctor, dentist, lawyer, physicist and accountant; and at the bottom of the list came the engineers and metallurgists. A comparable piece of research by Gareth Jones showed that academically able sixth-form boys clearly preferred to apply for university courses in pure sciences rather than engineering and technology. So, for perhaps twenty years the schools have been producing from the science side young men who believe that engineering, technology and production offer less good careers than the medical professions and the pure sciences associated with research.

There are two more serious aspects of this: the great dearth of girls taking mathematics and physics with the intention of training to be engineers or technologists in industry, and the preference amongst much younger pupils for sixth form education in languages and the humanities rather than in the sciences. Only in England and Wales does the education system enforce such irrevocable choices upon young people at an age before they can be expected to comprehend the vocational consequences. It is well known that medicine as a career is chosen at a younger age than almost any other and obviously boys and girls have some conception of the life and work of a doctor from a comparatively early age, even if they have no family tradition of entry to that profession. The engineering and other professions practised within industry have therefore to make a deliberate effort to put across to school pupils the intellectual challenge, fascination and rewards that await those who choose that direction because – unless young people happen to have an engineer or industrial manager in the family or amongst neighbours – they are less likely to think of these as a career.

Evidence provided for the Finniston Committee of Inquiry into the Engineering

Profession (1980) disposes of the belief that academically-able sixth-formers do not choose engineering: a significant proportion of undergraduates in engineering faculties had very good grades in their A-levels. Engineering is a popular career amongst boys leaving independent schools. But it cannot be denied that it is far easier for a young person of modest academic attainments to get a place in an engineering department than in pure sciences or humanities. This is mainly due to the enormous expansion consequent upon the development of the new technological universities and the thirty polytechnics; but it undoubtedly affects attitudes amongst school pupils and their teachers. Bright youngsters are not attracted to study for courses which they feel can be entered by persons of lower ability and so a vicious circle is established: the universities and polytechnics fill their places with under-graduates of modest attainments who then enter industry and perpetuate the image of rather mediocre professional engineers and technologists.

Many sixth-formers also apparently believe that to take an engineering degree does not of itself provide a rewarding career. Sixth-formers need evidence that engineers can achieve positions of high responsibility and influence if they are to be attracted to careers in industry.

This is in marked contrast with the situation in many other countries. There is no doubt of the very high regard in which engineers and industrialists are held in, for example, Germany. The Dipl. Ing. is generally reckoned to be entirely the equivalent intellectually and socially of the medical doctor or barrister, and the same could be said of the products of the Grande Ecoles in France, some of the most prestigious institutions of higher education anywhere in the world. In North America it is said that engineering students are drawn from the same enterprising, energetic, intelligent and attractive young men as are medical students. There is no doubt that the high regard in which North Americans hold those who, by engineer-ing skills, imagination and drive opened up a huge continent, reflects back into the schools so that able and ambitious young people choose careers in industry and an engineering education to fit them for it. In Japan 85 per cent of members of the boards of big companies in industry, as well as a high proportion of top civil servants and other administrators, have taken degrees in physics or engineering. This is the accepted route for those who want to get to the top and yet in this country an enormous change of attitudes will be required if we are to reverse this particular symptom of the British malaise – the comparatively low status of professional engineering in the league table of occupations suitable for able and ambitious youngsters. On the question of women entrants to industry there is absolutely no evidence of any biological reason why women should not be managers in industry or successful as engineers and technologists. In Eastern Europe it is com-mon for women to study these subjects and no Scandinavian would ordinarily consider it unfeminine if his daughter wished to study engineering or production management rather than medicine or dentistry. So, there is a real task to be accom-plished in changing attitudes amongst the general public, the media who frequently reflect the attitudes of the general public, and those who are influential on the destiny of young people still at school, that is the teacher of their best or favourite subject.

It is sometimes said that the situation would be improved if more teachers (or even all teachers) had had a period of work experience in industry before training to teach. Various suggestions have been put forward and there are schemes for students in teacher education to spend short attachments to industry. There are many teachers who have taken advantage of the CBI scheme of industrial attachments for three weeks or so to enable them to have a greater insight into industry and its challenges. Some school governors contend that careers teachers in particular should be chosen from amongst those members of school staffrooms who have had experience of work outside teaching, but this does not necessarily mean that they will be influential in persuading their more go-ahead students to consider careers in industry. Observing interviews for senior posts in careers teams, for example, it is clear that many teachers who studied mathematics or physical science at university and entered industry then decided to become teachers just because they found industry uncongenial. Since they were not likely to get to the top in their originally chosen career it seems unrealistic to suppose that they are going to advocate industrial careers for the bright and energetic pupils in their charge. Indeed, it is quite common for them to express strong views to the contrary when asked by governors whether their previous experience in industry predisposes them to advocate such careers for their pupils.

It is often argued that because there are no engineers or people with industrial or commercial experience on the staff of many schools, pupils do not have the opportunity of finding out more about work in industry. This argument seems weak, however, because it is equally true that the schools do not have surgeons on the staff or architects or barristers, to name just three popular careers. Greater knowledge of what happens in industry may cure ignorance but unhappy experience as an employee in an industrial or commercial organization is not likely to produce many more young people predisposed towards industrial careers.

There is a fashion in careers which has to be recognized. From time to time individual occupations appear to be much sought after by school-leavers or college entrants and it is certainly the case that in the last two or three decades many of the most energetic, able and imaginative young people chose to study arts and humanities subjects with the intention of pursuing careers in law, the civil service, journalism, broadcasting, advertising and those professions generally thought to be influential rather than activating.

Another aspect of the attitude of schools towards industry stems from the comparatively low regard in which the subjects of craft, design and technology have traditionally been held in the grammar schools. Universities expected undergraduates to have passes in mathematics, physics and chemistry if they wished to read engineering, and indeed this is still the case; though universities are happy to have design and technology as an additional subject it is not normally acceptable as an alternative to physical science. There is still an image of craft metalwork despite the great changes which have taken place in this subject in recent years. As a result very few girls take it at all, and those boys who do take it think of it as a subject preparing people for craft level employment. There is no evidence that those school-leavers who have done well in this subject necessarily do any better as craft and technician apprentices and some people do very well with only a minimal experience of this kind of activity in school. The academically able, pressed by the requirements of examinations, frequently drop these subjects just as they drop other creative, aesthetic, and three-dimensional educational experiences at a relatively early age. The advantage of good education in design and technology is that it inculcates graphicacy and three-dimensional concepts and this is important for a wide range of careers not only in design in industry but in marketing and sales, production, research and development, etc. The problem is exacerbated by the dire shortage of imaginative teachers of these subjects. It may be that with falling rolls, and more school buildings becoming available, some LEAs could establish technology centres to which students could go from a wide range of schools. The most inspiring teachers could be concentrated in these centres to give what is a valuable educational experience to all pupils regardless of their ultimate career destinations.

People who pontificate about teachers' attitudes towards industry often forget that not only is there a shortage in schools of teachers with a background in many industrial and other professions, but that the traditional poor attitude persists towards making and doing. That these skills should be encouraged in the early years of the primary school is demonstrated by an odd dichotomy: surgery is probably one of the highest regarded professions in the eyes of young people and yet it is essentially a career which requires enormous dexterity as well as qualities of intellect and character. Presumably this is because, regardless of the content of the job, the spiritual aspect of saving life is regarded as more worthy than the intellectual challenge of management in industry!

Of course it is up to industrialists and the organizations which exist to propagate industrial careers to overcome some of these attitudes. In Britain the Industrial Society with the 'Challenge of Industry' conferences has been successful in many schools in encouraging able youngsters to believe that a career in industry can be as interesting and rewarding as one in the independent professions such as accountancy, law or dentistry. The situation may be improved by a much greater willingness of schools to allow pupils to participate in those activities which come under the umbrella of school industry liaison. 'Understanding British Industry' is an obvious one and the examination syllabus for 'Understanding Industrial Society' another; the work of the Science and Technology Regional Organizations, such organizations as Young Enterprise, Project Trident, Index-link and the Careers Research Advisory Centre Insight Programme are all useful; and the activities of the Engineering Industry Training Board can particularly help girls by showing them engineering and industry could provide fulfilling careers for them. The media also has an important role to play: to portray industry in a more encouraging light than it has in the past.

More information needs to be available in schools as to the essentially intellectual nature of an engineering degree and to the interest derived from careers in management. So many parents still believe that engineering means craft-level work and that it is predominantly concerned with machines and materials, not with money and men, which is thought to be the province of accountants, lawyers and general managers. We know that undergraduates expect their careers to provide an intellectual challenge, early experience of responsibility, good prospects and a variety of activities. Industry so far seems to have failed to get its message across but that is exactly what it can provide.

Careers advisers have a responsibility to ensure that able youngsters understand the value of studying mathematics, physics and chemistry in the sixth form. They should ensure that their students realize that these subjects lead to a wide variety of careers – not only in technology, engineering, medicine and science – but also in administration, social work and those other fields commonly entered by the sixth-formers who have studied the arts.

Another attitude which can be detected in schools is connected with the difficulty of defining a professional engineer as distinct from a technician or craftsman. A belief persists amongst school pupils (and possibly some of their teachers) that industry is only interested in practical people with materialist attitudes, whereas the importance of industry to the national economy and the country's capacity to support the social services, goes by default. Recruiting teachers with industrial experience may be counter-productive because if they have enjoyed working in industry they would probably not have wanted to transfer to teaching. However, there is a lot to be said for increasing the opportunities for teachers to observe industrial operations, and in particular to sit with managers in order to appreciate the intellectual level of their work and the mental demands made upon decision-makers. The increase in organizations offering opportunities for school/industry liaison is to be welcomed.

In addition industry itself could perhaps do more by persuading the media to give more attention to its successes and less to the image of strife-torn and un-successful factories; better opportunities for young people to have work-experience during their holidays and for teachers of industrially-relevant subjects to discuss with people in industry, ways in which they might contribute to pupils' curriculum; the provision of project materials and perhaps help with machinery as well as encouraging employees to visit schools and communicate some of the interest that they get from their job and the importance of it.

There is an unfortunate dichotomy between the modern ethos of schools which tends to be less competitive than when meritocracy was a popular concept and boys and girls were encouraged to do well in examinations in order to 'get on' in their careers. A laudable compassion for disadvantaged pupils may have produced a 'softness' in schools which is markedly at variance with the competitive requirements of industry. So long as boys are encouraged because they have got seven out of ten in their mathematics whereas the week before they only got four problems right, they will be surprised when they find that only absolute ten out of ten standards are good enough in industry. The same thing applies to punctuality, time-keeping, respect for materials, working under pressure and other 'spiritual' aspects of school-ing which make industry seem less attractive and contribute to the general malaise.

The Navy used to have a saying that an efficient ship is a happy ship and it is unfortunate that industry is presented as an unhappy environment in which to work while schools are thought to be delightfully non-competitive and child-centred. Besides, in many cases pupils enjoy pitting themselves against their own previous standards or those of their fellows whether this be in the gym, on the games field, in the orchestra or other activities such as Duke of Edinburgh Award schemes. A desire to succeed by whatever criterion one sets should not be devalued out of a concern for those who do not have the abilities to enable them to compete successfully. It may be that this attitude which stems from teachers' own preference for the relatively non-competitive world of education to what they call the 'rat race' of industry is more responsible for the industrial malaise than many people recognize. One can only hope that greater contact between teachers and employers and employees in industry and commerce will reduce this psychological barrier too and inculcate in young people the sort of attitudes which lead not only to personal success and fulfilment in their careers but to an improvement in the general state of the British economy.

### Note

1 HUTCHINGS, D. (1963) *Technology and the Sixth Form Boy*, Oxford University Press.

# Scientists and Engineers

*Geoffrey D. Sims*

## Introduction

Britain entered the twentieth century ill-equipped to deal with the manifold problems which were to beset her future as a major industrial nation. By 1900 substantial movements towards mass production were already taking place elsewhere, associated with an expansion in diversity of consumer goods production which, in the second half of the century, was to become an explosion. In many fields however we still remained dominant, particularly in the area of capital goods, and foresaw little need to broaden our view or adapt our approach to the market. Still less at a later stage did we rush to embrace the sophisticated marketing techniques which foreign competition would necessitate and which would become essential for the more advanced technologies which lay ahead. In the years to come we were often to take satisfaction from our ability to lead at the point of invention of the new, yet seldom could the same be said of our success in developing and exploiting these ideas.

Not least among our problems was a conservatism towards novel techniques, which were often costly to introduce, and in the absence of industrial strategy, we tended to stand, xenophobically, uncertain of which way to face. It is true that many of the pressures which bore on our development were of an external kind and were difficult to counter. It is equally true that we often failed to diagnose our internal weaknesses, and, if occasionally we did, we found it hard to prescribe remedies for them.

Whenever our attitudes and competence were in question, so, *ipso facto*, was our education, for the way in which education is approached can be critical in fashioning both.

The discussion in this chapter represents an attempt to summarize the development of education in science and technology in the twentieth century whilst, at the same time, seeking to demonstrate the influence of the attitudes of schools and employers on the process. The account given is clearly incomplete, and in common with the foregoing remarks is a generalization within which there will be many exceptions. It does not, and cannot, therefore, include all of the important events of the period, but the sample given is reasonably illustrative of the prevailing attitudes of the time. It is, however, impossible to discuss education and the British malaise in the twentieth century without considering the past and it is to this that we must turn first.

### The legacy of the nineteenth century

Before the beginning of the century there were few centres of higher education in the UK and those which did exist had only relatively small commitment to science and still less to technology. At a lower level there were the 'mechanics' institutes', which were voluntarily supported and whose purpose was to enlighten the worker about the world in which he lived and worked, rather than to teach him his trade. The concept was right, though in the main the institutes failed for two basic reasons: first, the general prevailing illiteracy made it impossible for most to benefit from the books with which they were supplied whilst, second, discussion of religion or politics was generally barred and these were the two subjects in which the working man was often most interested. Most of these institutes were therefore soon transformed into technical institutes whilst a few – notably Finsbury Technical College, (later to become the City and Guilds College), Manchester Institute of Technology and Birkbeck College in London – were in time to become important centres of higher education in science and technology.

The first ten years of the twentieth century also embraced the foundation of the majority of the large provincial redbrick universities and colleges, in many cases with a greater orientation towards local practical objectives than their predecessor institutions. The good intentions underlying their conception were well expressed by Joseph Chamberlain, the first President of the newly-incorporated Mason University College, Birmingham when, at a luncheon before the first meeting of the Court of Governors in 1898, he said:

> To place a university in the middle of a great industrial and manufacturing population is to do something to leaven the whole mass with higher aims and higher intellectual ambitions than would otherwise be possible for people engaged entirely in trading and commercial pursuits.[1]

Sidney Webb was also a promotor of the civic universities and in 1901 he urged:

> Nothing would be more widely popular at the present time, certainly nothing more calculated to promote national efficiency, than a large policy of government aid to the highest technical colleges and universities. The statesman who first summons up courage enough to cut himself loose from official pedantries on this point and demand a grant of half a million a year with which to establish in the United Kingdom a dozen perfectly equipped Faculties of Science, Engineering, Economics and Modern Languages, would score a permanent success.

In the event the state aid given to universities at that time amounted to some £27 000 compared with his suggested £500 000, whilst Germany was giving more to one university alone than Britain was giving to all of its universities.[2]

At this stage however it must be remembered that Britain, with an already diminishing degree of justification, still saw itself as 'the workshop of the world', and as such had dominated the market-place for more than a century. Against this proud background education could be regarded disinterestedly and was seen by most as a pure 'good', whatever its nature; no other purpose nor justification was needed. The confidence which had sprung from the economic dividend following our lead into the industrial revolution had in no way been undermined by the clear warnings of rising foreign competition in the latter half of the nineteenth century. We remained complacent and as far as education was concerned our complacency was firmly underpinned by the growing heritage of our Public School tradition.

The stamp of Rugby's Dr. Arnold was still apparent in most schools and however laudable many of Arnold's ideas may have been, his early conclusion that science was too difficult to be taught in schools largely typified the system. The classics were predominant, whilst an accompanying disinclination towards modern languages was producing an elite future leadership of singular insularity. Indeed the road to respectability under the influence of 'education' led *away* from the workshop. This inhibition of our scientific development inevitably had more far-reaching consequences, for, inevitably, it was the products of the school system which subsequently filled the tutorial positions in the universities. The atmosphere which resulted was, sadly, one in which it might have been said that, even if *science* might be a fit subject for gentlemen to study, *engineering* was really not to be countenanced.

Despite the ups and downs of our economic fortunes there was very little connection in people's minds between educational background and industrial success. There were those who recognised the problem, for example, as early as 1853 Lyon Playfair published 'a little work' on 'Industrial Education on the Continent' and in 1867 commented 'as an inevitable result of the attention given to it (industrial education) abroad other nations must advance in industry at a much greater rate than our own country. I fear that the result is already attained for many of our staple industries'. At much the same time the distinguished Oxford humanist, Mark Pattison, was writing in scathing terms of the inadequacy of science education at the universities and Matthew Arnold saw the school system as having 'very naturally fallen, all into confusion' and further lamented that, 'though properly an intellectual agency it has done and does nothing to counteract the indisposition to science which is our great intellectual fault'. In 1872 a Royal Commission set up under the Duke of Devonshire recommended:

1 That in all Public and Endowed Schools a substantial portion of time allotted to study, should throughout the School Course . . . be devoted to Natural Science – and we are of opinion that not less than six hours a week on the average should be appropriated for the purpose.

2 That in all General School Examinations, not less than one sixth of the marks be allotted to Natural Science.

3 That in any Leaving Examinations, the same proportion should be maintained.

Notwithstanding the fact that by that time some 948 schools were receiving grants for science teaching and that a small flow of pupils with some scientific education had been created, our reluctance to really tackle the problem is well summed up by Ashby, commenting some seventy-five years later that 'alas, many of these recommendations would not have been acceptable to many headmasters in the 1950s'. However some seeds had been sown and would germinate in time, albeit in favour of pure rather than applied science.

Similar warnings have been reiterated regularly since then and a typical example is provided by Mr. G. Franklin, a Pro-Chancellor of the University of Sheffield, commenting in 1910 with a remarkable lack of 'sense of occasion' as he opened the University's new playing fields, that:

> He wanted to say quite frankly that the amount of time wasted in cricket and football might be very well applied to more useful purposes. In saying that, he did not want to undervalue for one moment splendid opportunities now opened up to them by the playing field, nor the necessity for that physical education which made them strong and able to do the work which lay before them. But there was reason in all things and when he went to Germany, the United States, and other countries he did not find that anything like the time was spent by the adult population in watching football and cricket matches and other games as in this country. He had a strong feeling that the educational systems of Germany and America were at least not inferior to ours and that they were turning out a race of commercial men today calculated to win and outstrip us unless we were careful in the steps we were taking in regard to our education.

### Science in the schools

To pass too quickly over the early deficiences of our school system and its relation to the needs of manufacturing industry, however, neglects the more fundamental question of the schools and their disposition towards the teaching of science in any form. Clearly this factor in turn is critical in determining what it is possible to achieve at higher levels of education and later in industry.

Whilst the comments made earlier about Classics in the nineteenth century remained broadly valid, it was also true that some of the independent schools, particularly those which were established following the repression of the Catholics during and after the Elizabethan period, did teach some science.[3] As for the rest, the secondary schools, which were still seen as schools for the more privileged classes rather than providers of an extension of elementary education, still catered only for a minority of the population.

Only 128 endowed schools replied to the enquiries of the Devonshire Commission and these showed that whilst some sixty-three schools taught some science only thirteen had laboratories whilst eighteen only had scientific apparatus of any kind. By 1872 Harrow, Eton and Charterhouse were either building or planning science laboratories and a few others were following at last.

In 1895 the Bryce Commissioners, whilst accepting the desirability of some science education, felt that the endowed grammar schools could not satisfy the demand for teaching time without unduly contracting their literary instruction, a sentiment echoed by the Headmasters' Conference in 1903 which lamented that 'by their organization, by their inspectorate and by their grants the Government had pushed scientific and mathematical studies and neglected to furnish any means to advance literary studies'. The task of the secondary school was above all seen to be to 'humanize' and only then to impart efficiency for life as it had to be lived.

The climate was still a resistant one therefore and many other influential bodies and commissions were to urge action in the decades to come. We were also slow to learn from experience for, as the Great Exhibition of 1851 had revealed, other countries' achievements were now often founded on an understanding of applied science, whilst ours rested mainly upon a superiority in natural resources and improvization. Similarly the First World War found us still well behind Germany in the applied science field, and yet again relying upon our remarkable ability to improvize to help us win the war.

By 1916, however, public concern was growing and following a memorandum to *The Times*, signed by many eminent scientists, proclaiming that 'people were being destroyed from lack of knowledge (of science) on the part of legislators and administrative officials' a conference was held by the Linnean Society after which a 'Neglect of Science Committee' was formally established. By this time, however, the Government had become alerted to the situation and the Prime Minister set up a committee under the chairmanship of J. J. Thompson to debate our position in relation to science education.[4] Not surprisingly it advocated the place of science as a necessary and integral component of a liberal education, with some recommendations, like those of the Devonshire Commission before which would still discomfort some of our schools today.

Yet again the humanities had already rallied in opposition and defence and a Council of Humanistic Studies, under the Chairmanship of Viscount Bryce, was formed to ensure that things did not get out of hand. Much discussion followed and though significant progress was made by the scientists the concordat which finally emerged represented a dilute form of what was really needed, and a telling demonstration of the entrenched strength of the 'opposition'.

In 1916 also The Science Masters' Association had produced a paper entitled 'Science for All' calling for the teaching of an undivided general science syllabus, which established a vogue which persisted for some years. In many respects general science was easy to accommodate since it required fewer hours in the timetable than the study of individual sciences in depth. Yet once the Higher School Certificate was established in 1918 it became apparent that general science was a poor preparation for these more advanced examinations and there was at last some evident expansion of science teaching accompanied by more laboratory accommodation and a better provision of both teaching and textbooks. Some measure of the slow rate of progress of science in state schools can be gained from a recognition that in 1926 only forty-seven out of 225 State Scholarships were awarded in science subjects and of these only four could be classified as relating to engineering (less than 2 per cent). Most of the state schools were now teaching physics and chemistry though general science retained its place, particularly in the public schools, some of whose earlier and more ambitious efforts had burned themselves out at a preliminary stage. Even by 1932, when some 1378 secondary schools were in existence, only about half were entering pupils for science subjects in the school certificate examinations. This perspective is further sharpened by the fact that the secondary schools at that stage catered for less than half a million pupils whilst the elementary schools were educating more than $5\frac{1}{2}$ million, from which it may be inferred that the regard paid to science was still unbelievably low. The standard of teaching, where it existed, however, was often commendably high as we shall see later.

As we moved towards the Second World War the Spens Report (1938) paid scant attention to science, yet the Norwood Report, commissioned in 1943, in circumstances similar to those which gave rise to the Thompson enquiry during the First World War, 'again showed the reaction of a nation emerging from the throes of a disastrous war, almost lost through a technological deficiency'. Once again it emphasized the absolute necessity for science as an essential factor in school education.

It was left to the Butler Education Act of 1944, which raised the school leaving age to fifteen, to at last recognise that only a literate population could benefit from a scientific education. It emphasized the importance of science education for the upper age groups in secondary and technical schools and the Act highlighted, more clearly than any of its predecessors, certain chronic weaknesses in the field of science. It drew attention to:

    i the shortage of competent trained teachers of science;
    ii a shortage of competent laboratory assistants;
    iii inadequate provision of science laboratory accommodation;
    iv inadequate supplies of apparatus and materials;
    v inadequate financial cover for the running costs of science teaching.

There is a sense of listening to a stuck gramophone record about all of this history for there have been many other reports and enquiries published both before and after 1944, which could have been quoted but which give the same message. The above, however, will suffice.

In the years between 1944 and the present time the schools have usually possessed adequate physical provision for the teaching of science, though there has been a marked disinclination on the part of young people to take the subject and it is reasonable to question to what extent this was a consequence of the quality of the science teachers at whose mercies they would sit.

Throughout the post-war years, whatever the conclusions of high level committees may have been, certain facts speak for themselves. For example, in the period between 1952 and 1960, whilst the numbers of pupils taking O-level maths more than doubled from 80 000 to 177 000 and A-level maths trebled from 11 000 to 33 000, with physics and chemistry showing similar trends, the numbers of mathematics and science teachers rose only by about 30 per cent and the annual vacancies for science specialists in schools rose by between 20 per cent and 30 per cent (according to discipline).

A further matter of concern was to be found in the ability levels of the teachers recruited, for whereas in the decade preceding the war the number of 1st and 2nd class honours grades recruited into teaching posts had constituted some 60 per cent of the total; in the decade following the war it had dropped to 40 per cent and showed every sign of continuing descent below this point.

The overall quality of science teachers was therefore decreasing and the total stock would undergo a sharp decline when the pre-war contingent retired. Seen against the background of a still sharply-rising birth-rate the position was serious indeed and in 1968 the report of the Dainton enquiry into 'The Flow of Candidates in Science and Technology into Higher Education', further underlined the continuing seriousness of the situation. As before no positive steps followed to remedy matters.

Notwithstanding the conclusions of the Dainton enquiry the numbers of science teachers and their quality had continued to be largely determined by (mostly adverse) market forces and political dispositions for, whilst in the years between the wars there were relatively few jobs for qualified scientists, the Second World War gave rise to a considerable industrial demand for people with scientific and engineering education. Invariably industrial posts were better remunerated than those in the schools and it was thus only in periods of recession, when industrial demands fell, that good quality graduates applied in any significant numbers for teaching posts and in consequence we still find ourselves in general with an ageing school science teaching population.

Clearly without the creation of a suitable climate of opinion within schools, it was unlikely that the Higher Education sector on its own could make good these deficiencies. Indeed the contributions of school and post-school educational development will always be so interdependent.

### The awakening of public consciousness

The movement towards science perhaps showed itself at its strongest in the Thirties, helped on the one hand by a substantial corpus of emergent good quality teachers in the schools and on the other by the stimulus of a spirit of adventure which science provoked among the young. It was still possible for the good amateur scientist to make some impact upon the world and any intelligent schoolboy could pursue scientific hobbies which might lead him to a career. He could make a radio set, could learn something of the problems of mechanical structures whilst enjoying his 'meccano' and, if he were of a more imaginative and discerning kind, could read popular magazines such as *Armchair Science*, which enabled him to wonder at the potential of atomic energy even though at the time few people had the slightest idea of how atomic power could be harnessed. The Thirties therefore saw a number of young people, within the grammar school system at least, who had a tremendous enthusiasm for science. It represented the still largely unconquered world about which it was possible to speculate and where research and exploration were bound to lead nearer to 'the truth'. Even though there were relatively few jobs available in research in industry at that time, those who qualified could always achieve respectability as teachers and their prospects were thus by no means unduly restricted.

That there was such a group of enthusiasts was to prove greatly to our advantage during the years of the Second World War for many 'scientists' who had emerged from the school and university system in this period found the opportunity to utilize their fundamental science in a way which was vital to the war effort. Electromagnetic theory formed the basis of electromagnetic wave propagation, as well as of the designs of the components which had to be realized and mastered before radar could become a reality, whilst the analysis of structures and structural mechanics, still at that time largely regarded as a 'basic' subject, had to be understood before our aircraft technology could become competitive with that of the alien countries.

We emerged from the war, therefore, encouraged that 'science' might be the answer to many of our future problems too, and indeed, at that time, there was little evidence from our export market that it would not be so. In particular our capital goods, not least those based on wartime technology, commanded respect throughout the world and many of our traditional industries also still flourished. We concluded that to invest in the production of yet more physicists was one of the best things that we could do for the good of the nation and large physics departments sprouted everywhere. Physics research, though often extremely expensive, was easy to defend for already the potential of atomic energy had been revealed as the most potent of all justifications for such investment, and other developments must surely follow.

By this time, however, we had entered the uneasy Sixties with the economic pendulum swinging rather more violently than we cared for, to reveal the balance of payments problems which were to dominate our lives for years to come. Our new apprehensions arose from the confluence of many forces and it was only at a secondary stage of the analysis that they may have been attributable to any over-dedication to 'science' rather than to 'engineering'. We were, however, starting to realize much more widely than ever before that, in the advanced consumer goods markets particularly, science alone was not enough. Great technological advances were hailed as *scientific triumphs*, when they succeeded, whilst our reverses were mainly seen as *engineering failures* and many a restive manufacturer started to look afresh at the output of the universities and ask 'Why is it that these places cannot produce the people that we need?'. That it was impossible to gain a clear picture of what the manufacturer really did need is perhaps not surprising as any possible deficiences at the educational level had not really been diagnosed, even if the evidence of prejudice, conservatism and neglect had been apparent to some for a century or more.

## New institutions

The early Sixties then, saw renewed demands for a more practical style of education which would provide the kind of professional that industry really required. Few people recalled the words of Playfair a century before, though this time the specification of the lacuna was rather more precise. What was needed was not a man versed in basic science – for he would not appreciate the realities of industry – but someone who could design and who was interested in and motivated by the problems of real-life engineering, rather than those of pure scientific discovery. Government at last recognized the truth of the situation and thus it was that the Colleges of Advanced Technology (the CATs) were born, dedicated to produce people to conform to this notional specification. The six CATs would not award degrees but instead would offer a 'Diploma of Technology' (the Dip. Tech.) thus emphasizing the fact that they were both different and moreover *useful*.

The concept was a good one and many of the CATs devoted themselves to their task with dedication and imagination. Soon, however, a fundamental problem arose. Why should those whose education destined them for industrial good merely have a diploma? Those who had been through university courses emerged with degrees (which were clearly better)! The CATs not unnaturally reacted positively and soon began to see their future place as technological universities, which, if they were different in conception and quality from their German counterparts, nonetheless fulfilled a clear need. Helped by the fair wind of the 1963 Robbins Report they soon achieved university status and were numbered alongside the conventional universities whose charters and statutes were disconcertingly similar. Indeed, whilst they retained some differences of character they were rapidly to become so much like the other universities that the difference soon became minimal. It is true that the ex-CATs provided their education, in the main, through sandwich courses with industry providing the training periods necessary to complete the sandwich, but the universities too were beginning to recognize the need and accept the force of the argument that properly 'formed' engineers were a species necessary for industrial survival.[5] The redbrick universities were thus reappraising their approach and the presence of the 'ex-CATs' coupled with the plaints of industry caused a much greater internal examination of their position than was apparent at the time. That the differences between the two forms of institution were to become further eroded was not the fault of the technological universities, for shortages of industrial training places in times of recession coupled with a general lack of good qualified applicants from the schools necessitated, in all cases, some degree of reversion to conventional course subjects and patterns which was neither wished for nor needed.

At that time the contrast between the British and the German systems must have crossed a number of minds for the Technische Hochschulen had enjoyed university status for a century or more in Germany. Moreover their graduates were seen as being in no sense inferior to those of other German universities: indeed their graduates were greatly respected by German society at large and by German industry in particular. The engineering profession enjoyed no such standing in this country, whilst our new technological universities could scarcely yet be expected to be of the calibre of their German counterparts, for none of them had been initially founded as a university and many of their staff, who had peopled their progenitor institutions, were scarcely of university calibre.

It is perhaps ironic that when 'science' crossed the Channel to industrial England, before the beginning of the century, it was in the form only of 'wissenschaft' or 'pure knowledge' and it was this that had caught the imagination and determined the response of our universities. Applicable science of the nature of that which was to be found in the European technological universities met with little enthusiasm in the UK and very few institutions, of which the Imperial College of Science and Technology was perhaps the most prominent, could have been recognized as in any respect comparable.

Notwithstanding the increased status of the CATs and the improving response of the universities, industry was still not receiving the attention it demanded either in numbers of technologically-educated students or in quality.

The Government's next response was to establish 'The Binary System'. As with the CATs, the new 'polytechnics' were produced by upgrading a number of selected technical colleges.[6] Their task would be to produce people for industry and they were conceived so as to complement the function of the universities. The polytechnic remit, though different, overlapped substantially with that of the universities and, at the professional level, the polytechnics and the universities were soon producing similar numbers of sandwich course students for industry.

It is not unfair to the polytechnics to state that although some of their degree courses were different in kind, the universities were still attracting the more able students and whilst some areas of industry preferred their product, it still failed in most cases to measure up in quality to what was needed. At the same time, however, the polytechnics were making a unique contribution in providing well-trained middle-level manpower. This contribution must not be undervalued even if the universities remained the leaders in technological thought. Whether or not this 'thought' was of the right kind for industry may well remain a matter of debate for decades to come, but all innovation needs to be underpinned by research and it was the universities which remained the primary sources of invention outside of industry itself.

The polytechnics had not achieved all that was hoped of them, not least because of the continuing disinclination on the part of school-leavers to take science-based courses. Fishing, with the universities, in a pool of entrants of limited size, many of them substituted arts-based courses in compensation. Nonetheless the fact that they were primarily locally-funded and controlled institutions had enabled them to make a singular contribution to local needs and their success on this count was more apparent than that of the universities. In terms of their educational input in the short post-experience course field the universities were, by 1980, outstripping the polytechnics by a factor of 7:1 in science and engineering. On the investigatory side however the polytechnics were catering for needs which the universities had often disregarded as inappropriate. Similarly the polytechnics catered actively for an increasing call for updating courses in the management field as well as in many areas of social administration. The fact that universities offered courses under similar titles misled many into believing that widescale duplication existed. In general this was not the case and with the exception referred to in the undergraduate field, the intended complementarity of the two sides of the binary system had been achieved with a greater degree of success than was often acknowledged.

### Education and industry – the missing links

At this stage, then, various pressures and interests had combined to provide at least a limited stream of people who would embark on careers in industry as productive engineers. They had been at least partially prepared for this by the educational process, but industry was still voicing dissatisfaction. How much this was of industry's own making only history can judge, but any deficiences of the new graduates were still habitually ascribed to the shortcomings of the educational system. The graduate, wherever he came from, 'was still reluctant to involve himself in production problems'.

Whilst many would argue that this was due to an absence of interest on the industrial side in bridging the gap between the preparation given by the tertiary sector and the realities of an intensely-competitive industrial climate, complicated further by all the problems of the shop floor, there remained more fundamental problems to be overcome.

Perhaps the most sinister of these was the persisting decrease of interest in science in the schools. The Robbins Report had provided for all qualified young people to read the subject of their choice at university. Their choice for the most part did not seem to lie in the direction of science or engineering.[7] As we have already suggested this must at least have been due in part to an absence of really able science teachers, but the social climate was also unfavourable to science which was beginning to be seen as something of an evil force in itself. Many young people were more interested in courses which they felt would help them to reform and heal society, whilst others sensed that they would experience a greater degree of freedom by taking courses for which there was a less rigid timetable. Clearly those subjects which did not involve practical laboratory studies offered a much greater flexibility of lifestyle, and were therefore to be preferred.

The proportion of science-based school-leavers was thus decreasing fast. Some educators, however, were alive to the need to produce more practically-inclined students and in some areas tremendous local efforts were devoted to encouraging sixth-formers to take part in project work of an engineering kind. In some regions organizations such as the Southampton Forum for Science and Technology developed, through university or polytechnic initiative, to aid the process. A typical 'Forum' might be a three-pronged organization in which industry, institutions of higher education and the schools participated jointly. Their objective was to educate the schoolteacher, as well as the pupil, in industry's needs and to make available resources and equipment to enable school-leavers to become 'practically' oriented during their final years at school. Notwithstanding the discouraging picture reflected in the preceding paragraphs, the success of these initiatives was manifest, for the number of engineers in training in the universities rose. The fact that it rose, however, at the expense of those who would otherwise have read physical sciences represented less than total success, as for a long period the shortage of engineers had been compensated by recruitment of scientists whose lack of engineering expertise was in due course rectified through their subsequent experience in industry. The transfer of a part of this cohort to engineering courses was nevertheless a clear gain, both in quality and immediate effectiveness.

We have already alluded to another basic problem which still remained to be mastered. The intense international competition to which British industry had been subjected in the post-war years had resulted in the disappearance of many major engineering manufacturing firms as they were progressively absorbed into ever larger consortia. For example, Metropolitan Vickers, which had for half a century possessed one of the most renowned engineering apprentice training schools in the world was to become part of the General Electric Company. With the merger the graduate training scheme which had produced such a dazzling list of world calibre engineers was soon to disappear, and, as the pace of industrial mergers quickened so too did many other prestigious industrial training facilities. Indeed, short-term financial pressures were seriously affecting longer-term provision, in a most sinister manner.

This trend, too, intensified the demands on the educational system to produce people who were trained, as well as educated, to be of immediate use in industry. In some ways this lack of formal industrial training may well have been one of the most telling factors in our inability to compete in the Seventies for it was at that time that the professional institutions also restricted the path to professional qualification by insisting that all future members should have undergone full-time education – something which ran totally counter to the broadbased British tradition of part-time study whilst gaining experience at work. It was believed that this decision would help to enhance the prestige of the profession and in time raise it to a level comparable to that in our European competitor countries. The hypothesis was to prove as ill-founded as it was practically damaging.

Whatever the truth of this analysis, the fact remained that, notwithstanding the movement towards industry of the universities and the polytechnics, industry had in large measure diminished the vital links which connected the educational system with its own real needs.

From the middle Sixties onwards many serious attempts were made by various bodies, including the Science Research Council, to try to strengthen this weak link in the education and training chain. The 'Bosworth' courses, initiated in the mid-Sixties, were intended to provide a matching of the graduate into his industrial specialism but they only enjoyed limited success for, once again, industrial recession drove industry from the partnership which was essential for such courses to succeed. The Science Research Council also produced the concept of 'Total Technology' courses, which implied a training based, not only on the fundamental basis of engineering and design experience, but which took into account cost, time and market factors, with the aim of producing engineers capable of project management rather than people who would be limited by the constraints of a conventional engineering education. But we were still only tinkering with the fringe of the problem.

It was not only economic problems, however, that hindered our progress.

Entrenched attitudes still presented serious difficulties and frequently the graduate, persuaded by his university that he could have a satisfying future in industrial production, soon returned totally disillusioned. The most common complaint was that he was tired of being told that when he too had been doing the job for thirty years, as had his fellow 'engineers', it might be appropriate for him to speak, whilst it was quite clear to him that in other countries young engineers carried substantial responsibilities at a very early age. It is easy to blame it all on industry but it is also true that many universities which believed that they were providing what industry needed were not sufficiently in touch with reality to be fully aware of what the need really was.

## Was it just education?

Whatever were the reasons for our economic decline, and our approach to education could only be held accountable for some part of it, attention had only to be paid to the way in which engineers were used in the total innovation process in Germany to realize that there was a radical difference of approach to that found in the United Kingdom. In the Sixties, for every two engineers engaged in research in the United Kingdom there was one qualified engineer employed in the development and production process, whilst in Germany for every engineer engaged in research there were seven engaged in the subsequent production chain. Clearly, therefore, Germany put a much higher value on the use of the educated professional in the production stages of a project, whilst taking much the same view of the importance of graduates in marketing.

There is little doubt that the origins of this problem lay back in the nineteenth century. As has been already stated, the engineer was an accepted and respected part of the German class structure, whereas in the United Kingdom he was not so. Qualified scientists and engineers had always been seen as important to the later stages of the innovation process in Germany, whereas in the United Kingdom they were not – it was against tradition, their prospects were limited, and they preferred to work elsewhere.

It is tempting to ask if it would have made any difference if our attitudes towards scientific and engineering training had differed and had corresponded more closely to that of some of our competitors. The answer to this must of course be 'yes', but it is inevitably a qualified 'yes' for other factors associated with financial management clearly played an extremely important part. It was significant, however, to note the reluctance of our motor industry to recruit graduates even to their design teams; it was significant to note that in the field of semi-conductor technology we started late at every stage of the development; it was significant to note that we believed that a satisfactory numerically-controlled machine tool could always be made by taking a conventional tool and buying a box full of electronics from Germany to control it.

We still had the proudest record of Nobel prizes of any nation in the world and so there was little wrong with our fundamental science. Our record in patenting new fundamental inventions of the widest significance was also impeccable. What we lacked was the ability to translate these ideas into marketable products. The marketability of a product depends not only upon the man who is selling it, but also upon its reliability, the technical and visual appeal of its design, and its ability, if not meeting an immediate need, to generate a need for itself.

In most of these areas we were less successful than our competitors though realization has at last come upon us. To capitalize upon that realization, at this time, presents a daunting task, as it always will for the heavily-handicapped starter. Not only does the climate of society have to accord respect to those who are engaged in the innovation process but that climate must be such as to generate enthusiasm in the young to follow engineering careers. The latter task is the most fundamental of all and the one which we do least well. It is furthermore the one where there has been the most reluctance to change. Only time will tell whether the present signs of a re-awakening to our real educational deficiencies are indicative of a genuine desire to do something about them.

## Notes

1  Notwithstanding these good intentions however, the 'redbricks' showed only a partial ability to connect with the realities of industry and later in the century they too were to suffer criticism for their isolation from 'real life'.
2  Government did in fact respond to this urging which was supported by A.J. Balfour (the politician) and scientists like Sir Norman Lockyer. By 1904 the University grant was doubled from £27 000 to £54 000 – still a staggeringly small sum.
3  When Stonyhurst moved to Britain from Belgium in 1794 it brought with it an active interest in science. Similar attitudes were to be found in the Quaker schools and others with links with the dissenters, e.g. Mill Hill.
4  J.J. Thompson was the discoverer of the electron.
5  'Formed'. The French 'formation' implies a blend of education and training for which there is no exact English equivalent.
6  By the end of the Seventies some thirty polytechnics had been established to which must be added another six 'Scottish Central Institutions'. This compares with some forty-four chartered university bodies – though, in many respects, the individual colleges of the Universities of London and Wales function as separate institutions.
7  The one area of science which remained strong in the universities was that of the Biological Sciences in an age where either ethical or financial reasons persuaded many young people that medicine was to be their career. (There were many who, failing to gain admission to Medical School, went into the Biological Sciences as second best.)

## Selected bibliography

AMA/ASE/AAM (1970) *The Teaching of Science in Secondary Schools*, (3rd edition), John Murray, London.
ARMYTAGE, W.H.G. (1955) *Civic Universities*, Ernest Benn, London.
ARMYTAGE, W.H.G. (1957) *Sir Richard Gregory*, Macmillan, London.
ARMYTAGE, W.H.G. (1976) A Social History of Engineering, Faber and Faber, London.
ASHBY, E. (1966) *Technology and the Academics*, Macmillan, London.
DAINTON, F.S. (1968) *Enquiry into the Flow of Candidates in Science and Technology into Higher Education*, HMSO Cmnd 3541, London.
EMMERSON, G.S. (1973) *Engineering Education: A Social History*, David and Charles, Newton Abbot.

JENKINS, E.W. (1979) *From Armstrong to Nuffield*, John Murray, London.

LAUWERYS, J.A. and SCANLON, D.G. (Eds.) (1968) *Education within Industry (The World Year Book of Education 1968)*, Evans Brothers, London.

LAWLOR, J. (1968) *The New University*, Routledge and Kegan Paul, London.

PRAAGH, G. Van (1973) *H.E. Armstrong and Science Education*, John Murray, London.

# Management Training and Education

*David T.H. Weir*

## The British Malaise

To talk of a malaise is not the same as to talk of ultimate failure. A malaise is a state of sickness from which the patient may hopefully recover.

So in the first part of this chapter we examine some of the broad structural features of British society, paying at least some attention to possibilities for recovery as well as the reality of sickness. Later, we outline the basis of a treatment philosophy.

### The economic environment

The United Kingdom has been known generally as the sick man of Europe in terms of its poor economic performance and growth rates lagging well behind those of major West European competitors. By universal agreement there is need for some radical restructuring of the industrial base. Skill shortages in key sectors, coupled with an abundant supply of unskilled and intermittently unemployed labour, a persistent brain drain of skilled managerial and technical manpower, and a chronic deficiency of investment in the manufacturing sector, are characteristic aspects of the British economy. The disappearance of some quite major manufacturing industries, such as motor-cycle manufacture, in which Britain was formerly a world leader, and the enforced reorganization of others, such as the car industry, combined with high rates of inflation, and low economic growth, to produce a crisis of national economic morale. But because this picture is so well known and the main dimension so widely understood, there is a danger of failing to identify the positive possibilities in the British economy.

Let us start by considering the British economy from the point of view of energy. The energy situation is favourable and likely to become more so. North Sea oil and gas may in the long term be seen to be among the less significant parts of the British energy base. Of greater significance, possibly, are the still unexploited coal reserves (for example in the Selby Coalfield, Central Yorkshire), some of it thick seam and thus susceptible to new exploitation technologies. The UK is centrally involved, of course, in the developing nuclear technologies. There are also substantial under-utilized possibilities of a longer-term nature in wind and wave power. Only in the solar energy field is Britain at a visible disadvantage compared to her Southern European neighbours.

In management terms, the implications of the British energy situation for the theme of this collection are considerable. The field is dominated by large nationalized public corporations. The British Gas Corporation, the Electricity Industry (consisting of the Electricity Council, the Central Electricity Generating Board, and the twelve Area Boards) and the National Coal Board are long-standing evidences of public sector involvement in the energy industry. The creation, in January 1976, of the British National Oil Corporation indicates the determination of the public sector to remain in a central position in the energy field. BNOC is, in fact, an oil company in embryo. It is involved in a series of participation agreements with the commercial companies operating in the field. It took over the National Coal Board's own stake in the North Sea programme, and it is intended that BNOC becomes a fully-integrated oil company. Its first Chairman, Lord Kearton, came from a considerable experience of leadership in large private sector enterprise. BNOC also took over the North Sea interests of Burmah Oil and is involved in research into offshore technology. If BNOC merely succeeds in two of its four principal aims, it will have failed. For besides aiming to secure ownership of a large part of the offshore oil and involvement in strategic decision-making about the exploration of oil resources in partnership with the commercial companies, BNOC is also charged 'to assist the development of a national exploration capability and to secure better technological and economic knowledge for offshore explorations.'

These last two are *managerial* objectives. They will depend for their fulfilment on BNOC's being able to generate or to influence the development of a cadre of managers trained to a high degree of technical and specialist sophistication. Public interest in the North Sea has largely been focused on its first phase, that is the extractive aspect. Arguably its greatest significance for the British economy lies in the development of second phase industries and managerial capability.

Undoubtedly the giant public sector corporations in the energy field recognize their obligations and needs in respect of management education. This is no new phenomenon and many directors of management and senior executive programmes in business schools and management centres in the UK have cause to feel considerable gratitude for the solid participation and support of these public sector enterprises.

The dominance of the City of London in the British economic and financial life, and its role as a market leader in such activities worldwide, is another stereotype, the truth of which is seldom questioned. Recently the City financial institutions have come under renewed attack for their apparent failure to direct investment towards profitable new areas of manufacturing industry, and for their over-readiness to capitalize on short-term phenomena such as the boom in office property in major cities. Such criticism, however, typically overlooks the fact that in terms of most criteria, this industry is highly successful in its own right. Although London is, of course, by far the dominant partner in the UK 'finance' industry, Edinburgh is by no means insignificant, and one of the leading success stories of Scottish business in the past decade has been the emergence of the Edinburgh-based firm of merchant bankers, Noble Grossart. This sector too has an excellent record, not merely of support for established management courses, especially at London Business School, but also for joint ventures with Business Schools in the development of tailormade courses such as the Barclays Bank Programme at Manchester Business School.

The image of Britain as a technologically-backward society, still resting foursquare on the virtues of Victorian manufacturing industry, is belied also of course by the computing industry and, in particular, by the worldwide dominance of British software houses. The relation between the public and private enterprise in this sector is particularly complex. In an information-based technology, one of the leading public sector activities is concerned with information. The National Computing Centre was established in 1965 'to provide guidance and informed advice on computing topics to all users.' NCC is charged also to promote the 'awareness of the UK as a major world source of computing expertise and to promote exports of hard and software'.

The future of the UK economy cannot be examined in isolation. The natural resource base is, however, strong and remarkably diverse. While attention is invariably drawn to the widespread phenomena of urban and metropolitan blight, and the perceived inadequacies of manufacturing industry, the overall picture is not unhopeful. Scotland, in particular, represents a largely under-exploited area in terms of both natural resources, potentially highly-skilled labour force, and productive agriculture. Many major multinationals have relocated successfully in Scotland in recent years.

### The socio-political environment

The main fabric of the socio-political structure of the United Kingdom is probably undergoing more rapid change at present than at any time in the past one hundred years. The foundation of the union between England and Scotland is itself being questioned by the growth of a political party, the SNP, explicitly committed to a nationalist posture. Despite the setback of the last General Election, future scenarios for Scotland at least must include the possibility of outright independence. These pressures are by no means irrelevant to the choice of Scotland as a location for a third national business school and for the remarkable consequential growth of management education in Central Scotland in the past few years. Moreover, the decentralized structures of the Scottish Business School, depending as they do on a matrix of operating networks, may constitute a model for similar developments.

To some extent the socio-political environment represents a set of countervailing tendencies. Public sector enterprise on the whole seems committed to the logic of economies of scale. So local government is succeeded by regional administration without a clearly accepted locational focus, for individual and collective involvement. To date the scale of organization has been much more apparent than the promised economies.

At current enterprise level the past four years have been notable for a considerable extension of governmental powers into industry, in the estimation of many senior managers and personnel officers. Chief executives often complain that such powers have passed the limit of bothersome time-wasting and become perceived invasion, not to say oppression. But this may be an over-statement for two reasons. First, much of the plethora of legislation initiated by the Trade Union and Labour Relations Act of 1974 – the Employment Protection Act, Redundancy Payments Act, Equal Pay Act, Equal Opportunities Act and legislation expected in the field of worker participation – have merely restated and reformulated rights already achieved for the labour force by the more effective trades unions. They also relate explicitly, through the doctrine of 'good practice', to the management styles and structures of the best companies. Arguably what has been achieved at ICI, or GEC, should be within the capabilities of the medium-sized engineering company. Predictably, though, in both cases there is a fairly immediate impact on management education. This may be triggered by a demand for technical expertise, for example, in the field of labour law, or personnel policy, to cope with legislative imperatives or it may be, for example, a request to provide management information in a form available for union scrutiny and use, under the Disclosure of Information provisions of the Employment Protection Act. But in either case the resulting activities are likely to lead straight into the more general fields of management and organization development.

## The cultural environment

C.P. Snow identified the source of many problems in British society and its educational system, in the existence of what he characterized as the two cultures. British institutions accept and encapsulate, according to this argument, the reality of a dichotomy between the two cultures of arts and science. Moreover, it is the arts-based culture which dominates. Its widespread hegemony throughout British society is associated, according to Snow, with Britain's failure to adapt to the reality of the twentieth century world. Since the late nineteenth century it is believed, other advanced industrial societies and in particular those of Germany, the United States, and the Scandinavian countries, have developed educational systems which attach more priority to science than to the arts. Their civil servants and their industrial leaders tend more frequently to be drawn from the ranks of engineers and scientists than from lawyers, accountants and arts graduates. It is argued by others that engineering is neither arts nor science, but a third culture, that of technik, and that those trained and expert in this third culture, the technicians and technologists, are even further down in the power structure of British society. So British educational institutions give priority to arts over science in general and pure science over applied science and technology in particular.

With this as the background, it is argued that Britain's industrial decline is readily explained. To these general cultural forms, there are institutional parallels. The most prestigious institutions of higher learning, the ancient universities, whose degrees and certifications are the most desirable, are the homes of the high culture of the arts and latterly of pure science. The technical institutions are lower in status, attract participants of a generally lower social class background and produce the occupants of lower places in the industrial hierarchy. These arguments are familiar and need not be developed too much here. That they come somewhere near the truth is readily admitted. What is not so clear is what positive programme of educational and institutional reform would radically transform this situation within a short enough time to improve in any significant fashion Britain's economic and industrial standing in the world league. Concern with Britain's poor performance in business and management in the early 1960s led to recommendations by the Franks and Normanbrook Committees to set up business schools on the American pattern. Here, however, the balance was even more generously tipped towards the practical rather than the academic. For British managers had in general had no theoretical or academic training in the principles of management, other than those of specific, already professionalized, disciplines such as engineering, accountancy, and possibly law. The creation of national business schools and of, for Britain at least, quite new qualifications was at that time seen as a radical step.

However, it is worth bearing in mind that there have been two phases at least in the evolution of the British business schools. In the first period most emphasis was placed on two quite distinct sorts of programme. For the recent postgraduate of high ability intending to enter industry or commerce and proceed eventually to a position of senior management, the preferred model was that of the full-time Master of Business Administration comprising both an introduction to business and industry and a training in certain selected skills of immediate relevance. The course content was theoretical and to some extent vocational. But arguably the orientation of most MBA programmes is scientific rather than technological (to revert to the two cultures kind of formulation).

The other programmes were characteristically for post-experience managers. Their content has been of two kinds. The business schools have offered high-powered but still scientific courses. Consultancies and the private sector colleges have offered more directly vocational though equally demanding programmes.

The second period of business school development has coincided with a downturn in the economy and with shortages of funds for training as well as arguably with a more realistic appreciation of the role of the business school in transforming managerial performance in declining sectors more immediately. To this period we owe the part-time Master's programmes on the one hand, and a rediscovery of company-based programmes on the other. In this latter category have come developments which create a new role for the business school academic as 'tutor', 'team leader', or (most recently) 'consultant' to an action learning programme. These programmes, too, impose different sorts of strains on their participants, both staff and students. For the 're-entry' problem we have substituted the problem of overload. For the problems of relevance we have substituted those of mutual credibility.

### The technological environment

Immobilities in institutional structures are a crucial problem for societies like ours which are becoming dependent on more and more complex technologies. As the rate of change of knowledge and its diffusion accelerates and as more complex capabilities and skills become more widely diffused throughout the population, one of the fastest-growing needs is for change itself. It is argued that no one leaving university or entering the labour market at the present time, can possibly expect to be earning a living in forty years' time from the skills he has learnt now. Indeed, some engineers believe that this change phenomenon can be quantified on the following rough basis – that the knowledge of engineering moves forward one year in fifteen. Thus what is taught now in the final year of a university degree syllabus in engineering will be taught in the penultimate year in fifteen years' time. Thus total obsolescence of knowledge occurs at present within the working lifetime of any one man.

There are other pressures too. Political and social changes accelerate in some ratio to changes in technology and indeed may themselves generate demand for new technologies. The past few years have seen renewed pressure for the introduction of new forms of work organization. The more flexible operation of man/machine systems is associated not merely with changes in technology that make more flexible operation possible, but also with political and social demands. Groups of workers in the labour force who were formerly apparently destined to monotonous, repetitive and non-developing work throughout the whole of their working life are now demanding control, flexibility, feedback, variety, responsibility and a chance of personal career development. But this demand for greater participation, almost universal throughout the Western world, is paralleled also by an accelerated growth of high technology, some of which has the potential effect of facilitating systems to control the environment without the use of human beings at all.

What type of educational system can cope with these demands? We simultaneously seek high performance and high participation. High returns to society and to the individual – immediate performance and long-term development. No other area of professional competence has achieved this at present. No system which hopes to survive can ignore the special needs of the very able. Likewise no society which wishes to survive can do without the skills of the moderately able, or more importantly, of those who are not only academically able, but also capable of turning their ability to practical account, and it is in this latter field that the British system has most characteristically failed.

If we were to characterize a system which might take over for the last quarter of the twentieth century, it might be that of *the opportunity-based high skills and high flexibility culture*. A system characterized both by its openness at the point of entry and by its having many points of entry, but also by its insistence on high standards of performance, regularly attested and equally regularly updated. This is the goal of management education as a whole.

If we accept the first section of this paper, at least in outline, we need to develop the argument in several ways. In particular, we need to identify the perceived deficiencies in the present situation which relate specifically to manufacturing and engineering management. However, the literature on this topic is generously larded with critical and historical analysis and this section will simply review some of the most widely quoted comments and beliefs without making any pretence at a systematic review of the evidence.

This chapter represents an attempt to take this analysis and critique a step further into a positive philosophy of education and training of relevance for engineering management in manufacturing industry. It draws in part on experience derived from planning and participating in programmes for engineers and managers in one of the most industrially deteriorated regions of Britain and Western Europe, the West Central area of Scotland centred on Glasgow.

Let us start with a definition, a readily understandable and acceptable one. An engineer is someone who makes, fabricates, or controls the manufacture of some complex object or part of a series or structure of complex objects using some technology to transform materials. He is thus both craftsman, entrepreneur, and necessarily scientist. He not only understands what he does, but why he does it. His trade, in a complex industrial society, is perhaps most akin to that of the doctor.

The analogy with medicine is a substantive but not entirely useful one. The engineer also typically functions within private enterprise industry. He has to be concerned as much with price and cost as with quality and perfectability, with markets as well as with raw materials, with personnel and human relations as much as with mechanisms and forces. In short, in most industrial societies an engineer is, by the age of forty, typically a manager as well as an engineer. It is with this mythical archetypical model engineer that this analysis deals. The analysis is thus principally concerned with the situation of engineers as managers in manufacturing industry though it may conceivably have wider implications.

If we examine the balance, though, between what we may call the practical and theoretical elements in engineering training, there has clearly been a change of emphasis during the past decade. The 'normal' progress to qualification as an engineer in the United Kingdom is now a three year academic course followed by an equivalent period of training generally under supervision. This pattern is varied by the sandwich course offered at some institutions which intersperse practical experience and academic teaching. But academic and practical education are normally split, the first being the responsibility of a specifically academic institution, the latter the responsibility of an employing organization.

Several characteristic problems can be identified here. It is argued that graduate engineers enter their first job with little appreciation of the environment in which they must work. Their contribution is thus necessarily limited. They are disappointed and disillusioned as are their employers. It is also argued that the quality of engineering education in the academic institutions suffers from their inability or unwillingness to attract engineers with practical experience to teaching positions. But many academic institutions would argue that this is not their prime need, and that it is right and proper and timely for them to concentrate on theoretical rather than practical or vocational training.

There is concern also about the *quality* of the training received by graduate recruits to industry. It is believed that half of such recruits receive little or no formal training but are left to learn 'on the job'. While the engineering institutions are becoming more active in supervising the training and early experience of their graduate members, this is by no means universally effective.

More seriously it is believed that there is no systematic supervision for engineers after their first few years in industry. Thus their own future progress depends on their own capability and knowledge of what the educational system has to offer, and perhaps also on variable interest taken in their personal career development by their employer. Companies have to keep their own balance between the needs of production and maintenance and future development of individuals.

Concern is also expressed about the quality of people attracted into engineering courses. It is believed that the academic qualifications for entrance to engineering are lower than for other subjects and that this becomes part of a regressive spiral as brighter students become deterred because of the low image of academic excellence represented in university and other courses in engineering. Also, given a lower overall entry standard, relatively more time must be devoted to remedial teaching and bringing students up to a common level of professional acceptability.

At any rate, some dies seem to have been cast – but not without regrets and possibly recriminations. Engineering *is* becoming an all graduate profession. While it was formerly possible to enter the profession through the more practically-oriented route of the Higher National Certificate, this is no longer acceptable. While many regret this fact, it is argued that the difference is not a fundamental one. Students formerly compelled to take the HNC route, it is argued, now stay on at school and are likely to go direct to university. Thus there should be, on balance, no net loss to the system.

Let us make some basic points in favour of the *status quo* or at least what is now emerging as a *status quo*. It is not self-evident that the search for qualifications is meaningless or corrupting. Historically most occupations which have achieved a sense of importance in the community at large have moved inexorably towards a more professionalized structure. They have attempted to control entry qualifications and to regulate standards of competence and performance. Some of the standards are monitored and policed exclusively by the profession itself, but most are at some point buttressed by societal regulations, embodied in formal legal structures.

The registration and licensing of competent practitioners offers society some guarantees and safeguards and, not unimportantly, some recourse against named individuals of institutions in case of non-performance. Such regulations characteristically involve restrictions on the practice of the non-qualified. These are not trivial benefits. Nor are they to be lightly cast aside in the case of societies which depend very largely on advanced technology.

But one does not have to be too much of a radical to see the high status and reward structures as being buttressed more by tradition and embodiment in legal support than in current value to society. And certainly all professions or would-be professions face similar problems of training, retraining and for different sorts of occupational career mobility. There may be no one model of the educational and training system which satisfies all these criteria. There is certainly no one set of institutions, neither universities, polytechnics, technical colleges, nor professional institutions which appears uniquely to act as the master integrative mechanism for whatever structures are proposed.

We can identify three phases in the development of the British educational system. (There are, of course, important differences between England and Wales on the one hand and Scotland on the other, but these are not such as to radically affect this analysis.) Before 1944 educational systems were largely class-based. Some institutions were specifically designed to train a ruling elite to take leadership roles at home and, more importantly, in the British empire. Others were to provide technicians and professionals to occupy subordinate positions to those held by the generalists produced by the élite institutions.

Since 1944, education has been based rather more on attributes than on class symbols. The system has been more closely geared to individual attributes, needs and development possibilities, than to societal needs *per se*. But the perceived inequalities and wastages built in to a too early selection system have escalated into a condemnation of the structures as a whole. Arguably this reaction has gone too far and some of the desirable qualities of élite institutions and of high-powered academic training have been lost.

We referred earlier to the 'opportunity-based high skill and high flexibility culture'. To support this we require a system characterized both by its openness at the point of entry and by its having many points of entry. In addition, what is required is an insistence on high standards of performance, regularly attested and equally regularly updated, as a basis for a new philosophy of education and training in the next period.

The most visible monument to the philosophy of *open entry* is, of course, the Open University. This has been a revolutionary institution in many ways, not least in the field of educational technology. But while the TV and radio components of the Open University courses necessarily attract most public attention, professionals have learned to develop a very high regard for the standard and quality of the Open University's more traditional materials. The textual and additional reading and the tutors' guides are in many courses definitive on their topics. Moreover the philosophy of joint course team development and regular updating is founded on a philosophy of teaching which serves to highlight how often and how sadly these qualities are missing in traditional university undergraduate teaching.

In terms of unit costs per student head, the Open University represents a realistic and acceptable use of scarce educational resources. In the early days of the Open University, anxieties were often expressed by academics in more traditional institutions that standards could not conceivably begin to equate with those obtaining in the existing institutions. It is widely admitted that these fears have been quite groundless.

But *what* precisely have we learned from the Open University? That the traditional institutions are inappropriate vehicles for undergraduate teaching in general? Surely not, for in many subjects the quality of the total learning experience must depend on the existence of equipment, laboratory space and time to utilize these resources. These are available in universities and also in industry.

What the Open University has revealed is that there is a tremendous demand persisting throughout people's *total lifespan* for education (much of it explicitly non-vocational, but some of it vocationally-oriented), of a kind that could previously only be obtained through immersion in a residential programme of two or three years at a university. In the field of management education this insight is also well understood. There is currently much enthusiasm for action learning. The growth points in management teaching are still in the post-experience field.

The Open University has shown that within the framework of an overall plan, it is possible to learn accretively. The Open University has its rules of performance and its standards of attainment but, and this is surely the crucial point, the total learning experience is not necessarily compressed into some arbitrarily-conceived timescale of two, three or four years. The experience can be, and is, spread to take account of the other life interests and concerns of the participant. Similarly in management education project-based learning develops a tempo and pace of its own. If a student's project, for example, is based on the introduction of group working in an assembly shop it is unhelpful to terminate the analysis at some arbitrary time period to coincide with a university submission date.

'Live learning' is the learning from and with live experience. This does not come in packages labelled Terms 1, 2 and 3. So our structures of education and training must be flexible enough to cope with this. Similarly as consultancy in the personnel field changes into organization development, the change is not one of emphasis nor of trendy nomenclature; the change in role is associated with a change in philosophy, from that of the outside expert, technician or salesman of specialist skills, to that of the wise, knowledgeable and trusted adviser and friend to a total system.

The individual is changing his role in the learning process too. The individual develops a responsibility for the management of his own learning, appropriately, for he is the one who stands to gain by it and who has to make the judgement about the opportunity costs of his own time and involvement in the learning situation.

Many of these developments are seen as explicitly or implicitly threatened by established institutions. It is possible to imagine that the Open University could in time (and possibly in a very short time) come to take prime responsibility on a national basis for undergraduate teaching in the arts. This might be more efficient in itself. It might also release the energies of the university-based academics in these subjects to involve themselves in the research which they often claim they are denied by the need to service large numbers of undergraduates. (In fact such a change would almost certainly be seen as threatening by that same body of people.)

But concern for the consequences of these changes in philosophy for the major educational institutions should not be allowed to overcloud the realization that these institutional structures are not themselves necessarily part of the permanent landscape. The recent fate of many colleges of education so soon after they had been encouraged by the Government explicitly to expand shows this all too clearly.

The history of developments since the war in the field of both engineering and management share some similarities. There is first a phase in which society becomes aware in a generalized and diffused sense that something is wrong. Some of the failure is traced to the inadequacies of the educational institutions. These are offered the opportunity of taking an interest in new areas. Some accept, others persist in their old ways. The ethic of academic freedom supports both these reactions. But for whatever reasons, and they are many and complex, the resulting reaction is not sufficient to amend the total situation adequately. So new institutions are grafted on or allowed to develop alongside the existing ones. Thus the colleges of advanced technology developed and in due course the polytechnics in the case of engineering and technological education on the one hand; so in their turn the business schools and thereafter polytechnic management departments came into being.

But this process cannot go on for ever: the institutional inertia is too great and the costs of maintaining obsolete systems too massive. However, the hardware is there, the institutional plant is there, and to some extent the personnel are there. Is there a philosophy of education and training in this field which will direct our attentions towards ways of utilizing these assets? Is there a manufacturing product and marketing mix which will make sense of an operation which in total does not seem to be serving the market adequately?

Let us accept at the start that it is wilful extravagance to simply create and proliferate new institutions *ad hoc* to meet specific needs on a one-off basis. What is needed is a philosophy within which several institutional forms can find their place. This philosophy will have to meet two quite distinct objectives. It will have to fulfil societal needs in the case of engineering and, in particular, of manufacturing industry. These are measurable, actual, and their non-fulfilment in the recent past has been closely associated with a process of total national economic decline. This is and must be the prime requirement. If this is not achieved there will be no sense in a philosophy of individual choice and an ideology of individual self-development. There will be no choices to be made; no surplus to be distributed.

The demands for such individual choices and for individual fulfilment are, however, very high and growing. They have been fostered and accelerated by a rise in living standards and more importantly by rising standards of primary and secondary educational provision. Thus the expectations held by participants in the educational process are for quality, not merely for quantity. They symbolize participation rather than submission, creation rather than dictation, mutual learning rather than pedagogic instruction. Individuals believe themselves capable of and having a right to participate in the direction, amount and – most critically – the timing of their own education and personal development

Both the societal and individual dimensions come together in a third requirement for any educational system in the last quarter of the twentieth century. It must permit change. Engineers will expect to become managers and to be trained as managers and not to be significantly disadvantaged in comparison with those who have had access to management training. They will also expect to move into a situation of parity with those who have traditionally dominated the general policy and strategic levels of organizational decision-making. Moreover, they will not wish to be inhibited by what they perceive as irrelevant institutional barriers from moving into and from the educational and training functions and, hopefully, vice versa.

Some of this, of course, is easier to predict than to specify. But some systematic parameters can plausibly be identified. There will undoubtedly be a need for a *plurality of institutions.* The job will not be the prerogative of the universities alone with their high tradition of academic excellence, or of the polytechnics with their concern for vocational relevance and practicality.

But there will be no room either for low standards. The system must be élitist in the best sense and also possibly in a sense which is currently often regarded as undesirable. There must be room for an élite to develop and to progress at an accelerated pace. There must also be flexibility of timescale. Institutions must match individuals' needs of flexibility on the one hand and should be aware that in providing flexibility they are permitting the development of excellence and specialization at the appropriate time.

Some disciplines, and more importantly some industries, recognize this. Some of the major *technical* innovations in electronic recording have been the work of very young men. In the field of popular music, revolutions are made not merely by the artists who are often young, but by the engineers who are young too. Thus the 'Wall of Sound' concept which changed the sound of pop in the 1960s was the work of Phil Spector, a man of 25. The model builders and camera crews of 'Star Wars' are young men in a young men's world because the pressure of the market demands the instant production of new technology. Ideas move direct from the drawing board or back street lab to full production. In this industry it is the garage workshops of the likes of The Beach Boys and Walt Disney which nurture the birth pains of new technology. Similar contrivances had to do also for Frank Whittle and Barnes Wallis.

At about this stage in the argument the good engineer starts to put pencil to paper and rough out a model. Let us take time to do this. But first let us briefly schematize some of the systems which we have been discussing and which seem to be more or less apposite to our discussion.

Model 1 is firmly engrained in British educational thought. It implies that there is a large field of practical knowledge, which is believed to be inferior to and to serve the needs of the theoretical knowledge. Theoreticians and practitioners are different men with different abilities. The theoretical abilities are more highly regarded and better rewarded. There is no or little movement between the one field and the other. This is the 'hierarchical' model (see Fig. 1).

The second model (Fig. 2) is similar but differs in that while there is little movement between the theoretical and the practical both are equally regarded. This 'apartheid' model underlies the binary view of education.

The third model (Fig. 3) is one which reverts to the hierarchical but allows for mobility through the grades. The older approach in which it was possible to move through apprenticeship to Ordinary National Certificate to HNC and thus into degree, higher degree, research and R and D is an example of this. The important thing is that the weight of reward and status is still on the side of the theoretical rather than the practical. Let us call this the 'mobility' model.

There is a fourth model (Fig. 4) which hardly exists at all in this country and possibly not at all elsewhere. It is possible to conceive of quite separate theoretical and practical worlds but with personnel rotating between them to take advantage of characteristically distinct but equally valuable types of experience. Let us keep

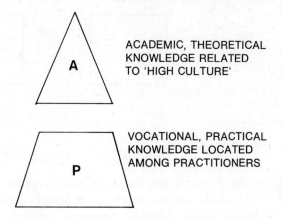

ACADEMIC, THEORETICAL
KNOWLEDGE RELATED
TO 'HIGH CULTURE'

VOCATIONAL, PRACTICAL
KNOWLEDGE LOCATED
AMONG PRACTITIONERS

**Fig. 1.** The "Hierarchical" Model

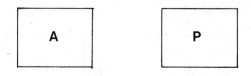

**Fig. 2.** The "Apartheid" Model

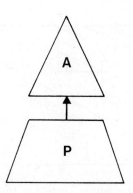

**Fig. 3.** The "Upward Mobility" Model

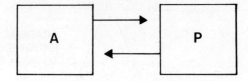

**Fig. 4.** The "Rotation" Model

this one in mind. It may have something to tell us.

In the traditional British schemes of higher education, the first twenty-five years of life are almost exclusively theoretical. Practical work is, however, the ultimate outcome. So schoolchildren become students, students become postgraduate students and are then ejected into a world of a quite different type. This too has its disadvantages. Let us not forget that it also makes some sense. Many things, and according to our previous argument, nowadays many more things, have to be learned to a high level. Professional practice depends on a high level of professional knowledge (see Figs. 5 and 6).

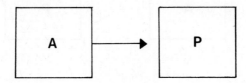

**Fig. 5.** The "Traditional Career" Model

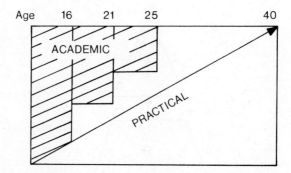

**Fig.6.** The contemporary system of training based on initial period of higher education followed by the 'reality shock' of sudden immersion into cold water of industry.

*The master objective of our educational philosophy is to allow us to plan a system which will produce men in mid-career who are both theoretically knowledgeable and practically competent, and who have the capability to develop further not merely into new areas of knowledge but into the mastery of new practicalities. Thus they will be not merely attuned to the likely needs of organizations and society in a rapidly changing environment, but they will be better attuned and equipped to take hold of those needs in their own interests, and provide opportunities to defend themselves, and their economic and psychic needs, within a rapidly-changing situation. It is crucial for the individual to control the timing and amount as well as the direction and quality of his own learning.*

The sandwich course is another method of organizing the formation process (Fig. 7). The formal periods of learning are alternated with industrial experience. The student applies academic wisdom gleaned in the period of formal instruction to understanding the practical application of these theories and concepts in industry. But more significantly his understanding of the application makes him more critical and aware of the bounds of relevance of the theories in the classroom. The sandwich course approach, either 'thin' or 'thick', appears to represent an almost ideal solution to the problem of balancing academic and practical learning. However, its widespread application has been vitiated for several reasons. Possibly the chief of these has been that the sandwich approach was adopted in institutions which were not in the front rank in terms of academic prestige. It may or may not be fair to infer that the academic standing of the students was in any way inferior. Indeed many companies still positively prefer to employ graduates who have come through a sandwich programme. But the general view of sandwich courses in the higher echelons of British society has been a rather negative, or at best a grudgingly dismissive one.

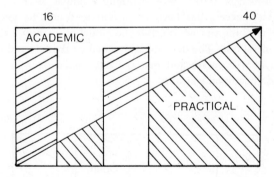

**Fig. 7.** The Sandwich Course Model

A growing phenomenon of the 1970s has been the return to work of married women. This return is paralleled in reverse by a growing demand for re-qualification and developing qualifications among those who have already had one bite at the academic cherry (Fig. 8). Master's courses, diploma programmes, and short courses designed to cater for the mid-career returner to the academic mill have never been more popular. And academic institutions have been under some pressure to organize

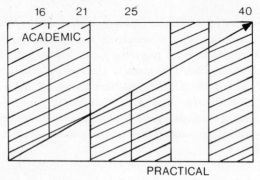

**Fig. 8.** Initial period of first degree followed by
practical experience. Re-entry to academic
stream for full-time postgraduate course later.

their courses and teaching structures to accommodate this demand. But even in the relatively prestigious fields of business and management education, a similar process to that which affects the sandwich courses has obtained. It has been the marginal institutions of higher learning, the newer universities, and the polytechnics which have been most responsive to this kind of demand. Many of the programmes which have been inaugurated in this way have been excellent. But there has been enough chaff in the mill and enough courses of a secondary nature, often in fact offered by commercial and consultancy interests, to make the would-be participant in such a programme uncertain about its particular standing and likely usefulness for his career development.

The Open University is the most stunning example of this process (Fig. 9). Arguably its chief success has been in providing routes to re-qualification for members of the teaching profession. But the model of learning exemplified by the OU is a very general one. The demand stimulated by the OU and rewarded by the professionalism of its courses and material has spilled over into other areas of professional and vocational learning.

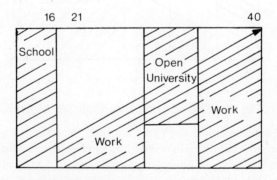

**Fig. 9.** The "Open University" Model

In 1975 we inaugurated the Master of Business Administration degree by part-time study at the University of Glasgow. This degree operates over a three-year period. Students attend courses on a Saturday morning, Monday and the two succeeding Monday evenings. Over a three-week cycle therefore the participant loses one day from work, half-a-day from his weekend, and two evenings from his leisure. Over a three-year period the equivalent of a one-year MBA programme is covered. All the participants are professional managers. All, with a very few exceptions, keep on their regular jobs. Indeed in many cases the course is punctuated by an increase in responsibility due to promotion. In the final year of the course the learning is largely oriented towards a project which the participant undertakes in his own company, usually on a problem of immediate practical relevance.

This course, unique when it was introduced, though rapidly flattered by emulation elsewhere, represents what I should like to call 'herring-bone learning'. Throughout the three years of the course a balance is kept *naturally* between the academic and the practical. The managers' responsibilities at work do not go away. If he is to make sense of the academic learning he has to relate it to areas in which he is under-taking the practice of management. And if he is to develop a concrete appreciation of the theories of motivation, assembly-line balancing, decision analysis, inflation accounting, or industrial relations structures, he will do so with an expectation that the knowledge is his to be *made* relevant.

The interplay between the academic and the practitioner becomes more vibrant in such setting. The cycle of feedback from the classroom to the factory and vice versa is fairly short. Ideas can be challenged, tested, exchanged, and put into a company's information system; colleagues have views, as has the collective wisdom of the organization, which can be returned to the academic. During the period in which the programme has been running, research and consultancy have developed and flourished. All of this puts pressure on the academic, but it is pressure which is usually enthusiastically welcomed because it leads to a refinement and strengthening of professional competence.

One vital argument in favour of the 'herring-bone' approach (Fig. 10), is that it

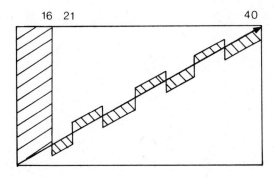

**Fig. 10.** Herringbone Learning

is a relatively inexpensive use of resources. Companies obtain the benefits of a high-level qualification without the attendant risks of losing the participant. Likewise, the home life of the participant has to be stretched to accommodate the demands of the programme, but this is in most cases much less of an inconvenience than the wholesale uprooting, or at least loss of salary through attending a full-time course.

But for me at any rate, the final justification of this kind of approach to learning is one that derives from our understanding of general systems and the logic of self correction. In British society we have tended to develop systems which are large, often massive, take time to learn and time to operate, and the operation of those systems takes place over a relatively long cycle. Indeed that cycle often represents the whole lifetime of an individual. The result is a compartmentalization and over-bureaucratization of British society. We need, and I believe we need urgently, to move towards systems of learning and of employment which allow for a multitude of small mid-course corrections. The individual needs to be able to base further learning on the skills he has already acquired. The academic needs to move out of the prison which separates him from the ordinary routines of industrial, commercial and professional life. The part-time MBA offers one model, a model based on general principles which permit the more continuous readjustment of the institutions of higher education and what those outside higher education sometimes call 'the real world'. Of course both worlds are equally 'real' but the structures of learning and practice in which both have been embedded for too long have continued to inhibit the learning of the one from the other.

# Industry, Society and Education – A Multi-National View

*Alexander Kennaway*

Much current comment on the decline and present poor performance of British manufacturing industry can be shortly expressed as follows:

> The rise of Union power has prevented management from carrying out its true role as entrepreneurs by obstruction to more efficient manufacturing methods and ruined the competitiveness of products, not only by such methods, featherbedding leading to over-manning, but also by demanding and obtaining wages that are unjustified by productivity. Union power has become a reality since it was bolstered by a succession of Statutes. Government has also further shackled industry by a spate of legislation that has forced upon it expensive and unproductive expenditure inspired by those who sought to protect the community from attack on its environment, the customer from exploitation, and the worker from arbitrary and unfair treatment. Government intervention in industry has merely distorted the free play of market forces which, left to themselves, would automatically produce positive action leading to recovery and to a prosperous nation.

The proponents of such views add, when considering the education process, that graduates of universities are not well trained for industry, that even the education of technologists and engineers is largely irrelevant and that the fledglings from such courses are not so useful as those who learned on the job.[1] If science and engineering is too specialized and 'academic' then, too, the education of 'generalists' those who graduated in the classics and humanities (even in geography and law) and who used to be recruited in the 1950s and 1960s with avidity by the major companies, are also not successful in industry.

Encapsulated – this view concludes that (left wing) intellectualism has ruined the country and prays in aid the 'Glorious Past' of Great Britain, whose Industrial Revolution was first and led to a dominant and prosperous economy based on free entrepreneurs, great men, and to a leading role in exporting manufactures, including engineering products. The *status quo ante* Left Wing Man and the Do-gooders was a vibrant, expanding economy. All that has to be done is to return to the conditions of the nineteenth century, restore to industry the freedom to make its own decisions, operate its factories as it will, make the Unions see sense and all will be better. British is best, and will prevail again.

This paper argues that this view is wrong, that its view of British history is incorrect, the premises are invalid and the prescription for recovery is irrelevant to a large degree and incapable of achievement in a democratic society. If one may label such views as typical of the Right Wing in politics and of the representatives of Employers, then there is also a conventional Left Wing view which is also inadequate and containing fundamental fallacies and whose prescription for recovery is equally wrong. Currently it avers that it is essential for recovery to include the Unions and the shop floor in the affairs of the Boardroom; to develop a partnership between Government and industry in planning ahead; it considers that modernizing production facilities, encouraging investment is crucial. It shares with Right Wing politicians an exaggerated fascination with productivity. Deficiencies in the management will be corrected by the combined wisdom of civil servants and trade unions. The extreme Left regard profits as wrong, an exploitation of the working class who are the sole source of wealth. Order will be maintained by policies for everything from pay to investment. This view is also wrong, in my view, and cannot lead to industrial recovery.

It is a pity that industry has become a playground for the amateur, especially when he has so much power to inflict damage. This paper offers a different analysis of success and failure of British business, looks at the different traditions, history and society as it has impacted upon the industry of our chief and most successful competitors. It suggests another way forward, one that is very largely, if not completely, within the authority of industrial directors to carry through. It requires that boardrooms be composed of directors, professional in every way, employing all appropriately-educated executives to the end of identifying market wants, and serving them with products that are fully fit for their purpose throughout their working lives, demonstrate value for money and appeal to customers. Performing service that people want enough to pay the right price for is at the heart of successful business. The more firms that do it properly, the more they will earn, the better will our position be relative to our competitors and the quicker will we recover from the recession. All else, however important, is secondary. In short: more firms have to become competent. The urgent task in Great Britain is to improve rapidly the performance of, say, the next thousand companies to be as good as the best.

What is the reason for their present relatively poor performance? Why are more and more goods replacing British goods both in the UK and in export markets? Let us take a short review of history and look for signs that point to the present condition of British industry.

## Some historical comments

The argument that British manufactures were pre-eminent and that they held a commanding share of world trade through the nineteenth century is so overstated as to be misleading. In fact, the commercial success of late eighteenth century and early nineteenth century British industry was based on the trading instinct of the British, much more than on the technical excellence of British goods.[2] The trading companies, such as the East India Company and its competitors, set free to exploit the colonies and to compete with the Dutch and Spaniards, assisted by British arms, ensured a monopoly for the export of British goods to the colonies of Britain and other countries, prevented local manufacture and ensured a cheap supply of raw materials to British factories. Cromwell also broke the monopoly of the guilds and set the process in motion that allowed greater opportunities for self-made men to set up in technically-based business. The rapid growth of manufacture, using the inventions of the few great practical engineers like Watt, Stephenson and Brunel (who was educated in France) depended also on the willingness of landed gentry, flush with bumper profits from several years of good harvests, to invest in labour-saving devices that led to the lowering of cost of manufacture while the price was kept high in colonial markets by monopoly.

Thus the pattern for British industry was set: ingenious mechanics supported by merchants and amateur bankers without involvement or expertise in manufacturing exploiting controlled markets with the lines of supply and monopoly protected by the Navy and Government. It must not be forgotten that the Industrial Revolution was primarily based on mass production of textiles rather than engineering products. These came slowly and were not pre-eminent in world markets for long. Education for engineers came very late to England. There were only two universities, Oxford and Cambridge, and they taught mainly divinity and the classics; not until 1875 was engineering taught. The consequences showed: the development that should have taken place from the happy combination of the location of iron, limestone, coal and water in Coalbrookdale was not what it could have been. British industry was rapidly caught and then overtaken by the French; the Paris Exhibition of 1855 seriously alarmed the thinking, British élite. A contemporary observer of the period wrote: 'The skilled industries of Great Britain with their irregular bands of workers trained anywhere, nohow, armed with fantastic scraps of empirical knowledge, are doomed.' (Sylvanus P. Thompson, 5th December 1879 to the Royal Society of Arts.)

The French have been at least as inventive as the British: for example, the Jacquard loom, and the quality of European textiles, ceramics and glassware owed much to the emigration of skilled craftsmen from France to escape the anti-Huguenot persecution. At the turn of the eighteenth century, French ships captured by the skill and seamanship of the British Royal Navy, formed the best of Nelson's fleet. The quality and inventiveness of French manufactures shown at the Paris Exhibition of 1855 were the envy of the world. It was the result of a century of deliberate policy in France which, alarmed by the defeats in the Seven Years War at the hands of the British and Austrians, determined to modernize its system of manufactures, roads, bridges and artillery and fortifications in order to raise the standard of its army, which by the Revolution and continuing into the Napoleonic era, was pre-eminent in its will to learn, its application and organization. Napoleon destroyed his General Staff, believing that he could do it all himself. Thus, well before 1870, the French Army was far less efficient than the German and utterly failed to appreciate the logistic and technical requirements of contemporary war. There is a moral here for the successful chief executive, who should take care to have competent advisers and executives, fearless in analysis and in offering opinion.

It was not only the French who demonstrated the value of the application of intellect to the identification and solution of real problems. The Germans were swift to found industry, as were the Americans, and they began rapidly to take trade previously considered by the British to be an exclusive preserve. The development of the motor car, begun in France and Germany, was enthusiastically taken up by the British. But no British firm made a consistent profit from the 1890s to the outbreak of the 1914 War – with the exception of Rolls Royce, who combined excellence of design and workmanship with commercial acumen. The French exported one-third of their production and were the world leaders.

The British General Staff failed to learn the lessons of the Crimea, the American Civil War and, indeed, the Russo–Japanese War. It was plain that war henceforth was not going to be romantic, a question of personal bravery, *panache* and class leadership. It was going to require the application of the industrial complex of nations, would be infinitely destructive and thus pointless as an instrument of national policy. If the politicians had failed to perceive this and were nevertheless bent on war, then it is also true that almost alone the German general staff and officer class saw it and prepared for it. The British did not.

The British chemical companies that were emerging, rather late, to challenge German competition, such as James Muspratt, had to send people to German universities to get an adequate training in chemistry and also appointed Germans as executives about the turn of the nineteenth and twentieth centuries.

The 1914–18 War itself exposed the weaknesses of British industry almost as cruelly as it did that of Tsarist Russia. The rudimentary nature of the British chemical industry brought the country perilously close to disaster through lack of ability to make nitrogen on an industrial scale, through lack of dyes and other organics – ironic lacunae in view of the British invention of aniline dyes a generation earlier. The failure of shells to explode on hitting German battleships at Jutland contributed to the dissatisfaction with that battle from the British viewpoint. The British Army never had a trench mortar equivalent in performance to the German; and so on.

The alarm following the identification of German superiority in industrial technology led to the formation of the DSIR in 1916 and the establishment of the Research Associations which were supposed to lead the technical competence of industry, an aim which, in the opinion of many, it has never succeeded in doing. It might have been more to the point had H.M.G. drafted some competent technologists into industrial boardrooms. In 1928 Lord Eustace Percy wrote in an official report that British exports commanded a lower added value per unit than the equivalent imports.[3] It is sad to note that this remark has been made repeatedly since 1945 as if it were just newly observed, but little improvement was noted over the period.

In the 1930s the Germans and Japanese were attacking the British home market with cheap goods, especially in highly technical spheres, such as watches and instruments. The policy may well have been motivated by the desire to smash commercially these industries upon which a modern future war would depend. The British (correctly) reacted with accusations of aggression against fledgling industries. But Britain in the 1930s should have been in a better condition to fight back. But British industry did not want to employ graduate engineers, nor to give them positions of authority where they might have taken steps to make goods that were competitive. By the beginning of the Second World War it was possible for the Dean of Engineering at Cambridge University to tell his freshmen (of whom I was one), 'Before you undertake this honours course in Mechanical Engineering reflect, no British employer will want you'. I had seen enough of British factories as an apprentice to grasp the truth of that terrible remark. Churchill was persuaded by men like Tizard, Lindemann, Blackett and C.P. Snow, that the conduct of the War depended on harnessing our brainpower. And so the men found themselves drafted into technical jobs. My role was fortunately not in a factory but in the Royal Navy, with a long tradition of educating engineers at degree level and of training them in the Fleet after graduation.

At the end of the War, I saw, as a research officer at the Admiralty, how little the engineering and shipbuilding firms had learned from the experience of war. My experience, together with those of my colleagues who also survived the War, made me realize that civilian shipyards and heavy engineering were not run by men who knew how to advance an industry by creative technical and commercial means. So we did not go, as we might well have done, into British shipbuilding firms. Instead we went into the process industries with a more progressive management. Sir Alfred Egerton reported some years later on the dearth of graduates in ship-building. One of my Naval colleagues became the marine superintendent of a major British shipping line and designed a standard modular carrier of advanced design and solicited tenders for their manufacture in the early 1950s. On the Clyde he was told patronizingly that he did not really want these things, what he really needed was what the Clyde had always done. 'British was best you know'. He then offered the designs to a Japanese shipyard where he was listened to by nearly 200 executives of the firm, all graduates in one form or another of engineering, who, within a week had offered him improvements in detail of his design and who later built the ships on time and competitively. The chemical industry had, by then, learned from the American and Continental experience, especially the German. Indeed, many of the key and successful enterprises both in and serving the process industries were created by immigrants from Europe, especially Germans, mostly Jews. Since 1945 these industries have become competitive with their foreign competitors, and amongst the most progressive firms in the country. Certainly they have proved to be amongst the most stimulating to work in.

But during this period, British engineering has continued its old habits. Product after product is imported; British manufacture ceases to be competitive or even ceases altogether. The foreigner is continually blamed for making better products – cars, television sets, washing machines, machine tools, aeroplanes, ships, plastics processing machinery. The representatives of industry, such as the CBI, play the same old tunes, now on imported tapes from BASF or discs, rather than the old

British 78s, but the message is the same. It is all the fault of:

1 the British workman and his unions;
2 the Government for interference and too much legislation;
3 too high a tax burden on the manager and entrepreneur;
4 too much devaluation of the pound sterling, and now its high value;
5 a devaluation of the American dollar; and *now*
6 irrelevant education of the engineer.

In general their view is that the decline began at the end of the Second World War and that it is everyone's fault except that of the directors of industries.

While this is not the place to argue at length the case against these propositions, it is worth observing:

1 That in the United States of America, the home of entrepreneurial capitalism, the role of government in legislating industry and in financing its activities and those of universities is at least as great as it is in the United Kingdom.

2 The tax burden on higher salaries and company profits is perhaps only marginally higher than in the countries of our chief competitors. In any event, one does not observe British directors, managers and company owners deliberately slacking because they feel over-taxed.

3 Germany and Japan, in particular, maintain high industrial activity and exports in spite of the strength of their currencies. This is because the strength of their currencies followed the strength of their industries, rather than here where the pound is bolstered only by the presence of North Sea oil, and has not been used to strengthen the industrial performance.

Following the cries for freedom from Government shackles, one is perhaps entitled to wonder how many British boardrooms are competent to respond to the challenges of a free market economy. It is ironic to note how often they ask for protection when foreign competition becomes too good! How good, indeed, is the run-of-the-mill British company director?

In this context it is instructive, if saddening to the point of despair, to read a report by Dr. McQuillan to the BIM on attitudes of engineering employers to graduate engineers. It simply demonstrates that they have learned nothing and thought nothing useful over the last one hundred years. It is a consequence of having industry run by Petit-Bourgeois Man, perhaps a half educated, former foreman, who can do no better than to apply poorly-grasped mechanistic principles to a job he was never educated or trained for. He is fearful and jealous of the graduate and adopts the standard reaction – the graduate should know practical things, theory is unnecessary, he needs to be immediately useful in the plant. What such people are really advocating is that universities should turn out engineers like them – with Ordinary National Certificate or Higher National Certificate and nothing better. They may not dare to be so explicit, so the view is dressed up with words like, 'make engineering education relevant to industry', but the result of their advice would be to teach people how to substitute numbers in formulae from the hand-books, know how to design from the British Standard handbooks, know what the currently available catalogue items are, to choose from them, know the systems of industry, how to apply the various statutes, how to fit in with other people just like themselves, but above all, not to be above themselves, not to challenge accepted practice; and not to require training by the firm and its managers who are far too busy. Universities exist to train and not to educate, according to this view; or even to do both, all in the same time. This is not a recipe for a creative professional approach – it is a technician's view – at best. Employers and managers with these attitudes are very successful at de-intellectualizing recent graduates. By offering them advice to, 'forget all that college theory and find out how things actually get done here – or more probably – 'ere – lad', they break the confidence of young people with inadequate self-confidence in the use of thinking; others simply leave and run back to college or to places like the UKAEA with a 'sense of intellect'. It is quite a task for the student looking for a job to recognize at an interview the lack of com-petence in the firm and to go elsewhere. There is no point in having engineers registered as competent if they are to continue to work for incompetent directors.

## The European tradition

When Peter the Great was searching for ways and people to help him to modernize his totally backward country about 1700, he decided to establish the first vocational educational school anywhere in the world – the School of Navigation in Moscow. He took as a basis the mathematical school of Christ's Hospital – eschewing the English public schools as he thought them too classical and irrelevant for his purpose (he had enough in Church schools of his own). But he founded his poly-technical institutes on the French model with the same clear emphatic directive to teach basic mathematics, physics and mechanics and apply them to the practical needs of the community. After the expulsion of the Jesuits in 1761 the French took the opportunity to remodel the education system for the same end. Indeed, in 1775 the school of Ponts et Chaussées set up, and probably invented, the first sandwich courses – six months in classrooms in winter followed by six months in the field during the summer for practical experience. The instruction was grounded in the best maths and science theory of the times, as were the other colleges, such as that in Navarre. When the Americans were founding their military academy at West Point – which gave the first engineering courses in the USA – they deliberately rejected the model of the Royal Military Academy at Woolwich on the grounds that it was not as successful as the French at marrying the theoretical education in maths and sciences to practical needs of engineering.

The whole of the continental tradition in engineering education was based on solid maths and sciences, with a leavening of languages, deportment and military discipline added to the military schools. Indeed, Peter the Great's institutions and the Ecole Polytechnique required uniforms and military discipline from the students and teachers – the French still do. *The attack on irrelevance was against the religious and classical teaching which formed the basis of instruction before the reforms, but which were still desired by the nobility in France, Russia and England.* A significant difference in the aspirations of the social classes in these countries was that in France and Russia the technical education route was the only one open to the poor nobility, the towns-people and minorities if they aspired to high rank in the Army or the state organiza-tions as in Russia. Successive Tsars provided automatic entry to the Table of Ranks – the civil service – governed by the level of education reached. The equivalent of a master's degree conferred automatically the title and rank of nobility in the middle of the nineteenth century in Russia (perhaps Fellows of Engineering should sit in the House of Lords *ex officio*, like Bishops!). Standard Soviet incentives of increased pay, holidays and the right to work in research establishments governed by higher degrees are in this tradition. Thus, in France and Russia the sons of those who would now be called the middle-classes eagerly sought technical education in écoles *polytechniques*, whereas in England they tended to ape the aspirations of the aristocracy and to seek a classical education. It would have been the Catholics, non-conformists and those dilettantes and amateurs of science who would seek education outside England, where the only universities were Oxford and Cambridge which provided only a classical education (and then restricted it to members of the Church of England until 1858). Telford had to learn Italian in order to be able to read books on hydraulics.

From about 1850 the equivalent classes in Germany went to *technischehochschulen* and received a grounding in applied sciences and engineering. There was no snobbery working against these courses in the classes below the 'von' and 'zu', although Liebig thought engineering much below chemistry in content. (We owe to him, incidentally, the founding of the Royal School of Chemistry, now part of the Imperial College of Science and Technology, London.) Germany had been the transit area for war during Napoleon's advances and retreats. Indeed, Leipzig suffered in 1813 the crucial battle that forced his pell-mell retreat all the way to the French frontiers. The German ruling circles saw very clearly that Germany had no natural frontiers of defence and set about organizing themselves into a military–social–industrial complex. By the 1830s, industry, especially heavy engineering, began to be professionally organized. A significant element was the close co-operation between the banks and industrialists. The banks, through direct invest-ment and participation in the boards of directors, became competent as 'banques d'affaires'. Thus Germany has a long tradition of banks as investors, not merely as lenders against security; and with people steeped in technology and business in the banks.

In France and Germany a very high entrance standard was required from applicants to the top schools. The emphasis on personal qualities and high academic attainment was made from the earliest days and is still maintained. Thus the French, the Russians and Germans created an intelligentsia that eventually ran the whole of their society. It could talk with a common language and a common understanding, regardless of which branch of the establishment it was in. This tradition is still maintained in France, and is being re-established in Germany. In England, by contrast, it would hardly be possible to conceive of such an intelligentsia. Our system of specialized education, coupled with the anti-intellectualism of industry, has made it difficult for people to move successfully across the boundaries of the establishment, and indeed for each segment of it to understand and appreciate the problems and aspirations and ambience of the others.

In Tsarist Russia, official attitudes considered the educated middle classes as disloyal to the autocracy – with some justice – but later in the nineteenth century this disapproval did not extend to engineering, which was avidly studied by the less privileged classes. (At a lower level the mechanics' institutes in England and Scotland were also full of craftsmen eager to broaden their general knowledge and deepen their engineering education). Attempts by well-disposed and enlightened officials toward practically-oriented teaching foundered when the few educated people refused to become students in the new institutions founded by Peter the Great and kept on by Catherine the Great. The professors did research to keep occupied and were reluctant to teach the students drafted in by the Tsar to make up the numbers. *The whole Tsarist experience underlines the fact that no central authority, however powerful, can make progress against apathy if widespread in the establishment classes.* It seems unlikely, therefore, that the Engineering Authority proposed by the Finniston Committee will be able to improve British industry. It will become just another outside body of the Establishment, listened to perhaps, but no more.

Certainly no British government has the power of the Tsarist regime, and however enlightened it and the educational authorities may be, it will be vital to improve the attitudes of those very people who have demonstrated an indifference over a hundred years toward proper standards and professionalism in industry – the employers, and the middle classes who still retain snobbish attitudes against industry, manufacturing and technology.

The criticism of lack of relevance of education for the needs of society in past ages in France, Russia, America and Germany was *not* directed against high standards of maths and sciences and intellectual analysis, but against too much emphasis on humanities and classics. The American criticism of the British was that they were not as good as the French at linking theory to practice.

*It is purely an English (and erroneous) criticism to attack analytical studies in engineering.* It is only the British who have this problem with the relevance of engineering education to industry. Everyone else solved this problem long ago and no one else says that too much theory in maths, mechanics and science is bad for industry. It is the British who are alone in despising academic rigour and intellect in industry. At the same time, they still have social hang-ups that restrain those with the intellect to opt for engineering rather than for the law or medicine, or even for 'the City'. Still further they want to prevent the advancement of those, upon whom they have depended so much as a class – the technicians – from advancing to professional status.

There is little point in holding up men of genius as examples of the pre-eminence of any one nation; they are few enough and no nation has a monopoly of them. The best will, in any case, survive any system of education. What we have to consider is how to get the best out of those who, falling short of genius, are yet capable of above average attainment.

It should be said that there is nothing fundamentally wrong with British engineering when it is properly managed. Under dedicated administrators British engineers designed and built some of the best railway systems in the world, in India and in South America; the Indian Post Office system was similarly built and was of high quality. British engineers and technical administrators today still have a high reputation on construction projects and in the management of complex industries across the world. It is also worth noting that the German, American, Japanese, French and Swiss companies who operate subsidiaries in the United Kingdom, report that these companies perform excellently, staffed as they are with British middle management, technologists and workforce. It is also reported that the most profitable pharmaceutical companies in Great Britain are those that are subsidiaries of American firms, followed by subsidiaries of European companies, the bottom being British owned and British managed. To my personal knowledge some of these companies are staffed with the best engineering and applied science graduates from the United Kingdom, but they work under the management systems of their parent companies, and of course under foreign top management. The conclusion seems to be inevitable: when British engineers are led and stimulated by the élite they perform outstandingly well. This, of course, is equally true for the best of British companies who perform extremely well in the world markets. It is the quality of mediocrity, advocated and championed by the mediocre that is too prevalent, particularly in British engineering firms, and has to be resisted and superseded by élitism in order to obtain outstanding professional performance.

This review invites the rejection of the hypothesis that all was well with Britain from the inception of the industrial revolution until the end of the Second World War. It is far more likely that Britain failed to exploit the opportunities created at the turn of the nineteenth century and that its manufacturing performance has been sliding downward ever since, with the exception of a few, very well-run firms, upon whom the main burden of performance, both at home and for exports, chiefly depends.

It remains to test the more natural hypothesis that the performance of manufacturing firms depends crucially upon the quality of its leadership, especially upon its boardroom directors and chief executives.


## Some crucial contemporary aspects


The recent report of the Finniston Committee links the performance of British industry to the quality and education of British engineers. This is a completely unproved assertion. However, it stems from the terms of reference of the Committee, which in themselves made this assumption. The Report of the Committee itself demonstrates the underlying unease of the Committee with the conclusion that it is required to draw.

The Committee permits itself a somewhat coy criticism of the leadership of British industry.[4] It would have been better if it had expanded the point and analyzed it as carefully as it has analyzed the attributes of engineers, for in fact the responsibility for the performance of industry lies, as it must, in the boardrooms of the companies concerned. As has been demonstrated in the historical section of this paper, British industry has steadfastly set its face against the proper marriage of professional directors, professional in every required sense, including that of technology. As has been stated many times elsewhere, the boardrooms of firms in countries competing with Britain, namely France, Germany, America and Japan, are staffed by graduate engineers who have been joined by colleagues from every discipline and in this way have provided a proper team, marrying the requisite business skills and understanding the basis of the business. This basis must, as Finniston says in his clever phrase, 'the Engineering Dimension', embrace marketing and technology.

Business has to be based upon a rigorous identification of what the market wants, and then to set about to meet this demand by a meticulous engineering specification in order to provide goods and services which people will be prepared to buy. For this reason, therefore, the products must clearly be fully fit for their purpose, throughout their working lives and be cost effective, as well as having an appeal including that of the visual. This short definition in itself explains why engineering products require the attention of a well co-ordinated range of skills. The ability to identify a market rigorously requires imagination, objective and dispassionate thought and the intellectual ability to analyse carefully. It is not good enough simply to assume that the past will extrapolate into the future, as so many companies do, and it is not good enough to be smug and assert that what we have always provided will go on being bought. A coincidence of view between potential customer and seller is essential if both are to be satisfied with the ensuing contract and product.

There are so many examples within British firms which suggest that they consider a frank and rigorous exposition of these issues to be ungentlemanly and unnecessary, and that they prefer to rely upon a casual contract, ambiguously expressed, and then wonder why law suits ensue between them when the product fails to meet what the customer expected it to do.

The definition also requires an alert perception of opportunities. These opportunities may be brought about in so many ways; a change in the market, an alteration or an extension of the operational requirements, a change in the supply of an essential raw material such as fossil fuel, a change in distribution habits from the traditional wholesaler to discount shops, an advance in basic technology (for example the invention of semi-conductors and lasers), the advent of the development of fracture mechanics, or, to take an even more apparently abstract example, the development of reliable statistical methods and operational research techniques. A business has to be alive to all these possibilities and recruit, stimulate and encourage people of the intellectual capacity necessary to appreciate all these issues. These men and women must not be so insecure and arrogant that they think they know everything on their subject and cut themselves off from the developing expertise in academic circles, in research institutes and in the laboratories of their competitors across the world. It is the mark of an educated man to know what he does not know and it is the mark of an experienced man to know who does. It is also the mark of a wise and humble man to identify his problems and opportunities properly and to seek co-operation with other people competent to contribute, and yet British industry is remarkable for its almost complete indifference to intellectual activity in universities and elsewhere. It is also true that a few companies who know how to develop a product competently and in good time, make the fundamental mistake of trying out their idea on their customer when they have an order to deliver something in which the customer is supposed to have complete confidence.

Why are so few graduate engineers in the boardrooms? Some argue that it is because few engineers exhibit skills of general management good enough to become company directors. They go on to assert that such deficiencies must be put right in extension of the first degree course to teach such skills. But not everything can be taught at first degree, nor indeed should it. The undergraduate without experience will be unlikely to relate properly what he is taught about complex organizations and about all the other facets than engineering that go to make up a rounded businessman.

It is worth remembering that our successful German competitors concentrate on engineering at first degree level, that their boardrooms have not only graduate engineers, but also chemists, physicists, commercial diplomés lawyers and so on. Perhaps we should look at the lack of educated people of whatever discipline in our boardrooms, then comment that the undereducated feel insecure with the better educated and reject them in favour of more like themselves. It is a self-perpetuating election of chaps like oneself. Given educated people at the outset, then it develops. Such boardrooms also pay proper attention to developing their people during their working lives and encourage them to attend courses to develop new abilities, do what they do now, but better. It is also instructive to note that in the British Armed Forces it is possible for officers and ratings to spend a significant proportion of their whole service life in courses. In industry it is a fortunate manager who gets more than a few weeks of systematic instruction, training and education, other than 'watching Nelly' during forty years of working life. Finniston very properly recommends that British engineers (and one supposes by extension, other managers) have a statutory right to paid study leave.

It is perfectly true that the education of engineers and of applied scientists could well be improved in some key aspects: especially in making clear the assumption that technology is larger than production, that science for industry is to be used in contexts larger than research, that business requires a strategy, a marketing policy, that industry is not an occupation for loners – it requires skills of communication and co-operation. It is essential, too, that schools are seized of the need to encourage more of their best people to seek further education to work in skilled capacities in industries, whether as technicians and craftsmen or as graduates.

The anti-intellectualism of British industry is not a secret that has been hidden from schools and society. Perhaps this is why so few people with the ability to graduate and to arrive at the top of a profession choose to go into industry.

How does this absence of all-round quality in the boardrooms show itself in performance of the firm? Some firms have no policy; they wait for the climate of business to improve. Inside such companies one may hear remarks like, 'There is nothing wrong with this firm that more sales would not put right'. It can be expected from such organizations that they will tend to be takers of orders at any price. If they think about it at all, tactics of price cutting are justified by remarks that such business pays the fixed costs and keeps skills together (often regardless of the fact that their labour turnover may be up to a third replaced every year). Such firms ruin not only themselves but also many of their competitors. Such tactics also prevent generation of enough funds to improve the products or productivity by up-to-date methods.

Another manifestation of a lack of marketing strategy is to go for anything regardless of the ability of the firm to supply that demand or that market. Obsession with volume or with market share as a touchstone of commercial virility is not unknown even in service industries. The results of many well-known High Street names have in decline attested to this blunder.

Another common fault is to consider smugly that past successes will automatically be extrapolated into the future. How many British firms failed to perceive that the Arab and Nigerian markets would run out of steam, one country after another? The euphoria of a big market in its heyday prevented them from analyzing critically that business was not steadily growing in each country, that it swung violently in the last decade. How many firms went on supplying the same product that captured a particular market without seeing that competitors had looked at their honeypot, come up with a better article and taken the market away? How many firms have offered products on a basis well-established on experience, but have studied too casually the specific conditions that a new customer requires and have produced a mismatch between them? Such firms often face not only the loss of payment but very substantial legal costs and damages. How many firms rely on an outdated design and fail to order a design audit, and then find that the product fails in a crucial respect?

Some firms are also deficient in co-operation between their sales and technical departments. The former may push for, and even get, an order that they cannot design a product to meet, make on time or even make at all, except by doing their development while attempting to satisfy the order. Some enter too casually into development of a new product range without adequate calculation of the cost and time involved to take it to completion. Some firms fail to develop enough funds to develop their processes or their product range, or to invest in proper sales and distribution organization and promotion. Some firms neglect their production facilities so completely that they are quite incapable of producing at a competitive cost.

Blindness to any one of these faults may well lead to slow decline, if not to disaster. A combination over some years certainly will – and does.

We can all produce far too many examples from experience to support each of these basic errors and many others. This is not to say that foreign firms do not show such faults, they do, but we have to compete with the best. It is not to say that all British firms are bad, they are not. Those that are well-managed, some well-known, show excellent results even in the current recession.

The types of company error mentioned, responsible for specific major loss or to the failure of the firm itself, could, but not in the context of this paper, be exposed by name and case examples. They have one thing in common – a failure within the boardroom of one kind or another. These failures all share an inability to identify the crucial issues to put appropriately competent resources to solve the problems in good time, and to direct the project through to success, both in commercial and technical terms. In no single case was it true that the necessary expertise was unavailable to the board of directors, had they chosen to look for it either from within their own organization or outside within the United Kingdom.

In my experience working abroad, whether in Germany, France or the United States, in companies comparable with those British companies whose performance has come under criticism, I have found a more integrated professionalism at top level. This has expressed itself in several ways. First of all, the boardrooms are composed of people who are largely educated in the appropriate technologies and at the same time have a complete grasp of the business. There is no divorce between those two aspects. In my experience, company directors in such companies are not anti-intellectual, many have higher degrees and some, indeed, have joint appointments with universities and polytechnics of the highest reputation. Their recruiting policies are clear and simple; they take graduates in applied science, technology and commerce, and they see to it that their staff are exposed to frequent contact with the universities. This is achieved, for example, by taking eminent academics as visiting lecturers, who give seminars, who sit in on discussions in the research groups and who discuss problems of all kinds. If these are extensive they are frequently awarded contracts to work on them in their own academic environment. Executives of such companies are encouraged to visit appropriate research institutes, universities and to obtain post-experience education by way of short courses and higher degrees. It is of interest to note that in the German chemical industry, for example, the employers' federation have advised the polytechnics that they do not want their graduates at *Diplome Ingineer* level to study management subjects or a foreign language. They would far rather that they graduated as competent engineers and they acquired these skills later on in life.

In America it is particularly noticeable that the graduate technical staffs of the leading companies are free from the very common attitude that one notices else-where: that they are sufficient unto themselves, know it all and will get by somehow without calling upon outside help. One of the other differences between the board-rooms of firms in these countries and of those in the United Kingdom is the presence of a large number of non-executive directors on the supervisory boards. These are usually men of wide business experience, still active in other companies. Some members of the supervisory boards will also be practising bankers connected with the firm. There is thus a considerable experience of finance, business, commerce and technology, and the experience of explaining the affairs of the company and of presenting its forward plans to such a body is a sharp one. Management practices and styles in such organizations are usually devoid of complexity, free of attachment to 'isms' and dogmas and are based on very simple principles which everyone understands. New graduates are rapidly indoctrinated with a business orientation to add to their own discipline and it is very rare to find a young scientist, even in a research department doing the most abstruse work, to be entirely free of this business orientation. The English stereotype of the boffin is hard to find in such companies. This is partly brought about by the unashamed purpose of undergraduate teaching which is to fit technologists and commercial graduates to work in industry. It is also to the credit of the directors and senior managers of the companies in which they work to reinforce this view.

### The way forward

I am not one of those who believes that the primary problem lies in industrial relations or in the re-assertion of management control over the trade unions, although both these factors must enter into the discussion. The solution to poor industrial relations stems from the establishment of a successful business strategy which produces a sense of stability and a confidence in advancing the prosperity of the firm.

It is noteworthy that in general well-managed and successful firms have very few problems with their labour force. Poor industrial relations do occur with managements, however good and however sincere, if they have inherited a long history of mutual suspicion and bad relations. On the whole, British trade unions and British working people consider that it is the role of management to manage. There is very little demand amongst the rank and file for unions to participate in management as there has been on the continent. It is tragic that British trade unions concentrate so much on the problems of production to the exclusion of marketing and of a business strategy, so much so that according to extreme left-wing opinions these latter are irrelevant and even parasitical. All wealth, according to this view, stems from the productive power of the shop floor. Indeed, when a firm has its back to the wall the unions offer to drop demarcation lines and to co-operate on the shop floor as if this is all that is required. Alas, the companies rarely fail for these reasons, and the offer comes too late. It would have been better if the unions had co-operated and indeed stimulated the management to develop a business strategy based on a market-orientated policy. The concomitant to this view is that working people have trusted managements to find profitable business, to carry out all the commercial, marketing and sales work and to ensure a decent standard of living on the factory floor. Much of the present problems can be attributed to the lack of business acumen and competence in many British companies, leading to a loss of markets. This is far more associated with the failure to perceive what the markets want in a changing world and with the inability and lack of resource to design and develop suitable products for the market, than it is with labour problems, or with a low productivity. This is because on the whole the choice between products depends far more upon their design than upon modest differences in price which reflect differences in labour productivity. This is not to say, of course, that the latter does not depend upon the former. Indeed, this reinforces the argument that competent managements have to invest in people with the technical ability to design products for the market and also which can be made economically. It is also true that to a very large degree it is the design and layout of production equipment that determines the cost of the products. It is becoming less and less true that decisions by the workforce affect the output of a modern production line (except when they refuse to operate it altogether).

It is quite wrong for the left-wing and for the trade unions to adopt a very old-fashioned British view that profits are a bad thing. (See, for example, *Your Employers' Profits* by Christopher Hird, published by Pluto Press.) Profits (plus depreciation) are the only source of internal funds from which all desired improvements can stem. How this resource is allocated is a question for management's decision. Increased profits lead to increased morale at all levels because there is now a choice as to what to do with the increased resources. By processes of added value wage bargaining, the workforce can see very easily how they themselves can benefit by the allocation of extra income and indeed can participate with management in the reduction of waste, the reduction of cost and therefore the increase of added value at all levels. The management become more interested as well because they can see that they can turn their professional skills to better effect.

It is also worth remembering when contemplating the apparently harmful effect of high wages that they may, in certain circumstances, have a beneficial effect. For example, according to Habakkuk the high standard of living enjoyed during the latter half of the nineteenth century by smallholders in the United States of America always forced factory wages to compete with them and thus impelled American capitalists to invest in labour-saving processes and equipment.[5] The easy access to productive arable land in the United States made this competition real, whereas in Europe land tenure and ownership were inimical to this process.

The search for the cause of low productivity purely in the amount of money spent on capital investment within the factory is also inadequate. There are many examples of expensive and erroneous investment on capital goods. Rather it is the quality of the investment within a business strategy that is important. From this argument it follows that the way forward for British manufacturing companies is to develop a market orientated business strategy and to equip themselves to carry it out. The decline has gone very far over the last one hundred or so years. The world outside Britain has also changed. Many countries have become far more competitive and far more capable of doing many of the mundane, technical things that Britain used to be good at. Successful business strategies are, therefore, now not so easy to find.

What kind of strategy is appropriate to the 1980s? It is clear that many of the formerly underdeveloped countries are now industrializing rapidly, indeed with the help of the most advanced industrial countries who are assisting them to put in the most modern productive resources. It is also clear that countries such as Japan, Taiwan, Hong Kong and others are increasingly capable of using their intelligence to identify what industrialized countries want, designing products for the mass consumer market and, indeed, for the industrial market as well. The average, run-of-the-mill products are assembled with great efficiency and put on to the markets of the industrialized countries at a cost with which the native product cannot compete. It cannot compete for several reasons. First of all, it is now late for such countries to attempt to copy the design of mass consumption goods because the Japanese and so on will always be one jump ahead. Secondly, there has been insufficient, and insufficiently intelligent investment in production systems and equipment in order to increase the added value per man. Thirdly, because such companies are run down, not only in productive resources but also in every other department, and most especially in morale (not only of the shop floor but of management, whence it all comes). The standard responses mentioned above lead to an ever lower level of activity, an ever lower added value, an ever lower opportunity to earn decent wages, a poor standard of the environment within which to work, and morale inevitably drops even further.

All this sounds very fine, but how on earth does one find a successful business strategy in the prevailing circumstances of reduced world industrial activity, increased competition from the developing countries in straightforward consumer goods, and the fact that Britain has been left behind in the industrial application of advanced technology and faces an increasing lead from our major industrial competitors?

The first essential is to identify what business the firm is good at, – if that market at which it is skilled is itself weakening then another must be found. If it can sustain continuing effort, then the prime thing is to do better what is already done, rather than to attempt to diversify. This requires on the one hand a continuous, rigorous look at the market, its wants and then design of products that will command a proper price. It is also good advice even in a depression. The answers for each firm are particular to it, for some the remedy is to go up-market, not to compete with the run-of-the-mill here or abroad. But all solutions have things in common: never to forget that the world changes; finding products and services in competition with those that exist; always to look at market opportunities first and then to devise and command with skill the means to satisfy them.

The successful development of a business requires an integral approach to the activities of the firm. It cannot be separated into activities such as product development, marketing, credit control, improving the asset ratio and so on. Some firms do not really have a business strategy at all and it shows in the quality of their performance. Many such firms complain that their foreign competitors are flooding the market and demand import controls from the Government. It is indeed astonishing how many people in private enterprise have been heard in recent years attacking Government interference and arguing that if they were freed from their shackles they would perform in a free market economy to the benefit not only of themselves but of the nation. Since business strategy can only be set by the board of directors, it follows that the key to the improvement of British industry lies in improving the performance of more British companies up to the level of the best of British companies and of their overseas competitors.

Successful companies, therefore, will ensure that they employ people capable of the highest intellectual effort and capable of recognizing that which they do not themselves know. These people will be aware of who does know, and will have the humility to go and ask such people, who may well be in research institutes, in other companies, or in universities. The collaboration between commercial engineering and technology and academics is of crucial importance and is certainly one of the keystones of success in Germany, France, America, Holland and, no doubt, elsewhere. It is sadly lacking in far too many British companies. A company can pull itself up by its own bootstraps; it can generate the funds in order to invest in all these activities if it tries hard enough and takes it slowly. There are examples of companies that a decade ago were small, struggling and on a downward path, who – by following policies such as these – are now highly successful and advertise the fact in the press. And they are right to do so. They are to be contrasted with the companies that have been quoted above as examples of failure and whose activities have led to so many disasters.

The question, therefore, must now be asked: 'How are more British companies to acquire such a professional business attitude, and how are they to become more successful in the uncertain world ahead?' There is no evidence to support the view that it all depends on the system of educating engineers, or, indeed, on the educational system itself. Except perhaps to assert that industry itself should do much more to change the social attitudes which are inimical today. It may well be necessary to have a much closer link between people who are working in industry and the schools. Very few schoolteachers, even those with degrees in science, have worked in industry. Means must be found to extend some of the excellent work by various bodies, including the City and Guilds of London Institute, to excite schoolchildren in practical things, and to persuade some of the best to fit themselves for careers in industry.

There is little evidence to support the assertion that the education of British engineers is deficient at the undergraduate level. Provided that industry makes it possible for its employees throughout their working careers to improve their qualifications, to go on post experience courses, both short and long, it will not be so necessary to extend the present three, or four, year courses. It is worth noting that the CBI in its response to the Finniston Report has *opposed* the statutory right of engineer employees to paid study leave! Mexico already has it. However, it must be conceded that the practice of engineering at full professional level may well require at least the five years of the German diploma in engineering. Engineering, after all, can be compared with medicine in that it requires a thorough grounding in a relatively wide range of sciences and then the application of those sciences to real and practical situations. This latter phase cannot be left purely to a practical period in industry after graduation. A proper engineering degree must require a grounding in science, followed by an academic training in its application. There is no evidence to suggest that the mere changing of the titles of engineers, or indeed their registration, will improve the performance of British industry. It seems unlikely that employers will be more inclined to recruit and promote such people when they have not taken people of equivalent educational attainment and intellectual ability in the past.

It seems inevitable that the right conclusion is that the responsibility for improved performance lies, as it does in other walks of life, at the top. This means that the boardroom must be composed of people who are truly professional and are prepared to identify and promulgate a strategy, to set a professional ambience and to will the means as well as the ends. Since it is unlikely to happen of its own accord, and to happen quickly, it would seem that some of the lessons from overseas should be quickly learned. This will require a much closer collaboration between industry and universities on the one hand, and industry and the finance houses on the other. On both sides of this interchange there will need to be an improvement in the understanding of the other and a competence to perform within the other's environment. There should, therefore, be a far greater interchange along the lines that Finniston has proposed between the universities and industry, and a much closer collaboration on education, on research, development and design projects. It will also be necessary for more institutions in the City of London to become *banques d'affaires*, and here it might be worth offering scholarships and the means whereby executives in the one work in the other. This should have the result that private enterprise could be financed directly by the primary banks, life insurance companies and pension funds who *must* then have the competence to protect and develop their own investment incomes in the companies concerned. If the British banks are reluctant to do this, it would seem logical to invite the closer co-operation of the many foreign banks in this country with such experience. These include the banks of the leading EEC countries, as well as America and Japan.

The City must change its attitude toward profits. City analysts drive firms to a short-term steady improvement in profits, which can often be at the expense of long-term growth and prosperity. Return on capital here has been above that of our competitors with a longer view and who as a consequence overtook us in trade and inevitably also in profitability. Japan is now accepting lower returns and thinks very far ahead. Germany is reported as putting first in business objectives, growth through market-led innovation and progressive product design based on the assumption that such an indirect approach to profit will bring its own reward.

## Notes

1 McQuillan, M.K. (1978) *Graduate Engineers in Production*, Cranfield.
2 Dobb, M. (1946) *Studies in the Development of Capitalism*, Routledge.
3 Percy, Lord E. (1928) *Report on Education for Industry and Commerce*, HMSO.
4 *Engineering Our Future*, Paragraphs 2.17, 2.19, 2.33, 2.34, 2.35.
5 Habakkuk, H.J. (1962) *American and British Technology in the Nineteenth Century*, Cambridge University Press.

## Bibliography

### England

McQuillan, M.K. (1978) *Graduate Engineers in Production*, Cranfield.
Dobb, M. (1946) *Studies in the Development of Capitalism*, Routledge, London.
Trevelyan, G.M. (1942) *English Social History*, Longman, London.
Cunningham, W. (1927) *Growth of English Industry and Commerce*, Cambridge University Press, Cambridge.
Shadwell, A. (1913) *Industrial Efficiency*, Longman, Green & Co, London.
Smiles, S. (1884) *Invention and Industry*, John Murray, London.
Bourne, J. (1865) *The Handbook of the Steam Engine*, Longman, London.
The Report of the Committee on the Education and Training of Officers of the Army (1902) HMSO, London.

BOND, B. (1972) *The Victorian British Army and The Staff College, 1854–1914*, Methuen, London.
The Letter Books of the RMA Woolwich.
RODERICK, G.W. and STEPHENS, M.D. (1979) *Education and Industry in the Nineteenth Century*, Longman, London.
HILKEN, T.J.N. *Engineering at Cambridge University, 1783–1965*, Cambridge University Press, Cambridge.
GUGGISBERG, F.G. (1900) *The Shop*, Cassell, London.
GOWING, M. and ARNOLD, L. (1974) *Independence and Deterrence, Britain and Atomic Energy, 1945–1952*, Macmillan, London.
Engineering our Future. The Report of the Committee of Inquiry into the Engineering Profession, (1980) HMSO, London.
HOBSBAWN, E.J. (1969) *Industry and Empire*, Pelican, Harmondsworth.
PERCY, Lord E. (1928) Report on Education for Industry and Commerce, HMSO, London.
Clark Report, 'Education for the Engineering Group of Engineering Institutes', (1929) HMSO, London.
Goodenough Report on 'Education for Salesmanship', (1931) HMSO, London.

### France

GAZIER, D. *Aperçu sur elevation de l'école des Ponts et Chaussees depuis sa création jusqu'a nos jours.*
ARTZ, F.B. (1939) *L'education technique en France au XVIII siécle, 1700–1789*, Alcan, Paris.
BIEN, D., *Military Education in Eighteenth Century France.*

### Russia

*History of Academy of Sciences of USSR (Istoriia Akademii Nauk USSR)*, Vol. I, 1724–1803 (1958).
VUCINICH, A.S. (1963) *Science in Russian Culture*, Vol. I, Stanford University Press, Stanford.
ALSTON, P.L. (1969) *Education and the State in Tsarist Russia (to 1860)*, Stanford University Press.
HANS, N. (1963) *The Russian Tradition in Education*, Greenwood, Westport.
HANS, N. (1951) Slavonic record 1952 on the Moscow School of Navigation in *Slavonic Review*, June 1951, Vol. 29, No. 73 'Moscow School of Navigation 1801'.
FARQUESON, H. (1959) *Pioneer of Russian Education*, Review by Nicholas Hans, Aberdeen University Review, Aberdeen University Press.
HANS, N. (1951) *New Trends in Education in the Eighteenth Century*, Routledge, London.

### America

FLEMING, T.J. (1969) *West Point, the Men and Times of the United States Military Academy*, William Morrow & Co, New York.
Proceedings of the Third Military History Symposium (1969) USAF Academy.
GRIESS, C.T.E., Professor and Head of the Department of History, US Military Academy, West Point, (Unpublished manuscript).

### General

HABAKKUK, H.J. (1962) *American and British Technology in the Nineteenth Century*, Cambridge University Press, Cambridge.
EMMERSON, G.S. (1973) *Engineering Education and Social History*, David and Charles, Newton Abbot.
Report of the Committee on the Training of Officers for the Scientific Corps of the British Army (1857).
KENNAN, G.F. (1979) *The Decline of Bismark's European Order: Franco-Russian Relationships 1875–1890*, Princeton University Press, Princeton.
WICKENDEN, W.E. (1929) 'A Comparative Study of Engineering Education in the United States and Europe', Bulletin 16, Society for the Promotion of Engineering Education, June, 1929.

## 3
## *Industrial Performance and the Effective Utilization of Manpower*

## Is Manpower Planning Necessary?
## Is It Possible? What Next?

*Lord Bowden of Chesterfield*

The number of scientists in the world has increased by about 12 per cent per annum, ever since the time of Newton. This means that the number has doubled every six years or so. The cost of equipping a scientist in real terms increases by almost 4 per cent a year, so the overall cost of science increases by 16 per cent a year and it doubles every five years. The same sort of thing has been going on independently in most other countries in the western world – in particular in America and in Russia. Clearly the costs involved expanded just as the numbers did. The inflation in the cost of science in most western countries took place at about 16 per cent per annum compound interest for many years. It was a rate four or five times as great as the inflation in the cost of ordinary goods and much greater than the rate of increase in the national income. It is only in the last four years that the inflation in the cost of science in England has been taking place at a smaller rate than the inflation in the cost of goods. Today the cost of science in real terms may even be declining.

When I was Minister of Science I went to see Mr. Rudnev who was the Minister responsible for manpower planning in Moscow. Mr. Rudnev said, 'In Russia we have an extremely complicated system of planning; we try to decide the optimum size of universities and distribute our students among the different courses so that industry will have the right people in ten years' time. We always get the answers wrong.' He added, 'You don't seem to make any plans in England and you get your answers wrong too'. We could not decide which of us was the more inefficient.

I must describe an example of manpower planning which is a terrible indictment of our system at its worst. For many years most of the men who were planning our towns and our countryside had graduated in architecture, geography or economics. Some of them had taken a one-year postgraduate diploma as well. But in 1970 the Government urged the universities to establish special undergraduate courses for the town and country planners. It takes a long time to organize a course, to recruit staff and to admit students. In 1974 the Social Science Research Council predicted a shortage of 2000 planners in 1977 – the annual output was about 600 – so universities expanded their departments. The first graduating class emerged three years ago, and they all got very good jobs. The third class which graduated July 1978 found there were no jobs in town and country planning to be had in the country. Government policy had changed. Public expenditure had been cut. There was nothing to plan, nothing for planners to do.

The story is not untypical. Twenty years ago I knew Lord Fleck when he was Chairman of ICI. I remember asking him what rate of growth UMIST should try to achieve in its schools of chemistry and chemical engineering if we were to satisfy the needs of industry and prepare our students for promising careers. He said quite firmly that both departments should grow by 10 per cent per annum for many years to come. So we built a splendid chemistry building and expanded our undergraduate school of chemical engineering until it was the biggest in Europe. Throughout the 1960s ICI recruited about 600 graduates every year. In 1969 their personnel director said in a public speech, 'We have learned our lesson, never again shall we allow our annual rate of recruitment to fall below a certain minimum figure' – which was never precisely specified, but was thought to be about 300. In 1971 they recruited thirty-two graduates. They seem to have decided that they had done all the research they were going to need for years to come. This astonishing change in their policy had a devastating effect on all the chemistry departments in every school and every university in the country and, to make matters worse, several other big firms cut their recruitment just as abruptly. If ICI do not want chemists, why should sixth-formers start a course in chemistry at school? For almost a decade every under-graduate school and every postgraduate school of chemistry in England was half empty. Before the 'fall' UMIST used to admit 140 chemists and 110 chemical engineers every year. For several years after we admitted only seventy chemists and forty chemical engineers. Thank goodness we have a few more now. ICI realised how much harm they had done. They have learned another lesson! Now every division is expected to recruit a certain minimum number of graduates, whether it wants them or not, unless it can get a waiver from the central board. I doubt if ICI will ever again recruit more than 350 graduates a year – this is about half as many as they used to recruit at one time; but I hope that they will never turn the tap off abruptly and stop recruiting graduates entirely.

### Estimates revised

ICL are the biggest computer manufacturers outside America. The Government had invested heavily in the firm and a great deal of our national future depends upon it. ICL used to recruit 400 or 500 graduates a year, most of whom were mathe-maticians or engineers. One year they recruited 490, of whom fifty-one were Manchester graduates. The following year (I think it was 1971) they recruited forty-two graduates altogether, of whom one was a Manchester graduate. He was a chemical engineer! Fortunately they want more men this year.

At one time the Post Office recruited no graduates at all, but took it for granted that a youth in training, by which they meant a boy who had learned to ride one of those red bicycles and deliver telegrams, would be able to design any piece of machinery the Post Office might need. As late as 1962 the Post Office had only fifteen graduates who had served a proper postgraduate apprenticeship. In 1971 they recruited 700 graduates and announced that they intended to recruit 900 graduates in 1972. This information was circulated to every appointments board in the country, but in the event they recruited fifty. Many graduates who had been led to believe the Post Office had jobs to offer turned down other opportunities. But, again, the Post Office announced its intention of recruiting 900 graduates. Three months later they revised their estimate by a factor of nearly twenty. This catastrophe was due to sudden unexpected cuts in the Post Office investment programme which were made by the Government which had already paid for the education of the engineers whom the Post Office was forbidden to employ.

### Essential services neglected

This is a perfectly appalling state of affairs. No country in the history of mankind ever became rich and prosperous by keeping its most productive people in idleness. The cutback in public expenditure has been so savage that some essential services are being completely and dangerously neglected.

You will remember that the Crown Agents managed to lose £200 million in the late 1970s through sheer incompetence in buying and selling property. There has been a court of inquiry to try and find out how they did it. In a sense it was fairy gold; they never lost any material object like a house, a road or a hospital. The amount which the Government's own policy costs the community every year through its inability to keep the civil engineering industry at work is at least twenty times as great as the total loss incurred by the Crown Agents. I believe that the system which creates such absurdities is wrong and must be changed. It makes manpower planning quite impossible.

Industry has always been used to the fluctuations in demand which accompany the trade cycle. These changes may be serious, but they usually take place fairly slowly, and a competent manager can usually foresee them and take action in time. The abrupt and totally unpredictable changes I have written about can only be produced by the Government. No industry can possibly cope with them or survive them. They seem to be the inevitable by-product of changes in Government policy, changes which have been intended to stabilize the economy and help British industry. We have all been very critical of drug manufacturers who persuaded women to use thalidomide as a sedative but did not realize what it could do to unborn children. We have been taught to accept the secondary effects of 'fine-tuning' as inevitable. However, I believe that the actions of sucessive governments have been well-intentioned, but arbitrary and completely irresponsible. Whitehall has ignored the consequences of its own policies.

The one profession which is booming at the moment is accountancy. No one foresaw the spectacular increase in its demand for graduates. Until ten or fifteen years ago people became accountants after leaving school at the age of eighteen and working in an office while they studied theory at night school or by correspondence courses. They served their articles, they were examined by the profession and admitted to its ranks. Since then two things have happened. Many of the big firms recruit graduates instead of schoolboys and several universities have created big undergraduate schools of accountancy.

In 1962 out of 5000 men who became accountants 500 were graduates. In 1977 there were 3000 graduates out of a total intake of 4500. In 1978 the four big firms (Peat Marwick & Mitchell, Price Waterhouse, Coopers and Deloittes) recruited 1100 graduates between them, which is twice as many as Shell, ICI and Rolls Royce want all put together. The shortage of jobs in production industry has driven many graduates in mechanical engineering and civil engineering to become accountants.

### Government policy?

I shall not say much about the effect of the inexplicable difference between the salaries of engineers in the public service and those employed in private productive industry, but I must at least mention the fact that an engineer employed by the Post Office, by a town hall, or by Whitehall can always expect to earn at least a thousand pounds a year more than his opposite number in a factory. Furthermore, he can expect complete security of tenure and an indexed pension, and he never has to work unsocial hours or take risks to earn it. What is the government trying to do? Has it got a policy at all?

There was a time when the universities were expanding and they recruited some of their ablest graduates as members of staff. Industry complained, but now that universities have stopped growing they cannot recruit any more, or promote staff they have.

Is it practical to organize a system of education when the opportunities graduates will have are so completely unpredictable? I would like to refer for one moment again to my conversation with Mr. Rudnev. I reminded him of a remark which was once made by the Duke of Wellington. He said, 'The French plans are like splendid leather harness which is perfect when it works, but if it breaks it cannot be mended. I make my harness of ropes, it is never as good-looking as the French, but if it breaks I can tie a knot and carry on.'

Graduates will have to be prepared to find a job wherever they can, whatever subject they studied at the university. All attempts that have been made to devise a rational system for predicting demand have utterly failed. How can anyone possibly decide how many chemists the country needs if our biggest employer of graduate chemists is so unpredictable in its demands? How big should our schools of electrical engineering be if the Post Office changes its policy so often and so profoundly.

Here is another example of the problems which make manpower forcasting so difficult. Consider the problems of the firms who make television sets; they are an important part of the whole electronics industry. The public spends about £500 million on sets every year. It is a fairly big industry, but not one of the giants. In 1972 and 1973 Mr. Barber (now Lord Barber) was Chancellor of the Exchequer in Mr. Heath's Government. He tried to inflate the economy – he removed restrictions on credit so that the demand for television sets suddenly and most dramatically increased. This was the twenty-sixth change since the war in the regulations governing the conditions under which people can rent or buy television sets, the twenty-sixth no less! No other country in Europe had experienced more than six changes, but our Government is trying to fine-tune the economy; it keeps changing the bank rate and the money supply – and the terms for buying houses, motor cars and television sets. Mr. Barber's inflation produced a boom in the price of houses and an enormous demand for television sets. We imported sets from Japan because we were unable to make them all ourselves. Several firms expected that the demand would continue. A large factory was built to make TV sets north of Manchester with money borrowed from the Government. Mr. Chattaway, who was the minister concerned, came up and opened it. Of course several years passed between the day some enterprising managers decided that the demand for television sets was booming and the day the factory started making them in quantity. Meanwhile, there was an economic crisis followed by a general election. Mr. Barber and Mr. Healey cut all non-essential spending. The demand for television sets fell overnight by a factor of five and Mr. Chattaway's factory closed almost before it had started work. What an example of government-aided investment and manpower planning! Pilkington's efforts to make the envelopes for TV tubes were abandoned soon afterwards and their £18 million plant was scrapped. Who will be a production engineer making TV sets again – whatever university appointments boards may say?

### Universities blamed

The Government seems to be trying to control the economy as if it were a servo system. They make use of inaccurate out-of-date information; the servo is sluggish so, as any servo designer could tell them, the harder they try to operate the controls the more unstable the system becomes.

Just think of the problems of universities. After a schoolboy decides to read engineering, he spends a couple of years in the sixth form preparing himself, then he has to go to university for three years, then he has to undergo that extraordinary experience which converts a college graduate into an engineer. After seven years or so, he is available as a useful member of the productive force of this country. Meanwhile, we have had a couple of general elections and half-a-dozen changes of national policy. There are either too many graduates, or too few, and people will blame the universities for lack of foresight.

We used to base our plans on the assumption that we should have full employment. For twenty years, unemployment never rose above 3 per cent – if it dropped below $1\frac{1}{2}$ per cent the economy overheated. But we now have 7 per cent or more of the working population unemployed. This is enough to upset all the manpower planners; but I want to deal for a moment with the problems of the civil engineers, builders, architects and their workmen who have been hit worse than any other industry of comparable size. A quarter of the workforce is often unemployed, nearly half a million men all told, and while they are idle, someone has to pay interest on the capital which has been invested in their huge machines. This industry is very dependent on the Government, and that is presumably why the Government has always used it as a 'regulator'.

Our civil engineering industry has to import timber for houses and oil to run its tractors and machinery, but not much else. Almost all its raw materials are dug out of the ground and made up by working men in this country. To keep half a million civil engineers out of work does very little to help the balance of payments. But if the half million were working, they would be producing roads and hospitals and factories and houses worth at least £4000 million every year.

## Accountants dominate

Accountants look after paper. Remember Mr. Slater's remark, 'I don't make things, I make money'. According to a survey that was made by Professor Stamp, the salaries of the partners in the big firms of accountants are bigger than the salaries of any other professional men in this country. The demand for accountants is virtually insatiable; their effect on gross domestic product is virtually nil. Nevertheless, the most important man in many firms is not the production engineer who gets things made, but the accountant who tells the firm how to survive after paying tax on the profits it hopes to make and has not actually made yet, and better still, how not to pay too much tax anyway. Meanwhile, the Department of Inland Revenue devises even more ingenious schemes for collecting cash from the citizens. It is an extraordinary and expensive battle which seems to be absorbing some of the ablest and most highly-paid men in the country. Do we really benefit from all this elaborate infighting? Today accountants dominate British industry. We have more accountants in this country than there are in all the other countries in the EEC put together. I believe that bad accounting has contributed more to the decline of British industry than recalcitrant unions or incompetent management.

Now I must turn to manpower in that great firm of Metropolitan Vickers AEI. When I first knew it, there were 27 000 people on the site in Trafford Park. I think it was the most remarkable concentration of engineering skill in all England, and the proudest factory in Europe. A man who worked at Met Vick in those days was a man of distinction. Met Vicks was regarded in Manchester with the same reverence as the Navy or the Bank of England. Its critics complained that it behaved with the arrogance of a nationalized industry whose losses would be underwritten by the taxpayer. Its engineers believed in their hearts that if they could maintain their position among the best engineers in the world, all would be well with them and customers would flock to buy the great machines they made. But loyalty, devotion and superb engineering were not enough. AEI was taken over by GEC. There are now about 7000 people on the site; three-quarters of the staff have gone.

## Financial pundits delighted

The extraordinary battle which destroyed the old AEI was fought between merchant bankers and accountants on behalf of shareholders. The views of the engineers were never considered for one moment. That financial wizard, Sir Arnold Weinstock, was able to convince AEI shareholders, most of whom were such people as the Prudential Insurance Company, that they would earn more on their investments if the GEC took the firm over than they would if it remained under its original management. The battle was fought out very publicly for six weeks in 1967. GEC increased its bids twice. The first offer for Met Vicks was £120 million. It would have cost five times as much to rebuild and re-equip the factories. Most of the shareholders know nothing and cared less about engineering. They agreed to sell the whole firm for £160 million. The engineers were horrified; the financial pundits were delighted. The lives of the staff, managers, engineers and workmen alike were transformed. Many men were shattered by the experience; but what does Trafford Park mean to the average City gent?

Willis Jackson had 980 people in the research department of Met Vicks when he directed it. Dr. Dodds, who succeeded Willis as director of research, once said to me, 'I have only 109 more days here and thank God I'm leaving. I have spent the last year sacking people I hired and have known all my life.' There are fifty people left in the department today. I have talked to scores who were fired. They never knew what happened, all they knew was that the end was near. It was a terrible experience for all of them. What sort of manpower planning can allow for the possibility of the virtual disappearance of the greatest firm of engineers in England? Half the industries in the North West have been treated in much the same way; it has been even worse for some.

Not very far from Met Vicks was the wonderful old firm of Bayer Peacock. They made locomotives which hauled trains up and down the Andes, all over Africa and all over Australia. After the Second World War the firm was bought by a financier who decided that the value of the site on which the factory stood was such that it would pay him to sell it as a housing estate, so Bayer Peacock of West Gorton disappeared after about a hundred years. Some of the staff, including several Manchester City Councillors, moved to Met Vicks just in time to see their world collapse for the second time. Their views about manpower planning are quite unprintable.

I have left the most depressing part of the whole Met Vicks story until last. When George Westinghouse came over here at the end of the last century to establish the British Westinghouse Company which became Metropolitan Vickers, he decided that he would have to educate the engineers he needed. Forty young men went (at their own expense) to Pittsburgh. 'The Holy Forty' they called them. They came home to vitalize British industry. Very early in this century the school for graduate apprentices was established in Trafford Park. Sir Arthur Fleming ran it until he retired and Willis succeeded him. It was beyond any doubt the most important and most successful enterprise of its kind this country has ever known. Young men who had graduated as engineers in universities in this country or abroad came to Trafford Park to learn how to be real engineers. In 1919 Fleming announced with pride that 'Metropolitan Vickers have now abandoned the idea of charging a premium to graduates who wish to join the firm. They pay them a wage which is almost large enough for them to live on.' I suspect that this particular tradition survived too long, and had something to do with the collapse of the apprenticeship school forty years later! A couple of hundred men came every year and every man served an apprenticeship for two years during which he saw every part of the factory. When they finished their training about 60 per cent of the graduate apprentices left Metropolitan Vickers to go overseas or into other British firms. We used to say, 'The best engineers in England can be divided into two classes: those who work in Met Vicks and those who used to work there.' Ex-apprentices were to be found in every country in the world which had railways, mines or power stations. They were the best sales force any company ever had. Arthur Fleming was once summoned to a board meeting. The chairman said, 'There are now thirty-two separate firms in this country making transformers and competing with us. You have educated the chief engineers of thirty of them! What are you going to do?' 'Educate some more', he replied and he turned on his heel and went out.

The whole of British industry depended on Met Vick men – it could never have prospered without them – and the success of Met Vicks depended on the prosperity of the rest of the industry of Great Britain. I remember when every professor of electrical engineering I know had served his time at Met Vicks. The system may have been too good to last. Other big firms copied it and the Industrial Training Act of 1964 came too late to save it. But the accountants got at it because they thought it did not pay. I doubt if any firm ever made a better investment, but goodwill and skilled manpower do not appear specifically in the books of manufacturing companies, although they may be more important than any of the items in the balance sheet. I have often wondered what effect they might have had on that 'take-over battle'. They might have changed the course of history.

I have often talked about that mysterious process which turns a raw college graduate into a professional man. I believe that no man becomes a professional engineer until he has been frightened out of his wits at least twice. There are some things that no university can ever do, but very remarkable things used to happen in Trafford Park. It is doubly ironic that the Met Vicks' scheme died just as the medical profession began to insist that medical graduates must serve a 'pre-registration year' in a hospital before they could practice on their own. They never called them graduate apprentices, but that is what they were. Young lawyers have always spent a few years in Chambers with their pupil master. Every good professional has to be apprenticed at some stage in his life and he must have been tried in the fire under the watchful eye of an older man.

## Engineering feat

The story of the turbo-generator industry in this country is quite extraordinary. Turbines were invented by Charles Parsons. The whole world copied them; they were developed and much improved. Met Vicks was one of the biggest manufacturers of turbines in this country for many years. They used to make complete turbo-alternator sets. Now they only make the low pressure cylinders of GEC turbines; the high pressure cylinders come from Rugby, and the alternators from Stafford.

Old Dr. Ferranti had noticed years ago that the demand for electrical power always increased by 10 per cent per annum, compound interest. After the war there was a pent-up demand for power. Everyone could sell every set he could make. In 1948, AEI manufactured a standard 48 megawatt set. In the intervening twenty years the power available from a single machine has increased more than tenfold, although the size of the machine has hardly altered at all. This is an extraordinary development. After the 1957 Suez crisis the Government thought that oil would not be available and that we would need more electricity. The demand for conventional power stations and for nuclear power stations was doubled. Then it was doubled again. The big companies undertook elaborate research programmes to design them and they built expensive new factories to manufacture them. Then, as you know, oil started coming around the Cape in enormous tankers and so the demand for power stations was cut by a factor of two. It was cut again by a factor of two and then, because the power stations themselves were so much bigger, it was cut by another factor of two, so the order book virtually disappeared. Some of the troubles of the electrical engineering industry are part of the price we are paying for Suez. The demand for electricity is not now increasing at 10 per cent per annum as it did for so long. Since the slump began in 1974, the demand has grown by 2 per cent per annum at most. The Central Electricity Generating Board, having planned for 7–10 per cent per annum is very much oversupplied with electric power stations. We have 70 000 megawatts of installed power. We would have had even more installations like Dungeness B had it not been several years late, but the maximum load that has ever been put on the grid is 42 000 megawatts. So for years no orders have been placed for power stations. How can any industry cope with an order book like that?

## Not needed for ten years

British industry could produce three times as many power stations as the country needs. The industry is struggling desperately for orders abroad. In the old days we could sell to what was then the British Commonwealth. Now this market is no longer reserved for us, so our people are trying to sell sets all over the world. GEC has, for example, recently sold one huge station to South Korea and another to Hong Kong.

What should we do with the most skilled workmen and the most skilled designers in the world if they have no orders from the CEGB, which is the monopoly buyer? How can we plan our manpower if the demand for turbo sets in one year is five times as much as industry can take and then for three years there are no orders at all? The Government ordered a huge coal-fired station – Drax B – from Parsons, to stop them from going bankrupt. We shall not need it for another ten years at least.

## Ambitious but unproved

Similar troubles hit the transformer business very hard. In one year CEGB orders for transformers dropped from £50 million to £9 million. Most companies which made them have gone quietly out of business.

We cannot afford to lose one of the greatest assets the country has, the skill and the group loyalty of some of the best engineers in the world. So the Government is trying to keep a great industry in being on the off-chance that sooner or later we shall be able to use it again.

A tragically similar problem faces the Coal Board. In 1914 we mined 285 million tons of coal, but it was decided to run down the coal industry in the 1950s because there was so much cheap oil. Lord Robens persuaded the miners to accept redundancies and allow pits to be closed. In 1977 we mined about 100 million tons; two-thirds of it came from pits more than seventy years old. The French closed their coal fields altogether and they are developing an ambitious and so far unproved nuclear power programme. When the oil runs out, what are we going to use for power? Will nuclear power see us through? There are two big users of coal, the steel industry which uses coking coal and the electric power industry which burns about 70 million tons of coal a year. Prudent men in this country think that we are going to need more coal, so the British Government is to be asked by the Coal Board to spend £400 million a year to modernize the industry and sink new pits. We may have more coal than we need in ten years' time unless the price of oil rises dramatically. The EEC is importing cheap coal from Poland and from Australia, but it has decided to develop its own sources of power as far as possible. Germany and United Kingdom are the only countries which produce coal in large quantities. The EEC is likely to give a subsidy of £20 a ton for coal mined within the EEC and burnt in electric power stations within the EEC. This will make it possible to build up the coal industry to supply a demand which did not exist for the past twenty or thirty years.

The concept of cost-effectiveness is never used these days about any of the great industries which the Government is supporting with the taxpayers' money. We may need them in the long term and they may be cost-effective then; but in the long term we shall all be dead. Can we afford to invest so much and expect such a small return for so long?

Two-thirds of our national effort in engineering is devoted to what is usually called 'defence' – armaments if you like – but we still have huge resources to devote to peaceful pursuits. We hope they will help our overseas balance of payments, but we have some very difficult choices to make. Should British Airways be allowed to buy Boeings or must they buy British? Should we build our own advanced gas-cooled nuclear stations, or ought we to copy the Americans, or even the Canadians? It has been estimated that developing Concorde and developing the advanced gas-cooled reactor each cost the taxpayer at least £2500 million, so £5000 million has been spent on developments in high technology which are not paying off. It is to this end that our best engineers have dedicated their lives.

### Artificially preserved

How do we begin to produce a rational plan for manpower? How do we decide what kind of engineers are going to be needed? British industry is in very bad shape.

Most of our great industries – ship-building, aircraft, coal and heavy electrical engineering – are being preserved artifically in spite of all ordinary commercial forces. Are there any prosperous industries left to subsidize the rest? If the shipyards had been closed in Clydeside, there would have been civil unrest on a scale the Government could not cope with, nor the army control. However, the decline of the great industries in Trafford Park has been ignored by politicians and public alike.

So much then for manpower planning in British industry. I believe an important underlying cause of our troubles to be a 'capital levy', which has bled industry white ever since the war although its very existence is unknown to parliament. The effective levy on capital results from the use of traditional accounting systems to calculate taxable profits in accordance with Treasury rules. In times of inflation, this practice has many deficiencies. In 1974, for example, nearly 60 per cent of the declared profit of British companies was due to the appreciation of the value of stock and work in progress. Half of the rest would have been needed to keep factories and plant properly equipped, so that less that a quarter of these dividends were real, three quarters came out of capital. Our future is problematical. Unless we can identify some of the causes of our troubles, we may never survive.

# Trades Union Influence on Industrial Performance

*Robert Taylor*

Britain's trade unions are often blamed for the country's relatively poor economic performance during the past thirty-five years. To a large number of people they have become the scapegoats for national failure. Paul Johnson, for example, gave voice to this widely held opinion in an article in the *New Statesman* in 1975. He accused post-war union leaders of being 'smug and self-assured, oblivious of any criticism', who encouraged their members' in habits and attitudes, in rules and procedures, in illusions and fantasies, which have turned the British working class into the coolies of the western world'.[1] Johnson went on to suggest that while Britain's slow growth rate had been blamed on poor management, lack of investment in new plant and machinery and Treasury economic policies of stop-go, behind all three lay trade union obstructiveness, 'the brotherhood of national misery' with resistance to necessary technological change and a refusal to accept new working practices that would produce higher living standards for everybody in the long run. It would be a mistake for union leaders to dismiss such comment out of hand as the mistaken, ignorant prejudice of a political apostate. During the past ten years, in particular, Britain's productivity performance, measured by output per person employed, has been appalling and the entire responsibility for this cannot be placed at the door of employers who fail to invest and governments who subordinate the needs of industry to those of finance capital.

The industry minister, Sir Keith Joseph, believes Britain's unions are especially Luddite in their attitude to productivity, more anxious to protect existing jobs in decaying industries than in the creation of new ones elsewhere, opposed to the profit motive and the making of money. As he explained to the National Economic Development Council's October 1979 meeting:

> Trade union attitudes make good management difficult. Many at shopfloor level seem hostile to the need for industrial efficiency. Many are encouraged to feel that reductions in working hours or increases in real pay are feasible without improvements in productivity, or that inter-union disputes which keep major new facilities idle do no lasting damage to employment in their industry. Just as important, negotiated labour agreements are less depend-

able in the UK and restrictive practices – reflected in a reluctance by labour to agree to the elimination of unnecessary work and rules – are too prevalent. Yet these practices all contribute to overmanning; to the inefficient use of plant and to a loss of competitiveness within industry.[2]

Graham Hutton in his Wincott memorial lecture in October 1979 argued that 'Our union leaders are preoccupied with job security (that is overmanning) to the exclusion of bigger wage increases for fewer, but more productive workers. They have thereby kept real earnings in Britain nearer the 'dole' than have unions in any other western country'.[3]

Such criticisms have become familiar in recent years, but they are nothing new. From their origins in the early nineteenth century, trade unions have been viewed with hostility by economists and employers, not merely as forces of potential subversion against the existing social and political order, but as dangerous monopolistic enemies of a free market economy where the laws of supply and demand among self-regarding individuals determined the price of labour. As the economist Alfred Marshall wrote of the 1897 engineering lock-out:

> Unless the ASE (the Amalgamated Society of Engineers) concedes to the employers the right to put a single man to work on an easy machine, or even two or more of them, the progress of the English working classes from the position of hewers of wood and drawers of water to masters of nature's forces, will, I believe, receive a lasting check.[4]

But can trade unions as reactive, voluntary, collective organizations really be held responsible for the existence of restrictive labour practices in so much of British industry today? The main argument of this essay is that the craft mentality remains deeply rooted in the traditional culture of the workgroup and the union represents the collective expression of an attitude of mind among workers. Our industrial system is dominated by 'the desire of one group of workers to attain and maintain privileges as against other groups of workers and to map out for itself a reserved area in which other workers are not allowed to trespass'.[5] In the *laissez-faire* economy of mid-Victorian England the trade union was regarded by workers as 'a device for getting more money for the same work; it was a joint stock company for selling labour; and, like any other similar undertaking, it hoped to make a handsome profit over and above the costs of supplying its product'.[6]

The restrictions on entry to a defined trade through the apprenticeship system were a legacy from the medieval guilds. In the name of job protection they were a way of maximizing the bargaining strength of the craft union against employers. A research paper for the 1968 Donovan royal commission defined a restrictive labour practice as 'an arrangement under which labour is not used efficiently and which is not justifiable on social grounds'.[7] But the commission was careful to distinguish between the union and the work-group for the persistence of such arrangements 'Where practices of this kind exist, insistence on retaining them usually comes from workers themselves, acting as groups which have certain interests in common which they try as best they can to further, rather than from trade unions', insisted Donovan.

'Most responsible union leaders deplore the habitual use of overtime. If time-keeping is bad, it is because management has been slack, not because trade unions have encouraged it. It is not trade union policy that mates should be under-employed'.[8] The 1969 the *In Place of Strife* white paper attempted to make the same distinction as well. 'There can be no doubt that equipment and manpower are not always used as efficiently in this country as in other comparable industrial countries', it admitted. 'This is partly due to customs and practices which restrict the efficient use of resources including manpower. On the whole such practices are operated, not by the unions themselves but by groups of employees, who see them as a way of protecting their jobs or of maintaining their earnings. Because of this, any attempt to get rid of such practices without adequate compensation is seen as a threat, either to earnings or to security of employment'.[9]

Many union leaders do recognize the obstacles in the workgroup to the change in labour practices required by technology. Len Murray, the TUC's general secretary, argued the point in his Granada lecture on 28 May 1980. 'It is less difficult for unions to win from their members acceptance of temporary wage restraint than it is for them to win agreement to changes in manpower practices', he claimed, 'Indeed, Britain's poor economic record since the war is due much more to the ineffective use of our resources than to excessive wage settlements'.[10] In the foreword to a TUC policy statement on new technology published in 1979 Murray asserted: 'Our message is a simple one. It is not just a question of accepting new technology or of fighting it. The issue is how we can maximize its benefits and minimize its costs and ensure that its benefits are equitably shared'.[11]

Union General Secretaries such as Clive Jenkins of the Association of Scientific, Technical and Managerial Staffs and John Lyons of the Engineers' and Managers' Association positively welcome industrial efficiency and their unions have co-operated in the introduction of new techniques. The Post Office Engineering Union took the initiative during the 1960s under its leader Lord Delacourt Smith to pursue genuine productivity bargaining with the Post Office. This produced impressive results, though the 1977 Carter Review Committee suggested that Britain's tele-communications remained 'significantly less efficient than the best of its overseas competitors'.[12] The Electrical, Electronic, Telecommunications and Plumbing Union under Les Cannon and later Frank Chapple co-operated fully with the modernization of the electricity supply industry, a point acknowledged by the 1971 Wilberforce Inquiry. During the 1960s the National Union of Mineworkers – despite serious doubts among its leaders – did not resist the sharp cutback on the coalfields and went along with the replacement of the piecework wage system by a uniform day wage for all miners. In the words of the Wilberforce inquiry: 'This rundown, which was brought about with the co-operation of the miners and their union, is without parallel in British industry in terms of the social and economic costs it has inevitably entailed for the mining community as a whole.'[13] NUM president, Joe Gormley, championed the principle of pit incentive schemes as a method of boosting productivity and they were eventually introduced in 1977–78 at area level. It has brought a clear improvement in output per manshift at the coal face and elsewhere underground, so that the British coal industry bears effective comparison in productivity performance with the rest of Europe. In 1979–80, overall output per manshift was 2.27 tonnes, the highest figure for four years.

These examples should qualify any picture of universal trade union hostility or indifference to improved labour efficiency, although it has been suggested that very few unions actually take much interest in the subject of higher productivity. C.F. Pratten discovered that 'union officials make little study of what constitutes labour productivity'.[14] 'Only one of the unions consulted had made any comparisons of labour productivity within or between international companies, or any international comparisons of labour productivity. The Transport and General Workers had obtained comparisons of productivity for wage claims it submitted to Ford and ICI'. Yet contrary to popular belief, unions are not formidable bureaucratic organizations with enormous power and discipline over their members or the running of industry. Trade unionists are not obedient foot soldiers in an army of labour. As Pratten comments: 'One of the more surprising features of this part of the study was the loose control shown to apply within unions. In some unions, local branches control a substantial proportion of the unions' finances and have a good deal of autonomy for determining policy for negotiations and in disputes'. Even twenty years ago very few union leaders were strong enough to dictate policy to a passive rank-and-file and their position has grown much weaker with the devolution of more and more decision-making down through the union hierarchy to the shopfloor itself, especially in wage determination and the ever-lasting struggle over 'the frontiers of control' at the workplace between management and workers. The resulting fragmentation has probably made it more difficult rather than easier for unions to win the consent of their members for changes in labour practices in the name of higher productivity. The rise in the independent autonomy of the work groups since the Second World War, with the resulting elevation of the shop steward and the recent appearance of combine committees outside the formalized structure of the unions themselves, has been shaped by the needs of industry. The Warwick University Industrial Relations Unit have found that there are now more full-time convenors and senior stewards at work in industry on the payroll of manufacturing companies than there are full-time trade union officers. Such developments have reinforced the tenacious persistence of restrictive labour practices in the workgroup and made it harder for a union to overcome craft or sectionalist attitudes at the plant.

Of course, where a trade union actually controls the supply of labour entering an industry, it might be more susceptible to the accusation of holding back productivity. A recent study at the London School of Economics suggests that as many as one in every four trade unionists in Britain are covered by a closed shop agreement, that is around 5 200 000 workers. About 14 per cent of that figure (837 000) are estimated to belong to pre-entry closed shops, where 'a union seeks to control the supply of labour to employers by restricting entry to the union and by insisting at the same time that job applicants hold an appropriate union card before being considered for appointment'.[15] Two industries are particularly involved in this arrangement: printing, paper and publishing; and shipbuilding and marine engineering. Neither has a good record for productivity performance. The national newspaper industry suffers from some of the worst restrictive practices in the country, operating in a jungle of high competing wage rates and overmanning, which were highlighted in the 1966 Economist Intelligence Unit study.

If anything the situation in Fleet Street has worsened considerably since that time, with the recent crises at Times Newspapers and the Observer. Power on the national newspapers rests primarily with the chapel (the work group) and not the trade union branch. Failure to comply with a union directive can incur fines on members and, in the final resort, the loss of the union card, which is a meal ticket for life, but although such sanctions are in union rule books, they are seldom used or even threatened. Time and time again union officials have their position with their members undermined by the willingness of weak Fleet Street managements to surrender to demands from chapels that possess the proven disruptive power to halt newspaper production.

As Keith Sisson admits in his study of Fleet Street: 'It must be obvious that the control which the chapels have been able to establish over the payment system and the demand and supply of labour goes some of the way towards explaining the high pay and overmanning'.[16] A survey carried out by the Advisory, Conciliation and Arbitration Service for the McGregor Royal Commission on the newspaper industry in 1977 discovered that of the production workers as many as 21.5 per cent were over the age of 60 and 6.5 per cent more than 65. With around 35 000 people working in Fleet Street, 12 000 of them production workers and 4600 casual part-timers, it is hardly suggestive of high efficiency. National print union leaders have recognized this, but they appear powerless to do anything about it. In 1977 they drew up an enlightened document – *Programme for Action* – which was a blueprint to bring the national newspaper industry into the new technological age, complete with generous severance pay for those workers who were no longer needed and a gradual, phased rundown on a voluntary basis in order to ensure no hardship. But only the journalists agreed to this union-inspired package, while the rest of the Fleet Street workforce turned down the programme in a secret ballot. Members of the National Graphical Association, in particular, face severe difficulties with the move away from mechanical typesetting to photocomposition and press-button, computer technology because their whole *raison d'être* as a craft élite is threatened and as a result they have responded in a militant, uncompromising manner.

The pre-entry closed shop in the shipbuilding industry is one of the reasons for the poor productivity performance in British yards. The whole future of the Boiler-makers Society is linked to the traditional demarcation lines that have existed in the construction of ships since the Industrial Revolution. In August 1971 the now defunct Commission on Industrial Relations published a hard-hitting attack on the organization of work in the yards.[17] As it argued: 'Because the work lends itself to self-supervision, the traditions of the industry protect the autonomy of the work group. It is a common feature of the industry that this often extends to some control over the times when the work actually starts and finishes. It also affects decisions about manning and about the allocation and distribution of overtime.' The CIR report continued: 'The extent and organization of the craft content of the work has led to the emergence of a large number of distinct craft specializations, each with its own skill, pride in work and control of much of the work process. Division into craft groups has been reinforced by union organization which coincides with craft organization, and by the development of social and work group attitudes within closely-knit communities.' The casual hire-and-fire attitudes of employers in ship-building and the economic ups-and-downs of shipbuilding since the inter-war depression hardened the independence of the sectionalist groups, who have naturally fought to protect themselves from job loss and to perpetuate craft distinctions, even when they no longer make any practical sense. In the words of the CIR, the result has been the continuation of 'the uneconomic use of labour'. Sectionalism stood 'in the way of wider job opportunities' and prevented 'differences over pay from being settled with the interests of all employees being taken into account at the same time'.

Improving productivity performance has been given a major priority by British Shipbuilders since the nationalization of the industry in 1978, through joint union–management initiatives in the yards. While a national industry-wide pay system has begun, replacing the fragmented, sectionalist bargaining of the past and the yards have much less labour disruption than they used to have, British Shipbuilders have still a long way to go in boosting output at a time of world recession. In March 1979 it was disclosed that British yards were only half as efficient as Japan's. An internal study showed that as much as three hours and five minutes of every working day was lost in production through the misuse of working time. A national pay agreement signed early in 1980 laid down a new emphasis on removing the obstacles to better performance through the end of 'one-in, all-in' overtime, the growth of job skill interchangeability, the introduction of work study, the abolition of archaic distinctions between boilermakers and other skilled men in the outfitting trades, between semi-skilled and unskilled, blue collar and white collar. The belated efforts of national union leaders in the shipbuilding industry to remedy performance are a welcome change, but the difficulties of translating good intentions from the bargaining table to the workplace remain considerable.

A similar problem exists in the nationalized British steel industry, for example. In 1976 all the steel unions signed an agreement with the British Steel Corporation to reduce labour costs and improve productivity. One clause said that there would have to be 'very significant changes in the organization and structure of work' in order to ensure that 'working practices match those of the Corporation's com-petitors'.[18] Another emphasised 'the need to man jobs flexibly in such matters as working light, broadening of job content and mobility, particularly in regard to the undertaking of alternative work without restrictions imposed by traditional union and branch boundaries'. At that time BSC released figures that showed it required only 64 000 Japanese steel workers and 87 000 American to achieve levels of output of liquid steel it took 182 000 British steel workers to produce. Yet four years later, BSC management was complaining that the 1976 joint agreement had simply failed to stick down at plant level, despite the attempts of union officials to win the co-operation of workers to carry through the necessary changes.

Comparative studies carried out by the iron and steel sector working party for the National Economic Development Office between similar plants in Britain, Holland and Sweden during 1979 revealed substantial differences in performance, although the lower labour costs in this country helped to balance the picture. 'The clearest difference between the United Kingdom and the continental plants was in the relationship and demarcation between production and maintenance employees', argued the report.[19] On the continent production workers are trained to be flexible enough to move around the plant to carry out different kinds of work when needed to do so. 'The benefits of such flexibility were in the ability to cover for those not at work without recourse to overtime and in increasing the job interest by job rotation', said the NEDO study. At the British steel plants surveyed, a separate group of semi-skilled maintenance hands or labourers are employed to fetch and carry for the craftsmen. These do not exist at all at the continental plants, where production workers carry out such work. Moreover, the continental plants have far fewer workers performing separate craft skills. 'Typically a mechanical craftsman combines the skills of a mechanical fitter, pipe fitter, welder/boilermaker'. In Britain we have many varieties of craftsmen inflexibly working in a given, narrow skill. Unlike this country, staff and blue collar workers at continental plants are treated the same in fringe benefits and status. All of them are salaried and rules for clocking on and off are the same for each group. The lack of demarcation in labour practices between production and maintenance at continental plants is also reflected in the absence of separate trade unions for both groups. In Britain we suffer from a multiplicity of different unions in the steel industry that adds to the complexity of the pay structure and the organization of the work at the plants.

Similar inefficiencies were discovered by a study team from the National Economic Development Office in 1972 who contrasted working practices at British chemical plants with broadly similar ones in West Germany and Holland. The report argued that manning levels for production workers were broadly the same in all three countries, but in the maintenance area UK plants compared unfavourably, needing 50 per cent more men per unit of output than on the continent. The NEDO study suggested the reasons for the differences lay in less shift working on the continent; all workers on the continental maintenance team were fully skilled; there was greater labour mobility between plants on the same site because of the centralized organization of maintenance; more freedom to use outside contractors when necessary and much greater flexibility between process operators and craftsmen. The craftsmen's mate is an unknown figure at continental plants, because all workers are trained 'to as high a level as their abilities allowed'. As the NEDO survey explained:

> The result of continental companies having such a high proportion of skilled men among maintenance employees was enhanced efficiency. For example, on small repair jobs requiring two men, both would be skilled and both would be allowed to do any part of the job, thus ensuring a quick finish. This increase in flexibility resulted in an overall cost reduction despite the greater use of more expensive skilled labour.[20]

In steel and chemicals the unions mirror the customs and practices imposed by work groups, and the same is broadly true of the motor car industry, where low productivity is now a major problem. In 1975 the Central Policy Review Staff bluntly stated: 'It takes almost twice as many man-hours to assemble similar cars using the same or comparable plant and equipment in Britain as it does on the continent'.[21] Low productivity in car plants was firstly blamed on overmanning, where 41 per cent more workers are needed in Britain compared with the continent to trim, finally assemble and dress the engine and as many as 69 to 78 per cent more plant maintenance workers are required. In the words of the CPRS report: 'Overmanning in maintenance is also an example of the impact of trade demarcations on efficiency. For example, if a multiweld machine used to weld body panels together breaks down in Britain, six maintenance men would be required to repair it – an electrician, jig fitter, pipe fitter, mechanical fitter, tool man and repair man. On the continent only two men, one mechanical and the other electrical, would accomplish the same job'. But even when production lines in car plants are manned at competitive standards output fails to reach high levels. The CPRS highlighted the 'slow work pace' as a major handicap with 'slower line speeds, late starts, frequent stoppages between and during shifts and delays in correcting mechanical problems'. Other obstacles to improved productivity were given as shortage of materials due to disputes affecting suppliers, poor quality control (plants in Britain need twice as much rectification time as continental car plants) and poor maintenance. Most of these problems can be blamed on management or the power of the work group, but the unions cannot entirely escape from criticism either. The CPRS report highlighted the 'fragmented union structure' in the car plants and concluded this was a factor 'which affects the continuity of production by provoking disputes over recruitment and demarcation'. Extremism among militant minorities was also put down by the CPRS as a reason for poor performance. The study argued: 'There is little doubt that the visibility and importance of the car industry and its vulnerability to action by relatively small groups (a dispute involving no more than four or five men can easily stop the track in an assembly plant) have led to the workforce being subjected to extremist pressure both from within and from outside'.

The British construction and allied industries emerges very badly from international comparative studies. A joint working party from the National Economic Development Office in 1976 concluded that British construction projects in the power, chemical and oil industries took far longer than similar ones either in the United States or in continental Europe, requiring more workers and taking more man-hours on site. The report found the ratio of unskilled to skilled was worse here than elsewhere and more supervision was required. It also recorded that less than a third of the working day on the British sites examined was actually spent on construction work, while a substantial amount of the day in some cases was spent 'not on plot'. The study concluded that construction workers in Britain were less ready to work in the rain, had prolonged tea breaks and their proneness to industrial disruption was greater than their contemporaries on the continent.[22]

A NEDO study of comparative productivity in the construction equipment and mobile cranes industry revealed a similarly depressing picture in 1979 when UK company performance was contrasted with the American. The joint union–management team was impressed by the three year labour contracts in the United States which ensures job security and a one union plant structure that helps to avoid inter-union rivalry and demarcation disputes, with a flexible use of labour.[23]

Nor is the picture very different in the engineering industry. In a 1979 study the Engineering Employers Federation concluded that 'the greatest barrier to productivity is inefficient practices within individual firms', although it was also stressed that the level of demand in the economy was the major constraint to improvements. Of the twelve firms that currently reported depressed markets for their products, as many as ten reported 'inefficient levels of labour utilization described by most as overmanning – which held down current productivity levels'.[24] A 1975 research project by the Department of Engineering Production at Birmingham University examined the distribution of time during a working day by operatives and machines in forty engineering and metal working firms during the 1968–72 period and a further forty-five firms in 1970–74. It discovered that the machines were idle for half the working time and on average operatives spent 16 per cent of their day simply 'waiting'.[25] A study carried out by Christopher Saunders of Sussex University between 1973 and 1975 which looked at the efficiency and competitiveness of our engineering industry by comparison with the West German found that while West Germany had 50 per cent more workers employed in their engineering sector, they enjoyed a level of labour productivity which was more than half again the British level, and a quantum of output more than double the British.[26]

Britain's railway system has some of the lowest productivity in Western Europe, argued a Commons Select Committee in April 1977. There was particular criticism of the use of second men in railway cabs on high speed trains (a relic from the steam age); the use of guards on freight trains; the low amount of driving time achieved by drivers (between $3\frac{1}{2}$ and $3\frac{3}{4}$ hours in an eight hour shift); and the large number of ticket and station staff.[27] An internal study carried out of railway productivity comparisons by British Rail in March 1980 concluded that 'the longer hours worked by British railwaymen do not, in general, lead to equivalent higher levels of output per man than those achieved by the other railways considered',[28] mainly because in this country the standard working week runs from Monday to Saturday and not seven days as on the continent. The study found productivity performance on passenger trains compared favourably with others, but alongwith Italy we had a poor level of efficiency on freight and parcels service, with the need for twice as many train crews to run a freight train as the most efficient, mainly because others have abolished guards and/or drivers' assistants on their freight trains. Persistent efforts in tight financial circumstances to make British Rail more efficient have not been very successful, mainly because the three rail unions find it hard to reach common agreement.

This selective examination of some of the sectoral evidence on low labour productivity suggests that the problem remains widespread and its ingredients (restrictive practices like overmanning, craft inflexibilities in demarcation, and limitations on output) are common.

A primary common cause of poor productivity performance in Britain lies in the system of time-served apprenticeships that covers industrial training. Here the old craft spirit lives on, even in areas where such a system makes no sense at all. But as the Donovan Royal Commission argued: 'In the context of technological change the drawbacks of the craft system become even more marked. If the only normal method of entry into the craft is via an apprenticeship, supply will respond slowly and inadequately to demand. Where expansion is required it will be delayed. Where technological innovation reduces the demand for a given craft then there will be waste and suffering among the men whose livelihoods and expectations for the future are bound up with its continuing existence.'[29] In fact, dilution agreements in the building industry have undermined some of the exclusivity of the craft system, but there is still a long way to go before British industry has a flexible, mobile work-force where the skill distinctions are obsolete. The May 1980 Central Policy Review Staff Report on Industrial Training suggested that:

> Control of the pattern of training has become a means, often with manage-ment acquiescence, of maintaining restrictive labour practices. A number of key skilled trades – notably in the engineering industry – are effectively reserved to workers who have undergone apprenticeship or similar training at the outset of their career; these trades are not therefore generally accessible to those who seek to acquire skill by any other route or at any other time in their career. A corollary of this is that adult training and retraining is relatively neglected; much of industry's training effort is concentrated on young new entrants to the labour force and systematic provision for upgrading and updating of skills is given relatively little encouragement or support from the education and training institutions which establish the framework for training in industry.[30]

An added scandal that perpetuates the inefficient use of labour is the concentration of formal training on the lucky few sixteen year old school-leavers, leaving the majority of young workers with no chance of acquiring any qualifications at all.

Can the unions be blamed for the perpetuation of Britain's archaic training system, which results in this country having the least skilled workforce in the western industrialized world by leaving training to the whims of employers and giving only a marginal role to the state? There is evidence that some unions do discriminate against adult workers who are trained in government skill centres. The Boiler-makers Society actually has an official policy not to accept any such entrants into the workplace, regarding them as 'dilutees'. And most craft unions are always ready to defend the principles of the time-served apprenticeship system from attack. But national union leaders, even in engineering, take a less intransigent position in public. They have concluded national agreements with employers which require trainees employed to serve a period on reduced wage rates before being fully accepted as skilled workers. Richard Berthoud in a study of skill centre trainees in Dundee and Stoke-on-Trent found only 13 per cent of his sample believed that the unions had any effect on their job chances and 68 per cent said they made no difference. He concluded that 'the union bogey has had little effect on the men's prospects. If union opposition has had an effect it is an indirect one. The majority of trainees (at least in a time and place of a healthy employment market) manage to secure a first job using their skills'.[31] In their training study Kenneth Hall and Isobel Miller argued: 'Clearly-defined rules and regulations governing the acceptance of trainees into membership of a trade union are no guarantee of producing a situation where the trainee feels that he is accepted. This is an example of the wide breach which can exist between union officialdom and membership: official rules may then not be adhered to because they are not the kind of rules the members want'.[32] However, their book concluded that 'the majority of trainees experienced or perceived little resistance to dilution'.

Union leaders are well-nigh universal in their hostility towards overtime working, a fact of British industrial life showing little sign of going away. The New Earnings Survey for April 1979 revealed that an average 6.3 hours are worked in all industries and services by manual male workers on top of their average basic of 39.8 hours. Over the last decade, between 28 per cent and 37 per cent of operatives worked an average of from 7.8 hours to 9.2 hours of overtime a week. In many industries even the ups-and-downs of the economic cycle seem to have little impact on the amount of overtime being worked. Indeed, there is abundant evidence that employers provided extra hours of work to overcome skilled labour shortages. Around 23 per cent of the gross weekly earnings of male manual workers derive from overtime payments, which have become a necessary ingredient in the wage packets of millions. In his research paper to the Donovan commission, E.G. Whybrew explained the different attitudes to overtime working between union leaders and the work group. 'To the central officials overtime appears to increase the supply of a particular type of labour with which they are concerned without bringing any compensation increase in their influence', he wrote. 'On the other hand, an extra employee while increasing the supply of labour is a potential recruit for the union. The individual worker, however, sees an extra employee in his department as increasing the supply of his type of labour with few compensating benefits. For him, however, an increase in overtime supplies the extra labour but raises his earnings and gives his workshop organization the possibility of using a cheap industrial weapon – an overtime ban'.[33]

There is little doubt that overtime working remains an inefficient way of using labour and its social effects with the reduction of leisure time are real enough. Whybrew's detailed investigations revealed that overtime is at its highest incidence among maintenance workers and lowest among general production workers. In his view, 'overtime encourages people to waste time at work in order to obtain a living wage'. Any future decline in overtime is more likely to reflect worsening economic prospects than any sudden improvement in labour productivity. As Whybrew explained twelve years ago, where employers took the initiative to eradicate overtime in the Post Office, electricity supply and Esso 'trade union co-operation was readily forthcoming if asked for', but the initiative for change must come from management since 'they alone have the power and means to provide alternative ways of doing things'.

A more fundamental obstacle to higher labour productivity (though difficult to estimate with any precision) lies in the inequality of treatment between white-collar and blue-collar workers.[34] The social stigma of manual labour is far more tenacious in Britain than almost anywhere else in the western world. In industry a form of social apartheid persists, where workers have different canteens, toilets, car parks, depending on their job classification. Perhaps more fundamentally, employers treat their manual workers as inferior to their office staff in fringe benefits such as pensions, holidays, basic hours of work, sickness benefit, and work disciplines like clocking on and off. In recent years some progress has been made to remedy these degrading reminders of our antique industrial system, mainly thanks to the pressure from some of the big general manual unions, but there can be no doubt that they have a deleterious effect on efficiency.

Along with the training apprentice system, they prevent the development of a more flexible, adaptable workforce. In 1977 a NEDO study of the machine tool industry found that 'for manual employees there were no real prospects of promotion beyond foreman or superintendant level and few vacancies arose at this level because of the long service of most foremen. There was little promotion in most plants from craft to technician grades'.[35] A survey of engineering firms carried out by NEDO in 1979 discovered that most managers agreed that 'the disparity between the status of craftsmen and non-manual employees was indefensible'. They found it difficult to justify a situation in which a 'school-leaver joining the company as a clerk receives better conditions of employment than his father who may have worked with us all his life'.[36]

The persistence of skilled labour shortages during an economic recession has clearly had severe consequences for manufacturing output and efficiency, but the lack of employment security for many manual workers is a major drawback for those companies who are trying to recruit labour. Both short-time working and redundancies may be necessary because of falling demand, but the workers who suffer from the uncertainties that follow are less inclined to take jobs in the manufacturing sector, if they can find safer employment elsewhere. As the machine tool study explained: 'There was wide agreement among employees that redundancy has led to a reduction of skill levels on the shop floor. Employees said it was unusual for many of those who were made redundant to return to the industry.'

Industrial disruption remains a serious obstacle to a more effective industrial performance as well. The image of strike-prone Britain is a serious exaggeration. By international standards this country ranks no more than sixth or seventh in the league among western democratic nations, far behind the United States, Australia and Canada, but such figures should provide no grounds for complacency. The vast majority of strikes in Britain are concentrated in a relatively small number of industrial sectors – the docks, car manufacture, shipbuilding and iron and steel. Large plants suffer from strikes much more than medium or small size plants. In an average year perhaps about 2 per cent of all plants employing around 20 per cent of the manufacturing workforce are hit by stoppages. A study carried out for the Department of Employment in 1978 found that while workers who do not belong to a trade union make up nearly half the labour force only 3 per cent of them struck between 1966 and 1973.[37] However, the overwhelming majority of strikes in Britain remain unofficial and do not enjoy the support of the unions whose members are in dispute. A survey by Industrial Facts and Forecasting Ltd (IFF) for Warwick University Industrial Relations Research Unit carried out in 1978 suggests that other forms of industrial action that fall short of an actual strike, such as overtime bans and work-to-rules, are far more in evidence in manufacturing industry than the official statistics might suggest and these different expressions of militancy can have a damaging impact on a plant.[38]

Nearly a third of the manufacturing plants covered in the IFF survey had experienced a strike by their manual workers between 1976 and 1978, while 46 per cent of establishments experienced some form of industrial disruption. While the interim report suggested that 'perhaps surprisingly, the density of trade union membership seems to have little effect on the proportion of establishments experiencing industrial action' the existence of shop stewards and combine or joint union committees at the workplace had an appreciable effect on the other kinds of industrial action. Clearly the disciplines and tactical consideration of overtime bans and work-to-rules are more familiar to those who are activists in the unions than non-unionists.

The IFF survey concluded that 'although it may be true that the 'strike problem' in terms of total days lost is concentrated in a few plants, the findings of the survey suggest that the use of some form of industrial action is surprisingly widespread'. Moreover it is also worth remembering that the overall strike statistics prepared by the Department of Employment do not include stoppages that involve ten workers or less, those strikes that last under a day except when the aggregate of working days lost exceeds one hundred, or workers who are affected in other establishments beyond where the strike has occurred. No doubt, there is much exaggerated reporting of Britain's peculiar strike 'disease', but it would be wrong to underplay the appalling consequences for productivity in many companies such as BL where between 1972 and 1979 industrial militancy became a way of factory life. Vital export industries such as vehicle manufacture and shipbuilding have suffered more from stoppages than more quiescent sectors like whisky distilling and food and processing.

It is customary to lay the blame for all these manifest obstacles to efficiency at the door of the unions. Yet as Guy Routh has pointed out: 'trade unionism is only the outward expression of a general tendency for people with common interests to ally themselves for their mutual advancement'.[39] The power of the work group remains central to an understanding of the problem. But this does not mean that unions are entirely immune from criticism over low productivity. Demarcation disputes between groups of workers have become less frequent during the past decade but the existence of separate unions to represent craft interests can make it difficult to push through genuine productivity bargaining.

While inter-union disputes, such as the Isle of Grain power station and the Hunterston terminal in 1980, do reflect genuine divisions of occupational concern the organizational difficulties of separate unions does add to the problem. Moreover, union bargainers are not always ready to see the value of improved productivity as a way of improving the living standards of workers in the long run rather than in the here and now. It remains a depressing British habit of mind to buy out restrictive practices at too high a cost so that the fruits of change can be enjoyed before any hoped for improvements in efficiency occur. The incessant competition for union members makes it hard for some unions to relish the idea of trading jobs for money, or co-operating with a company to boost output per head if it means fewer employment opportunities and not more. Dislike of the profit motive among full-time union officials can often blind them to the merits of innovation.

But the removal of bad labour practices must rest with the employers. The resistance of workers in Britain to change is not really very surprising. As one recent economist has pointed out:

> Since the managers tend to place much greater emphasis on productivity than job security, a real and important conflict of priorities may easily arise. It seems that managers in Western Europe and Japan have been more successful than the UK's managers in reconciling these two priorities by coupling relatively faster labour-saving innovation with faster product innovation and greater marketing effort, so that, in parallel, to a high growth in labour productivity and (therefore real wages) also a high ouput and (therefore) job security have been achieved.[40]

As Len Murray argued in his 1980 Granada lecture:

> Workers can only be got to accept changes in manning and working practices if they are convinced of the need for and benefits of change, and if they are protected against its adversities. They ask – fairly in my book – why they should accept the adverse consequences of decisions made for their own purposes by faceless boards of directors or by managements, or indeed by governments.[41]

It is worth remembering that only in the past sixteen years have workers begun to develop legal rights at work through statute law, as the voluntarist industrial relations system has been undermined. The legislation of the 1974–79 Labour government period gave workers many minimum rights that are commonplace in continental Europe, and the evidence does not suggest these have been exercised very effectively.

The 1965 Redundancy Payments Act and the 1975 Employment Protection Act have done something to modify the old hire-and-fire powers of employers, but not to any radical extent. Most companies continue to give a low priority to manpower planning: A NEDO working party report in 1975 concluded that 'industrial relations training for managers was not adequate in scope or quality' for 'too often industrial relations was subordinated to other functional areas of management'.[42] The obstacles to the creation of a more efficient, and wealth-creating economy are not just the fault of workers organized in work groups or trade unions. As one wise observer of our industrial relations scene once wrote:

> Trade unions may be a force for progress, but in their actual functioning they are, in the literal and unusual meaning of the word, 'reactionary' bodies. They react very closely to the members and their members in the main react to their everyday industrial experience. That is how union traditions have been formed over the years to express the lessons of group experience. They can only be changed by different experience that teaches different lessons. But different experience will only be forthcoming when those who carry out the final responsibility for running industry

and politics, that is management and governments, are willing and able to provide it. Trade union leaders, who have the force of mind and character to challenge outmoded traditions, cannot work miracles and make bricks without straw.[43]

The present harsh economic recession is a difficult time to expect any reforms in working practices. Workers are understandably anxious to perpetuate their jobs at almost any cost to avoid the dangers of unemployment. But Britain's unique combination of high unit labour costs and low real wages remains a direct result of our archaic system of industrial relations. Workers and their unions can respond to the challenge, if they are treated as partners in a national effort and not as enemies or outsiders. During the Second World War this country achieved levels of industrial output that became the envy of the Nazi war machine through the suspension of demarcation lines, the dilution and mobility of skilled labour and the establishment of joint production committees and works councils, with the full co-operation of unions with management. The mobilization of the economy for total war produced impressive results that ensured victory. Tragically, in the deceptively easier years of peace, custom and practice, over-manning and all the other familiar restrictive habits of British society once more became a fact of working life for millions. The central dilemma remains with no obvious solution: how to achieve a miracle in productivity when we lack the urgent stimulus of a nation at war to motivate necessary change.

## Notes

1 JOHNSON, P. (1980) *The Recovery of Freedom*, Oxford, Blackwell, p. 21.
2 JOSEPH, Sir K., memorandum (October 1979) National Economic Development Council.
3 WOOTTON, G. (1980) *What About Productivity?*, Institute of Economic Affairs, London, p. 26.
4 Quoted by Lord ROBBINS in 'Economists and Trade Unions 1776–1977', p. 9 *Trade Unions: Public Goods or Public Bads?*, Institute of Economic Affairs, London, 1978.
5 KAHN-FREUND, O. (1979) *Labour Relations: Heritage and Adjustment*, Oxford University Press, p. 43.
6 CURRIE, R. (1978) *Industrial Politics*, Oxford University Press, London, p. 31.
7 Donovan Royal Commission on Trade Unions and Employers' Associations, Research Paper 4, p. 47.
8 Donovan Royal Commission Report, HMSO (1968) p. 77.
9 *In Place of Strife*, Government White Paper, HMSO (1969) p. 12.
10 GRANADA (1980) *The Role of the Trade Unions*, pp. 75–6.
   HMSO, p. 52.
11 Employment and Technology – a TUC interim report, (May 1979) p. 5.
12 Report of the Post Office Review Committee, (July 1977) HMSO, p. 19.
13 Wilberforce Inquiry, (1972) HMSO, p. 3.
14 PRATTEN, C.F. (1976) *Labour Productivity Differentials within International Companies*, Cambridge University Press, Cambridge, pp. 58–9.
15 GENNARD, J. *et al.* (January 1980) 'The extent of closed shop arrangements in British industry', *Employment Gazette*, p. 19.
16 SISSON, K. (1975) *Industrial Relations in Fleet Street*, Blackwell, Oxford, p. 167.
17 Commission on Industrial Relations Report 22 – Shipbuilding and Shiprepairing, (August 1971) HMSO, p. 52.
18 Joint Statement on Reductions in Employment Costs and Improvements in Labour Productivity – British Steel Corporation, (January 1976) p. 1.
19 A Hard Look at Steel: International Comparisons of Steelworks Efficiency – General Summary, (January 1980) NEDO, p. 4.

20  Chemicals Manpower in Europe, Chemicals EDC, (1973) NEDO, p. 19.
21  Central Policy Review Staff – The Future of the British Car Industry, (1975) HMSO, pp. 91–2.
22  Engineering Construction Performance, (1976) NEDO, p. 22.
23  Productivity: the Findings of Visits to UK and US Companies; Construction Equipment and Mobile Cranes Sector Working Party, (July 1979).
24  Engineering Employers Federation – A Pilot Study of Performance and Productivity in the UK Engineering Industry, (July 1979) p. 44.
25  Midlands Tomorrow: West Midlands Economic Planning Council, No. 8, (1975) pp. 3–5.
26  SAUNDERS, C.: Engineering in Britain, West Germany and France: Some Statistical Comparisons, (1978) Sussex European Research Centre.
27  Select Committee on Nationalised Industries 1976–1977. The Role of British Rail in Public Transport, and also see DODGSON, John and PRYKE, Richard, (1976) *The Rail Problem*, Martin Robertson, Oxford.
28  European Railways Performance Comparisons, (March 1980) British Rail, p. 18.
29  Donovan Royal Commission Report, p. 87.
30  Education, Training and Industrial Performance, Central Policy Review Staff, (1980) HMSO, p. 17.
31  BERTHOUD, R. (April 1978) *Training Adults for Skilled Jobs*, Policy Studies Institute, p. 80.
32  HALL, K. and MILLER, I. (1975) *Retraining and Tradition*, Allen and Unwin, London, p. 121.
33  Donovan Royal Commission, Research Paper No. 9, WHYBREW, E.G. (1968) Overtime Working in Britain, HMSO, p. 51.
34  See the author's contribution to *Labour and Equality: A Fabian Study of Labour in Power 1974–1979*, (1980) Heinemann Educational Books, London, pp. 108–20 and TOWNSEND, P. *Poverty in the United Kingdom*, (1979) Pelican, London, pp. 432–75.
35  *Machine Tools: The Employees' View of the Industry*, (1977) NEDO, p. 20.
36  *Focus on Engineering Craftsmen*, (1980) NEDO, p. 27.
37  SMITH, C.T.B. *et al.* (1978) *Strikes in Britain*, London, HMSO, p. 33.
38  IFF (1978) *Work-Place Industrial Relations in Manufacturing Industry*.
39  ROUTH, G. (1980) *Occupation and Pay in Great Britain 1906–1979*, Macmillan, London, p. 200.
40  GOMULKA, S. (1979) *Britain's Slow Industrial Growth- – Increasing Inefficiency versus Low Rate of Technical Change*, edited by BECKERMAN, W. *Slow Growth in Britain*, Oxford University Press, Oxford, p. 190.
41  GRANADA (1980) p. 39.
42  Management Training in Industrial Relations, (1975) NEDO, p. 25 and p. 1.
43  FLANDERS, A. (1975) *Trade Unions and the Force of Tradition; Management and Unions*, Faber, London, p. 286.

# Research, Development and
# Technical Decision-Making in Industry

*T.L. Banfield*

## Comparative performance

Prophets of doom are rarely silent, though not often heeded. The breast-beating that has accompanied Britain's relatively lower economic growth rate in recent years has been unusual, in the sense that it has indeed become a fashionable part of conventional wisdom. The Jeremiahs are having a field day for a change.

It is therefore important to be quite clear about the extent of our so-called industrial shortcomings before attempting to analyze whether a cure is possible, necessary, or even desirable. This in turn hangs on what is meant by 'relatively lower economic growth rate'. Relative to whom? Lower than what?

Table 9.1 shows industrial production indices and growth rates for the UK as compared with the six original members of the EEC taken together as a group (ignoring the national boundary changes after the 1914–18 war). The choice of a common base year of 1938 does not of course imply that real wealth was equal in any absolute sense in that year, but in no others. The point of equality in standard of living was in fact probably reached some time in the 1960s.

Two points emerge very clearly in this long time-span. Firstly, Britain's performance since the 1939–45 war has certainly been better than its own record for

*Table 9.1   Industrial production indices (1938 = 100)*

|  |  | UK | EEC-6 |  |
|---|---|---|---|---|
| 1901 |  | 50 | 42 |  |
| 1913 |  | 68 | 71 |  |
| ∴ | Growth | (2.6) | (4.5) | %/yr |
| 1920 |  | 68 | 48 |  |
| 1938 |  | 100 | 100 |  |
| ∴ | Growth | (2.2) | (4.1) | %/yr |
| 1947 |  | 118 | 67 |  |
| 1970 |  | 276 | 430 |  |
| ∴ | Growth | (3.8) | (8.4) | %/yr |

the first four decades of the century. Secondly, although the continental European economies have consistently grown faster than the UK in peacetime, they have also suffered massive reductions in both wars which have been conspicuously absent in the UK. Reconstruction has inevitably distorted the continental growth rates in the few years immediately after each war, and at the same time has provided a springboard for sustaining future growth based on new factories and ports.

Nevertheless in the broad sweep from 1901–70 industrial output in the EEC six has grown at an average rate of 3.4 per cent per annum as against Britain's 2.5 per cent per annum. In 1901, Britain's economy was undoubtedly richer and more mature than on the continent, with in particular a much lower proportion of the workforce engaged in agriculture. In 1981 we know that our national place in the sun has been well and truly lost; that we have been edged into the shade by others, in spite of winning the two wars which wreaked such industrial havoc elsewhere. But to have continued alone in the sun would have been untenable. As recently as 1955 the UK held a 19 per cent share of total exports of all manufactured goods, though barely 2 per cent of the world's population lives here. By 1975 our share of all exports had fallen to 9 per cent, and nobody should have been surprised.

It is important here to distinguish between the depths of the current recession, which is essentially a short-term phenomenon, and Britain's lower performance when measured over decades. We are the subjects of a politically inspired monetarist experiment, that appears to have been designed to squeeze inflation out of the economy with no thought for unemployment consequences. This happens to have coincided with a world recession following the 1979 oil price rises. At the same time the value of sterling reflects the strengths of North Sea oil rather than the weaknesses of our international industrial productivity.

Such a combination of circumstances would have shaken the most robust of economies. Accordingly it is not the aim of this contribution to reflect on Britain's shorter term illnesses, serious though these are. Rather, it is the longer run British malaise which is under consideration; and regrettably it appears on this analysis to be based on envy. Relative to our own past standards we are doing well. It is only when we cast our eyes across the English Channel (and to a lesser extent across the North Atlantic) that we get a measure of what might have been. It is an emotion and a not altogether pleasant one at that, rather than statistical differences in, say, steel output per capita, that causes us even to need the term 'malaise' to describe the UK's international performance and standing.

## History

It is my contention that, in industry at least, this 'British Malaise' has developed essentially out of a deficiency of attitude. Undoubtedly this situation has been exacerbated by, *inter alia*, our national misfortune in having to make some pioneering mistakes in the Industrial Revolution, and by the survival as noted above of much of our earlier investment in heavy industry through the period 1914–18 and 1939–45. However, these factors are unlikely of themselves to have caused the UK to have underperformed so significantly in economic terms over the past thirty years. The basic reason in industry appears to be twofold: an individual resistance to change, and to a lesser extent, a deep-seated lack of trust between managers and managed.

It is not hard to see how our national economic history has encouraged and reinforced such attitudes. By a happy combination of circumstances, the UK found itself at the end of the eighteenth century with a rapidly growing population, abundant domestic supplies of coal and iron ore, men of technological inventiveness and application, and an Empire prepared to trade food for manufactured goods. This was backed up by a financial system which was sophisticated for its time, and was able to divert accumulated wealth away from its historic association with land into new industrial enterprises. It was helped further by an emerging middle class becoming aware of its political strength, and being encouraged rather than disturbed by the republican and liberal/democratic notions abroad in France and elsewhere.

With hindsight, it was probably the inability of the UK to feed itself (in spite of substantial improvements in agricultural practice) which provided the final spur. The contrast with France is instructive. Whereas the legal and social upheavals there from 1789–1848 were more far-reaching than in the UK, France was able to feed itself with no problems; and moreover it lacked the easily-worked coal and iron found in Britain. As a result it lagged behind in economic terms for over a century.

It is sometimes forgotten how slow the pace of industrial change was during the nineteenth century. The generation and utilization of steam was carried out by heavy over-designed machines of low efficiency but long life. The worker entering the Lancashire cotton mill in, say, 1830 for instance, would see few if any technological developments there from his youth to his old age. The mill-owners had found something profitable to do, and they simply carried on doing it. The wealth so generated was rarely devoted to developing faster or more energy-efficient machines. Instead it went partly to buy status for the owners, partly to fund municipal undertakings to improve the workers' environment, and only lastly into the workers' pockets. Nemesis when it came was swift and painful; it took little more than a decade at the end of the nineteenth century for local manufacture of cotton goods in India to make vast inroads into the previously secure exports from the UK.

This pastiche of one particular industry, brief though it is, nevertheless illustrates the two basic attitudes mentioned earlier. The mill-owners could for three generations say: we're doing very nicely as we are – why should we change? Even the workers could derive some security from being part of one of the most apparently stable and successful nations ever known; and if the hours were long and the wages minimal at least the local water supply did not now actively spread disease, infant mortality was falling, railway travel was cheap and widespread, and they were building a splendid new gas-lit Town Hall next to the public library!

The good was the enemy of the best. Reaching a moderately happy state and pressing on no further was attractive. The owner did not need to listen to his workforce, even when they perhaps had ideas for mechanical improvements. They resented his high-and-mighty style of living, and did not see why they should go out of their way to improve it still further. In short, the owners and the workforce shared a resistance to change and an inability to communicate with each other, yet neither felt particularly disadvantaged by these attitudes.

The mid-twentieth century has seen a radically different environment for UK industry, in which such attitudes are outdated and inefficient. The pace of technological change has increased, as has the importance of international trade. The long-standing bargain between the UK and the Empire has become irrelevant in the light of the independence and industrial development of the former dominions and colonies, and the increasing importance of Western Europe, as the UK's supplier, customer, and competitor.

There are two questions to be considered. Have the attitudes described above contributed to the post-war British malaise in the particular field of research, development and technical decision-making in industry? And, if so, what can be done to improve matters in the future?

## The present situation

Most lay observers of the industrial scene would be able to pass rapid yet fairly accurate judgements on the health of Britain's major industries. In the public sector there are efficient and (currently) profitable energy supply industries, resting on a combination of geological good fortune and a monopoly position in the domestic market. Included here is the coal industry, which is well placed to survive and expand following the Robens manpower cuts of the 1960s and the OPEC-induced oil price-rises in 1973–74. The steel industry is faced with massive social problems arising from too many small old plants, a high level of special steel imports, and a static level of industrial production; but France and Germany each have their troubles, and not even Japan and USA could be said to be doing reasonably well. The ship-building industry, formerly an important and profitable customer of the steel industry, shares with many of its international competitors the devastating effects of a glut of existing ships and low-price competition from Korea and Eastern Europe.

There is a similarly mixed bag in the private sector. The oil industry has long outgrown mere national boundaries; although two of the seven sisters have British roots, their success cannot be ascribed to purely British factors. Thus though the Forties Field in the North Sea is important to the UK as a nation, to BP it is one more field to be managed – and rather smaller and more accessible than the Alaskan North Slope. The UK chemical industry, though increasingly multinational, has grown at least as fast as its continental competitors, and generally with a higher level of profitability. The aerospace industry, following some spectacular failures and mergers in the 1960s, is by dint of international collaboration now ready and able to participate in the huge replacement/expansion market forecast for the next ten to fifteen years. The British computer industry, again following a spate of mergers, is the only one in Europe with a real chance of remaining viable in the shadow of the US giants. The heavy electrical industry has had to tighten its belt, but is surviving. The heavy construction industry, after a hesitant start in the North

Sea, is now doing well on an international basis and especially in the Middle East.

By contrast, the mechanical engineering industry has lost out heavily to European competition, especially from Germany; the prospect of Vickers pulling out of Tyneside would have been unthinkable thirty years ago. The shelves of consumer electrical and photo-/electronic shops are dominated by Italian or Japanese goods, and even those items with British brand-names often turn out to have been manufactured in Taiwan or Malaysia. The motor industry is not only British Leyland and Chrysler: Fords have been profitable as part of a very well-planned European-wide operation; and Vauxhall, whilst maintaining its small share of the UK car market based increasingly on continental GM models, is a much more respectable force in the commercial vehicle market.

The fact remains that, as we have seen, British industry has not shown the growth of its main competitors. In most of the specific industries described above, the one common feature of the less successful is a slow pace of change relative to the competition. That of course is merely a symptom; diagnosis is much harder, and prescription for a full cure practically impossible. Nevertheless, it is important to look more closely to see how and why an industry goes about changing itself, in order to highlight those areas where improvement is feasible.

### Industrial change

All industries evolve. All to some extent need an input of new ideas and new technologies, or they will eventually fail. This truth is independent of the social system in which the industries are operating. Failure in the capitalist system comes when individual companies are unprofitable enough for long enough to cease attracting money from banks or even governments. In the state run economies the process is seen more by the stroke of a bureaucratic pen, when the next Five Year Plan prescribes annihilation! The end result is the same; society chooses to fulfil its wants by a different means, or alternatively realizes that the wants are simply no longer there.

Different industries organize their evolution in different ways, governed primarily by the time-scale of change. In electronics it is not uncommon for up to 40 per cent of sales income to be devoted to research and development effort, since what is the 'state of the art' now will very likely be superseded in only two to three years. As a result research departments must contain highly-motivated and energetic idea-generators if the flow of new products is to be maintained. In pharmaceuticals a really successful drug may do well for eight to ten years in advanced countries, though only after many years of internal trials and clearance with appropriate national authorities have eaten into the precious patent life. Again, companies tend to be dominated by their research departments.

In the petrochemical and plastics industries, by contrast, most basic methods of producing the main building blocks are nowadays similar to those first employed around twenty five years ago; steady developments in catalyst technology continue to improve efficiencies, though the really big savings grasped in the 1950s and 1960s arose from economies of scale rather than new chemistry as such. Today perhaps 1–2 per cent of sales income is devoted to research in these areas, and much of that is technical support to existing products and processes.

At the other extreme there are industries like printing and steel. Although modern photographic and computer-based techniques are poised to take over in many areas (workforces permitting), until recently Gutenberg or Caxton would still have recognized the prime operations and machines in a print room. Steel-making has essentially only had three major technological shifts in the past century, though here too the Japanese have gained from economies of scale with great effect. Research in the former case has essentially come from outside the industry altogether and in the latter has concentrated successfully on different grades of steel with special properties. Railways too have seen a very small number of basic changes in motive power, from steam to diesel, diesel-electric, or electric; and although modern materials have transformed coach design, London Transport still run some pre-war rolling stock on the Underground.

But research by itself is not enough. The most brilliant new idea will lie fallow, or actually prove to be a drain on a company's resources, unless it can be transformed into a reliable product which confers benefit on the customers at a profit to the makers. This development stage can easily cost ten times the original research. At the same time, many more functions are involved and there is more scope for misunderstanding. Frequently there are purely technical difficulties associated with scaling-up what works well on the laboratory bench; the production and engineering functions may decide that a pilot plant is required to solve these, which takes both time and capital. Safety and environmental considerations impinge, for what is new and unfamiliar is frequently set higher standards of social compliance than the existing way of doing things; to steer a clear course in these difficult waters may need an imaginative collaboration between lawyers and engineers within the company, together with civil servants and society's locally or nationally elected representatives.

Again, a new development may require new skills to be taught to an existing workforce, or new and differently qualified recruits altogether; the personnel function will therefore need to be drawn in, especially on questions of wage levels. Nor must the role of the accountancy function be under-rated; far from merely adding up the forecast debits and credits, they can advise on the company's eligibility for development grants, show the effect on its tax position, and display the complex choices open in structuring the balance sheet to actually fund the new development.

The purchasing function, too, must be in from the start if new raw materials or components are envisaged; clearly, long-term supplies at an economic price must be assured in principle before the company commits itself to new investment. Indeed, an intelligent prediction of those materials likely to increase their real cost, for whatever reason, may be an important factor in setting research targets in the first place, as well as influencing development decisions as such. The over-riding example here is of course energy: OPEC-led price increases in 1973–74 and again 1979 may be uncomfortable, but they nonetheless do remind us that crude oil availability is finite at any given real cost level. During the 1950s and 1960s the developed world had access to rapidly-increasing quantities of oil and oil products at decreasing real prices. Unprecedented economic growth was stimulated as a result, but at the same time it was clearly uneconomic to invest in, or even do much research into, elegant ways of conserving energy. Now the situation has reversed. It is not merely good sense but also financially profitable for companies throughout British industry to pay far more attention to energy savings than they did a decade ago. Our temporary good fortune in having North Sea oil and 'cheap' natural gas must not be allowed to reduce development efforts in this direction.

It is clear then that development is a highly complex, expensive, and uncertain group activity. Its effect on a company far outweighs that of research. Development must ultimately be linked, however, to the one function so far not mentioned; that of marketing. Unless the company can successfully sell its new development to the market it has in mind in roughly the right numbers and at roughly the right price, then all the hard work described above will prove to have been a costly and time-wasting irrelevance.

## Industrial marketing

Marketing industrial goods is very different from selling soap-powder: customers simply do not respond to free plastic daffodils. Before the post-war development of advanced and very competitive industries in Japan, Europe and USA, industrial marketing was rarely recognized as such. A product was priced on a cost-plus basis, and the customer could take it or leave it. He usually took it, having nowhere else to go. But imaginative marketing consists of perceiving a new (or even an existing) need, and fulfilling it in a novel way.

British industry has not always been good at this. The Italians, and later the Japanese, correctly gauged the hitherto unrealized demand for light-weight but reliable motor-bikes, for instance, leaving the British industry plodding on twenty years out of date. Yet BMW proved that a finely engineered heavy motorbike, properly advertised to appeal to well-heeled customers, could still maintain a profitable place in the market. Even the market for the mundane plastic bucket was not foreseen at first: until the advent of synthetic detergents in the early 1950s most household buckets were placed directly on top of the stove at least once a week to boil the washing, and the idea that people might buy buckets that melted under such conditions was unthinkable. As a result, the first peacetime polythene plant in the UK was to cater only for the known but small demand in radar insulation.

There have, of course, been significant success stories in which technical achievement has been of obvious market value right from the start. A prime example here is the Pilkington float glass process, which gives a flatter product and totally eliminates the former grinding stage. Another is ICI's halothane anaesthetic, which for the first time enabled surgical operations to be carried out without unpleasant side-effects from the anaesthetic itself. Both have rightly enjoyed worldwide success. Nonetheless, it is an interesting comment on national attitudes that ICI's Dr. Charles Suckling, who was closely associated with the Halothane project and is now General Manager for Research and Technology, should be recently quoted as saying 'Scientists are expected to be able to tackle everything but are expected to fail; whereas marketing men are free to turn anything down initially, but are not expected to fail once they are in'. Too often, however, the market leader in area after area turns out to be German, French, American or Japanese. They are usually not selling at the lowest price, but their reputation for prompt delivery, reliability, back-up servicing, and superior design exceeds the reputation of the comparable British competitors. It is an uncomfortable truth that reputations can be more important than actual performance in this field; the British dog is the one with the bad name!

It is important for industrial marketers to realize what it is the customer wants when he considers purchasing their product. At a trivial level, the householder who buys a $\frac{1}{4}''$ drill bit at his local DIY store doesn't really want that bit as such – what he wants is $\frac{1}{4}''$ holes! Indeed, he probably only needs the holes as a means to locate screws for joining two pieces of wood or chipboard together, and if he could do that entirely with adhesives the drill bit would remain unbought. In essence, the customer has a problem – to construct a single piece of furniture or whatever out of separate components – and he will turn to whatever system offers him the most appropriate combination of cost, convenience, reliability and appearance.

The company which recognizes the customer's problems, and offers him a novel way of solving them, has made the vital first step in marketing a new development. Too often, however, the solutions appropriate for one set of circumstances are not capable of change when the problem itself changes. Thus the British motorcycle industry mentioned above seems to have ignored the fact that many of its sales in the 1950s were to people who needed personal transport, but whose main problem was lack of money to buy a car. Increasing real wealth, and better availability of economic small cars, enabled these customers to solve their problem with a Mini or an Imp rather than a BSA or a Norton. The constructive response was to segment and attack that market which still had financial constraints, such as the sixteen to twenty year olds; this needed differently designed machines which the Japanese supplied rather than the British.

## The way forward

For industry to escape the British malaise, it must be so manned and organized that profitable change is encouraged in response to market needs. This is no easy matter. It involves education and recruitment, management and financial training, imaginative planning by cross-functional teams, and a willingness on occasions to go against conventional wisdom. Sometimes the most implacable enemies of change are the revolutionaries of a generation ago, whose very success then has made them emotionally committed to preserving the 'new' *status quo* they helped to create, and has at the same time put them in the senior organizational positions to do just that.

The position is by no means hopeless, however. The British malaise has never extended to basic research. At the very highest levels the UK has provided a disproportionately large number of Nobel prize-winners, both in relation to its population and its national research budget. Then the Science Research Council has encouraged and funded joint research links between universities and industries. Some of the work of the specific Industrial Research Associations has been at a level far beyond the mere solution of annoying production problems. And industrial research itself, although obviously dominated by the big battalions, has produced a continuing flow of high quality ideas.

It is rather the development step which has seemed to cause such national trouble. Some companies have simply not realized how rapidly their international competitors are evolving, and have thereby not seen the need to devote money and effort to development – shades of the mill-owners! Others have tried hard, but have fallen into the trap of believing that a change which seems good for the producer must necessarily be good for the customer too. That may be so, but it is not a good guide to success in that it ignores the marketing input highlighted earlier. Only a minority of companies, in a minority of industries, have successfully assembled that blend of good luck and good organization, good ideas and good timing, that has brought new wealth and prosperity to themselves and the nation.

The Advisory Council for Applied Research and Development (ACARD) has argued cogently in a recent report that the competitiveness of British industry has diminished over the last two decades because we have, as a nation, failed to take maximum advantage of technological developments. More unemployment results from loss of market share following a failure to innovate, than from the introduction of new technology. Furthermore, attempts by firms or whole industries to avoid competition from technologically more adept foreign countries are doomed to fail in the long run. This is true whether the avoidance takes the form of a concentration on defensive market specialization, a continuation to pay lower wage rates, or the adoption of restrictive trade practices. In other words, there is no substitute for a ready acceptance of change.

It is more than coincidence that those same attitudes which we detected from the nineteenth century appear to be still at work today. 'Ideas good – execution moderate; could improve' is a mid-term report that surely reflects an individual reluctance to change and an inability to communicate successfully within a group of managers and managed. As a nation we seem to have perfected the art of 'satisficing'.

The individual elements needed to improve British industrial performance in the field of research and development decisions do not need to be invented. They are there but must be assembled correctly. The training of scientists, engineers, and managers is undertaken well at the initial full-time phase, and ample opportunities are available thereafter. Quantitative aids to decision-making are widely known and are usually applied where appropriate. There is an increasing number of business school graduates (and others with 'technological economics' training) moving into responsible positions in parts of British industry. Finance for new ventures is in principle available from a variety of sources; and although the lone inventor trying to set up a small manufacturing company may curse the short-sighted bureaucrats who are denying him capital, properly presented cases which illustrate well-planned ways of minimizing risk will usually be funded by the private sector and/or Government in one of its many guises.

In spite of all this, the level of Britain's industry-financed R & D fell in real terms between the mid-1960's and the late 1970's; whereas the same measure for our major OECD competitors (with the surprising exception of the USA) advanced significantly. The USA however was buffered by its high absolute level to start with, and by its huge assured markets in defence technologies.

What one cannot escape from, however, is the effect of individual attitudes. The answer to the question posed earlier in this essay – has resistance to change contributed to the British malaise? – must be an unequivocal 'yes'. The owner of a small engineering firm that has never employed graduates, for instance, and doesn't see why he should start now, has missed an important demographic change: a vastly higher proportion of young people are receiving some form of higher education in the 1970s than in the 1930s, so the bright school-leavers that used to join such firms are simply not now looking for jobs until they are older and better qualified. Again the materials buyer who is afraid of a new computer system, that will take the drudgery out of his job, has missed the opportunities it should bring to buy better given more time to explore alternative sources of supply.

Change is bothersome, and creates tensions. The industrial decision-maker who can nevertheless encourage changes in his organization that take account of real market need is well on the way to success. Yet paradoxically that type of skill requires qualities that cannot be taught. A good leader of a development team may not be the best qualified, or the oldest, or the most senior. Rather he (or she) will be the person best able to combine the various different ideas for change which individual team members may feel comfortable with, and then able to sell the resulting scheme to the directors and employees of the company.

There is then a way forward for British industry. It will not necessarily eliminate the envy with which we may look in future to our international industrial competitors; the grass is usually greener somewhere if you look behind enough different fences. No doubt there will still be ample material for a book with the same title as this one in fifty and a hundred years time, lamenting our failure to seize the opportunities presented by the microprocessor revolution.

I believe the solution to the British Malaise rests not primarily on better basic research, or cheaper venture capital, or different tax rebates, or more/less Government interference in various areas, important though these factors are. It certainly requires adequate R & D funding; it equally certainly requires a better appreciation of good international marketing. But above all it needs a willingness to understand what makes people tick, whether they be colleagues, competitors, customers, or cabinet ministers. British industry cannot avoid change. It must learn to welcome it. If it can understand and use the many social processes which are involved in creating and managing change, then it will survive and prosper, to the benefit of the whole nation. In the last analysis people matter more than technologies; for only people can create and accept change.

# Author Index

Albu, A. 58, 60
Alderoft, D.H. 3, 7, 60
Allen, G.C. 6, 8
Alston, P.L. 126
Armytage, W.H.G. 86
Arnold, L. (*see Gowing and Arnold*)
Arnold, M. 75
Artz, F.B. 126
Ashby, E. 76, 86
Ashworth, W. 7
Austin, Lord 25

Bagrit, Sir Leon 28
Bairoch, P. 34, 59
Balfour, A.J. 86
Barber, Lord 132, 133
Barnett, C. 2
Beckerman, W. 60, 156
Bernal, J.D. 28
Berthoud, R. 150, 156
Bien, D. 126
Bond, B. 125
Bourne, J. 125
Bowden, Lord 27
Boyson, R. 5
Briggs, A. 8
Brittan, S. 30
Byce, V. 77
Butler, R.A. 42

Cairncross, Sir Alec 59, 61
Cairncross, Sir A, Kay, J.A., and Silberston, A.
     60
Callaghan, J. 7
Campbell, R.H. 61
Cannon, L. 143
Carrington, J.C. and Edwards, G.T. 59
Chamberlain, J. 74
Chapple, F. 143
Chattaway, C. 133
Christie, C. 7
Coleman, D.C. 57, 60, 61
Cornwall, J. 36, 59
Cunningham, W. 125
Currie, R. 155

Dainton, F.S. 86

Devonshire, Duke of 13, 75
Dobb, M. 125
Dodds, Dr. 135
Dunning, J.H. 56, 60

Eden, Sir Anthony 26
Edwards, G.T. (*see Carrington and Edwards*)
Egerton, Sir Alfred 111
Eltis, W. 45, 46, 60
Emmerson, G.S. 86, 126

Farqueson, H. 126
Ferranti, Dr. 137
Finniston, M. 117, 118, 125
Flanders, A. 156
Fleck, Lord 130
Fleming, Sir Arthur 135, 136
Fleming, T.J. 126
Forster, W. 15
Franklin, G. 76
Freeman, C. 52, 60

Gazier, D. 126
Gennard, J. 155
Gomulka, S. 60, 156
Gore, G. 14, 27, 28
Gormley, J. 143
Gowing, M. and Arnold, L. 125
Griess, C.T.E. 126
Guggisberg, F.G. 125

Habakkuk, H.J. 122, 125, 126
Hall, K. and Miller, I. 150, 156
Hans, N. 126
Healey, D. 133
Heath, E. 42, 132
Hilken, T.J.N. 125
Hill, T.P. 59
Hird, C. 122
Hobsbawm, E.J. 7, 126
Hoggart, S. 7
Hutchings, D. 66, 71
Hutton, G. 142
Huxley, Sir Julian 25
Huxley, T.H. 1, 7, 13

Jackson, W. 135

Jenkins, C. 143
Jenkins, E.W. 87
Jenkins, P. 4
Johnson, P. 141, 155
Jones, G. 66
Joseph, Sir Keith 141, 155

Kahn-Freund, O. 155
Kaldor, M. 48, 60
Kay, J.A. (*see Cairncross, Kay and Silberston*)
Kearton, Lord 90
Keegan, V. 7
Kennan, G.F. 126
Kindleberger, C.P. 36, 59
Knox, F. 36, 59

Lauwerys, J.A. and Scanlon, D.G. 87
Lawlor, J. 87
Lengelle, M. 60
Leverson, I. and Wheeler, J.W. 60
Lockyer, Sir Norman 86
Lowe, R. 13, 14
Lyons, J. 143

McCloskey, D.N. 7
McQuillan, M.K. 112, 125
Maddison, A. 32, 59
Magnus, Sir Philip 11, 21, 22, 24, 28
Manison, L.G. 59
Marshall, A. 142
Martin, J. 61
Maudling, R. 42
Maunder, P. 60
Miller, I. (*see Hall and Miller*)
Miller, T. 2, 7
Mond, A. 25
Mottershead, P. 51, 60
Muir R. 24, 28
Murray, L. 143, 154

Norman, M. 41
Nossiter, B. 6

Paldam, M. 40, 59
Parkin, M. 60
Parsons, C. 136
Pattison, M. 75
Pavitt, K. 60, 61
Payne, G.L. 8, 29
Payne, P.L. 8
Percy, Lord Eustace 110, 125, 126
Playfair, Sir Lyon 12, 27, 75, 81
Pollard, S. 32, 41, 59
Praagh, G. Van 87
Pratten, C.F. 144, 155

Rippon, G. 60
Robbins, Lord 155
Robens, Lord 138
Robertson, J. (*see Wragg and Robertson*)

Roderick, G.W. and Stephens, M.D. 28, 125
Rose, F. 23, 24, 28
Roseberry, Earl of 13
Routh, G. 153, 156
Rudnev, 129, 132
Rutherford, Lord 25

Sadler, M. 15
Sander, G. 23
Sargent, J.R. 60
Saunders, C. 149, 156
Scanlon, D.G. (*see Lauwerys and Scanlon*)
Schumpeter, J.A. 56
Shadwell, Sir Arthur 4, 7, 21, 28, 125
Shanks, M. 51, 60
Silberston, A. (*see Cairncross, Kay and Silberston*)
Sisson, K. 145, 155
Smail, J.C. 19
Smiles, S. 6, 125
Smith, D. 45, 46, 60
Smith, Lord Delacourt 143
Snow, C.P. 7, 92, 111
Snow, Lord 3, 27
Stephens, M.D. (*see Roderick and Stephens*)
Suckling, C. 163
Swords-Isherwood, N. 57

Taylor, R. 156
Thirwall, A.P. 38, 42, 60
Thompson, Sir J.J. 24, 77, 86
Thompson, S.P. 109
Todd, Lord 27
Thornton, J.S. 60
Townsend, P. 156
Trevelyan, G.M. 125

Vucinich, A.S. 126

Wales, H.R.H. the Prince of 4, 5
Webb, S. 74
Weinstock, Sir Arnold 134
Wellington, Duke of 132
Westinghouse, G. 135
Wheeler, J.W. (*see Leverson and Wheeler*)
Whitehead, A.N. 11, 28
Whitehorn, K. 8
Whitworth, J. 18
Whybrew, E.G. 151
Wickenden, W.E. 126
Wilson, Sir Harold 27
Wootton, G. 155
Worth, F. 6
Wragg, R. and Robertson, J. 60

# Subject Index

academic/practical balance, in training 100–106
accountancy 131–132, 162
accountants 134, 136
AEI 135, 137
aerospace industry 160
agriculture 36, 139, 158, 159
aircraft production 48, 139
apprenticeship 19, 22, 135, 136, 149, 150
*Armchair Science* magazine 79
artizans, courses for 17–19
Austria 4, 33, 38, 39
Australia 27, 33, 34, 152

balance of payments 38, 40, 41, 42, 43, 46, 47,
    49, 50, 58, 138
Bayer Peacock 135
Belgium 1, 33
Birkbeck College, London 74
BL 153
BMW 163
Board of Education Report (1926) 25
boardroom
    lack of educated people, 118
    incompetence, 119–120
Boilermakers Society 145, 150
'Bosworth' Courses 84
'brain drain' 27
Brazil 1
'British Malaise', the vii, 6, 36, 67, 89, 158, 160,
    164, 166
British National Oil Corporation 90
British Rail 149
British Steel Corporation 146
British Westinghouse Company 135
BTR 56
business schools 91, 93, 99
Butler Education Act (1944) 78

Cambridge University 7, 12, 17, 19, 20, 109,
    111, 114
Canada 3, 27, 33, 34, 152
Canadian Royal Commission on Industrial
    Training and Technical Education 19
capital
    goods 73
    investment 40
    stock 39, 40

careers teachers 68
cars (*see motor industry*)
Carter Review Committee (1977) 143
catalyst technology 161–162
CATs (*see Colleges of Advanced Technology*)
Cavendish Laboratories, Cambridge 25
Central Electricity Generating Board 137
Central Policy Review Staff 147–148
'Challenge of Industry' conferences 69
Charity Commission 15
Charlottenburg Technische Hochschule 23
chemical
    engineers 130
    industry 23, 56, 110, 111, 147
        German 120
chemistry, in school 22, 70, 130
Chile 1
City and Guilds Central Technical College 20,
    74
City and Guilds classes 15
City and Guilds of London Institute 18, 124
civil engineering 134
Civil Service 6, 26
coal
    cutting machinery 54
    industry 139, 143, 160
    reserves 89
closed shop agreements, 144, 145
clothing industry 55
Colleges of Advanced Technology 81
colleges of higher education 26
Commission on Industrial Relations (1971) 145–
    146
Common Market (*see EEC*)
communication systems 12
competition
    industrial 2
    international 1, 7, 13, 84
Competitiveness, of British goods 52
computing industry 91, 160
Concorde 48, 51, 138
construction
    equipment industry 148
    industry 148, 160
consumer
    boom 42
    credit restrictions 43

cotton goods 159
Council of Humanistic Studies 77
Courtaulds 56
'craft mentality' 142
craftsmanship, tradition of 12
Crown Agents 131
cultural environment 92–93

Dainton Enquiry 79
defence 41, 45, 47–48, 138
demand, for British goods 53
demand management policies 42, 46, 50, 52
demarcation lines 145–146, 147, 148, 149, 153
Denmark 28, 33
Department of Inland Revenue 134
Department of Science and Art (founded 1853)
    18, 20
design and technology 68
Devonshire Commission (1872) 20, 75
'Diploma of Technology' 81
docks 152
Donavan Royal Commission on Trade Unions
    and Employers Association (1968) 142,
    149, 151, 155, 156
Dunlop 56
dyestuffs 23

economic
    decline 31–59, 89–91
    growth 36, 50
    progress, pursuit of 58
    recession 155, 158
education 44
    Act (1902) 11, 16, 17
    binary view 100·
    Butler Education Act (1944) 78
    elementary 15, 16
    engineering 22
    full-time 84
    higher 5, 6, 15
    investment in 28
    military 17
    naval 17
    possibilities of 11
    private 6–7, 75, 78
    in science and
        technology 73
    secondary 15, 16
    state 45
    system 5
    technical 15, 17, 18–19, 25, 26
    university 16
EEC 28, 59, 138, 157, 158
electrical
    engineering 56, 139
    industry 160
electricity, demand for 137
electronics 48, 161
emigration 23
Empire, British 2, 159, 160

employer responsibilities 154
employment growth 37, 38
Employment Protection Act (1975) 92, 154
employment by sector 44
energy 89
    problems 36, 48
engineer, role of 95
engineering 22
    as career 66–67, 75, 96
    courses 27, 83–84
    disillusionment with 85
    education in 73–86
    educational models 101–106
    employers' attitude to graduates 112–113
    Employers Federation 149
    firms 55
    as graduate profession 96
    Industry Training Board 69
    sector 149
    societal needs of 99
    status of 66
    training 113–115
        in Royal Navy 111
engineers
    educating 124
    reputation of British 116
Esso 151
Europe 34, 158
    Eastern 35, 36, 160
    Western 149, 154, 158, 160
    (*see also under name of country*)
European educational tradition 113–116
evening class study 19, 23, 25 (*see also night study*)
exporting 45

female engineers 27, 66–67
Finland 33
Finniston Committee of Inquiry into the
    Engineering Profession (1980) 5, 27, 66,
    115, 116–117, 124, 125
firm
    identification with 5
First World War 24, 110, 158
Fleet Street 145
foreign investment, by UK firms 56
foreign workers 36
France 1, 3, 7, 17, 19, 21, 28, 31, 33, 40, 55, 67,
    109, 110, 114, 115, 117, 132, 159, 160, 164
fringe benefits 152

GEC 56, 134, 135, 136, 137
Germany 1–5, 7, 11, 13, 14, 17, 19, 21, 23, 24,
    28, 31, 33, 38, 40, 47, 50, 51, 52, 54, 55, 61,
    67, 74, 81, 85, 86, 112, 114, 115, 117, 120,
    138, 147, 149, 160, 161, 164
government 6
    aided investment 133
    grants 14
    intervention, in education 13, 15
    intervention, in industry 107, 112, 123

policy 41, 58–59
spending 43, 49
support for science 14
Government School of Mines (1851) 12, 20
Great Exhibition (1851) 12
Greek 17
gross domestic product 3, 33, 34, 37
gross national product 34, 35
growth rates 157, 158

Higher National Certificate 77, 96
Holland (*see Netherlands*)
Hong Kong 122, 137

ICI 130, 132, 163
ICL 130
Imperial College of Science and Technology 18,
    20, 21, 82, 114
*In Place of Strife* publication 143
income, per capita 31, 32
industrial
    chemists 24
    decline 2
    efficiency 143
    management, German 52
    marketing 164
    production 157
    relations 4, 92
    revolution 3, 4, 12, 17, 107, 109, 158
Industrial Society, the 69
industry
    co-operation with universities 118
    liaison with
        finance houses 125
        with schools 124
        with universities 120, 125
    teachers' image of 65–66
Industry Technical College 18
inflation 36, 48, 89
innovation
    in industry 39–41, 52, 54
institutes of higher education (*see colleges of higher
    education*)
inter-union disputes 153
inventions 86
investment 38, 45
    deficiencies in 52
    in industry 39–41
    in UK, by foreign firms 56
iron and steel 146, 152
Italy 3, 21, 31, 33, 34, 55, 149, 161, 163

Japan 3, 5, 7, 11, 31, 33, 38, 40, 47, 51, 67, 111,
    112, 117, 122, 146, 154, 160, 161, 162, 163,
    164
joint union committees 153

King's College 20
Korea 137, 160

laboratories, science 76–77
labour
    contracts 148
    flexibility 149
    inputs 36
Labour Party 60
*laissez-faire* 142
legislation 154
Liverpool College 20
Liverpool Engineering Society 23
Liverpool University 23
Local Taxation (Customs and Excise) Act (1890)
    18
London Business School 91
London County Council 20

Master of Business Administration (*see MBA
    programme*)
MBA programme 93, 105, 106
McGregor Royal Commission (1977) 145
machine tools 3
Malaysia 161
Malcolm Committee (1926–28) 25
management
    conservatism of 58
    education 90, 92
    failure 3–4, 41, 52–58, 148
    mistrust of unions 4
    performance 58–59
    status of 5
Manchester Institute of Technology 74
Manchester University 20, 23
manning levels 147, 154 (*see also overmanning*)
manpower
    planning 129–139, 154
    problems 26
    shortages 36, 38
manufacturing vii, 44, 107
    societal needs of 99
marine engineering 144
market needs, identifying 86, 108, 117, 119, 121,
    123
marketing 163
marketing strategy, lack of 119
markets 1, 7, 13
mathematics
    in school 70, 78
    status of 26
mechanical engineering 53
mechanics' institutes 18, 74
media, the 65, 67, 69
merchant bankers 134
Mesopotamia 1
Metropolitan Vickers AEI 134, 135, 136
micro-chip
    industry 7
    technology 51
Middle East 161
middle management, recruitment 57
militant minorities 148

mobile cranes industry 148
models, for learning 101–106
monetarism 158
monetary
   control 49
   growth 48
money supply 49
morale 123
motor vehicle industry 51, 55, 110, 147, 152
motorcycle manufacture 89
multinational industries 160
Museum of Economic Geology 20

National Coal Board 138
National Economic Development Office 146,
   147
National Graphical Association 145
National Union of Mineworkers 143
natural resources 12
'Neglect of Science Committee' 77
Netherlands 33, 39, 146, 147
New Earnings Survey 151
newspaper industry 144–145
'night schools' 23
'night-study' 22 (*see also evening classes*)
nineteenth century 1, 2, 4, 7, 11–19, 31, 32, 85,
   107, 108, 109, 159
North Sea oil 31, 50, 89, 112, 158, 163
Norwood Report (1943) 78
Norway 33

*Observer*, the dispute at 145
OECD 166
oil 137, 138
   exports 47
   price rises 160, 162
Open University, the 97–98, 104
output
   growth 39, 53
   per capita 32
   per employee 36, 37
overmanning 38, 39, 142–143, 145, 148, 149 (*see
   also manning levels*)
overtime 143, 145, 151
   bans 152, 153
Oxford University 7, 12, 17, 19, 20, 109, 114

Paris Exhibition (1855) 109
participation, worker 94, 108
part-time study 84, 93, 105, 106
'payment-by-results' 15
Percy Report (1945) 25
petrochemical industry 161
pharmaceuticals 161
physics
   research 80
   in school 70, 78
   status of 26
plastics industry 161
polytechnics 82

creation of 26
   management departments 99
population growth 36
Post Office 130–131, 132, 151
power stations 137
printing industry 144, 162
private sector service employment 44
productivity 36, 38, 39, 45, 52, 122, 141, 142,
   143, 144, 146, 149, 153
professionalism, lack of 57
professions, school pupils' attitudes to 66
profit motive 52, 153
profitability 40, 56
profits, seen as harmful 122
*Programme for Action* document 145
public expenditure, cuts in 131
public schools (*see education, private*)
private sector 47
public sector 40, 43, 44
   borrowing 48
   employment 44, 45
   spending 46

Racal 56
railway system 149, 162
redundancies, in coal mines 138
Redundancy Payments Act (1965) 154
religion
   effect on growth 58
   effect on teaching 113–114
Research and Development 53, 161, 162, 164–
   166
restrictive practices 58, 150, 153
Robbins Report on Higher Education (1963)
   27, 65, 81, 83
Rolls Royce 110, 132
Royal College of Chemistry 20
Royal Commission on the Depression of Trade
   (1886) 18
Royal Commission on Education (1895) 16
Royal Commission of Scientific Instruction and
   the Advancement of Science (1872) 13
Royal School of Chemistry 114
Russia 113, 114, 115, 129

sandwich courses 19, 81, 103, 104
Scandinavia 4, 92
school
   compulsory attendance 14
   geographical distribution of 16
   grammar 16, 17
   and industry 65–71
   leavers 150
   leaving age 78
schoolteachers, lack of 5
Schools Inquiry Commission (1868) 16
science
   fellowships in 20
   importance of 12
   laboratories 76–77

neglect of 24
pure 27
scholarships in 20
in schools 76–79, 83
students 22
teaching of 17
'Science for All' 77
Science Research Council 84, 165
scientific
education 13
research 14
skill 12
scientists
cost of equipping 129
number of 129
shortage of 25
Scotland 91, 95
Second World War 25, 34, 80, 155, 158
self-help
belief in 6, 13
service sector 45
shipbuilding 51, 111, 139, 144, 145, 146, 152
Sixties, the 80
skillcentres 150
skilled : unskilled ratio 148
Social Science Research Council 129
social services 47
Society of Arts 18
Southampton Forum for Science and
    Technology 83
Spens Report (1938) 78
standard of living 31
state expenditure (*see public spending*)
state interference (*see government, interference of*)
steel industry 3, 51, 146, 147, 160, 162
strikes 152, 153
study leave 124
supply management policies 50–51, 60
Sweden 31, 33, 34, 39, 146
Switzerland 11, 14, 17, 19, 33, 34, 54
synthetic dyestuffs 3

Taiwan 122, 161
taxation 46
teachers, experience of industry 68
technical institutes 74
Technical Instruction Act (1889) 18
technische Hochschulen 21, 81, 114
technology
courses in 27
growth of 94
schoolteachers' attitudes to 26
television 2
televisions
demand for 132–133
textile machinery industry 54
theoretical knowledge (*see models*)
Thirties, the 79
Thompson Enquiry 78
Times Newspapers, dispute at 145

town planning 129–130
trade unions 2, 4, 107–108, 121, 141–156
control within 144
mistrust of management 2
obstructiveness 141
power 107–108, 112
Trafford Park 134, 135, 136, 139
training 150
transfer payments 46
transformer business 137
transport systems 12
Treasury, the 41, 42, 139
turbo-generator industry 136
Turner and Newall 56

UK firms operating abroad 56
UMIST 130
'Understanding British Industry' syllabus 69
unemployment 36, 38, 48, 133
unions (*see trade unions*)
United States 1, 3, 5, 11, 19, 21, 27, 31, 33, 47,
    52, 55, 67, 92, 111, 115, 117, 146, 160, 164,
    166
universities
American 24
British (*see under name of university*)
endowments to 24–25
German 21, 22, 24
redbrick 74, 81
University College 20
Uruguay 1

voluntaryists 14, 15

wages, high 122
wage-income ratio 40
war (*see First World War and Second World War*)
wartime technology 80, 110
welfare security 44
'whisky money' 18
White Paper (1956) 26
Whitworth Scholars 18
Wilberforce Inquiry (1972) 143, 155
women, return to work 103
workers, underemployed 45
work-experience, during holidays 70
work organization 94
work-to-rules 152, 153
'workshop of the world' 2